ANATOMY OF A CONFRONTATION

The Rise of Communal Politics in India

ANATOMY OF A CONFRONTATION

The Rise of Communal Politics in India

Edited by

SARVEPALLI GOPAL

ZED BOOKS
LONDON & NEW JERSEY

Anatomy of a Confrontation was first published in this edition by
Penguin Books India (P) Ltd, in 1991 and in rest of the world in 1993
by Zed Books Ltd, 57 Caledonian Road, London, NI 9BU and 165 First Avenue,
Atlantic Highlands, New Jersey 07716, USA

Copyright © Penguin Books India (P) Ltd., 1990, 1991

Cover design by Andrew Corbett
Printed and bound in India

The rights of the authors and the editor of this work has been asserted by
them in accordance with the Copyright, Designs and Patents Act 1988.

A catalogue record for this book is available from the British Library
US (cataloging-in-publication) data is available from the Library of
Congress

ISBN 1 85649 050 5

Contents

Preface

Differences between Hindus and Muslims have dominated public life in India for about the last hundred years. Artificially contrived at the start and drawing strength from divergence of social habit, these differences widened out to become the phenomenon of communalism, unknown almost anywhere else in the world. A few Indians felt genuinely that their religion was under threat; many more used their religious commitment to battle for jobs, secure political concessions or strengthen their reactionary interests. So widely did the virus spread in the penultimate years of the Raj in India that, despite the efforts of staunch nationalists in the modern sense, freedom came to India along with partition of the country. The areas where Muslims formed a majority of the population and wished to secede were thrown together to form the new state of Pakistan.

The fact of division was monstrous enough, but it was accompanied by the miseries of mass migrations and human beings slaughtering each other in a mad frenzy. The crowing tragedy was the assassination of Mahatma Gandhi by a Hindu fanatic. It was clearly a desperate situation and, if India were to turn away from a steep descent into savagery, sound principles of national cohesion had to be reasserted. Indian nationalism was still obviously brittle and free India had to pick up broken pieces to put together the jigsaw of nation-building in a fresh context. So in 1947 a slow, at times faltering, but steady effort was set in motion seeking to divorce religion from public life and to assure the minorities that the faiths they professed would have no bearing on their civic rights. Secularism would be the binding cement of Indian society.

The progress that the country was making in this respect has been severely menaced in recent years by a sharp recrudescence of political aggressiveness among diverse groups of Hindus, Muslims and Sikhs claiming religious sanction. The focus of the belligerence of the Hindu group, claiming to represent the majority community in the country, was the Babri Masjid in Ayodhya in Uttar Pradesh. Alleging that this mosque had been built in the sixteenth century after destroying a Hindu temple standing on the site of the birth of Rama—one of the avatars of Hindu belief—the Hindu communal party, the Bharatiya Janata Party (BJP), and the Vishwa Hindu Parishad (VHP), serving as its militant wing, were set on destroying the mosque and replacing it with a temple. Bricks were transported from various parts of India and, with great fanfare, large crowds converged on Ayodhya in October 1990. The result was clashes between Hindus and Muslims all over the country, with over a thousand deaths in a few months. In Ayodhya itself law and order were at a discount with police firing on Hindu volunteers. As a consequence of the arrest of its President, the BJP withdrew its support to the Union Government which had to resign. But the crisis was not over. Urns alleged to contain the ashes of those killed at Ayodhya were carried to all the villages, and it was planned to recruit a million volunteers and to demolish nearly 3,000 mosques in various parts of the country. Hindu revivalism was sought to be dressed up as Indian nationalism and the mosque at Ayodhya was denounced as a "Symbol of national shame".

In the first edition of this book published in April 1991, it was feared that were this movement to succeed, secularism would be strangled and India would be heading for a Fascist take-over. It is melancholy to report that, in the months since then, events have continued to move headlong in that direction. In the general elections in the summer of 1991, the BJP increased considerably its strength in the Lok Sabha and continued to whip up public opinion in the country; and the climax was reached on 6 December 1992, when its volunteers, defying all the assurances given to the Union Government and the Supreme Court by the BJP government in the state and manifestly well-trained for the purpose, demolished the Babri Masjid.

This would suggest that the Babri Masjid–Ramjanmabhumi issue is now a mere matter of academic debate. In fact, the crisis of which it was the focus, has deepened and gained greater political urgency. The siege to the basic concepts on which free India has striven to build herself has become more intense. So it has seemed worthwhile to bring out a fresh edition of these articles, first published in 1991, on various aspects of the problem with its wider implications, written by those who are specialists in their own fields and who have taken into account the extant evidence. No attempt has been made to impose a particular viewpoint and the reader will notice different shades and nuances of opinion and approach. It is hoped that the whole work will enable a proper understanding of this threat to the survival of a modern, democratic India.

Madras
February 1993

S. Gopal

ANATOMY OF A CONFRONTATION

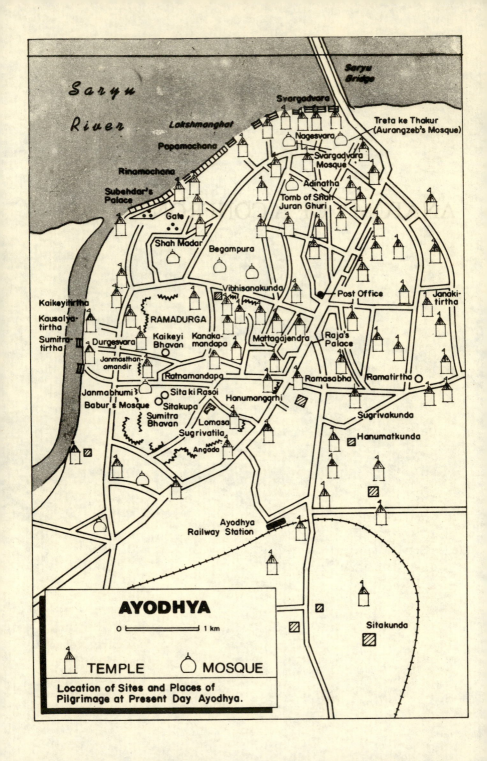

Location of Sites and Places of Pilgrimage at Present Day Ayodhya.

Introduction

Sarvepalli Gopal

The Ramjanmabhumi issue, the demand by a militant section of Hindu opinion for the demolishing of a mosque in Ayodhya and the building of a temple to Rama on that site, brings into sharper focus than at any time since 1947 a sickness which free India has not been able to shake off and demands reappraisal of many basic features of our society. But the issue itself (as well as the atmosphere in which it thrives) has been, as the essays in this collection show, contrived in recent times and with no historical basis. If, even so, considerable attention is given in this book to claims said to be grounded in history, it is because so much is being made of them in current propaganda. The identification of present-day Ayodhya with Ramjanmabhumi is a matter of faith and not of evidence. There is again no conclusive proof that the mosque, built at the time of Babur, was on a temple site or that a temple had been destroyed to build it. It is true that the mosque incorporates pillars which have non-Islamic motifs; but the explanation for this may well lie in the employment of Hindu craftsmen in the building of mosques or the incorporating of material from any derelict building in the vicinity which could have had a non-religious function or even have been associated with non-Hindu sects. In fact the style of these pillars is thought by some to be more Jaina than Hindu, and it is possible that parts of the mosque may have been picked up from Jaina buildings. Ayodhya had been a Buddhist and then a Jaina centre before followers of the Rama cult started settling there in large numbers in the eighteenth century and building temples under the patronage of the Muslim nawabs of Avadh.

Visitors to Ayodhya, such as Tieffenthaler in the late eighteenth century, have recorded a rather garbled version of a local story that either Babur or Aurangzeb destroyed a temple and constructed a mosque on its site and that this temple had been at the birthplace of Rama—incidentally, one among many with claims to have been located at his birthplace. But, as can be seen from the essays of Sushil Srivastava and K.N. Panikkar, it was only in the nineteenth century that British officials and writers began to give wide circulation and lend authority to the story that on Babur's orders a temple had been destroyed and a mosque built on the site. This fitted in with the British understanding of India. To cite the restrained language of Judith Brown, the British tended to break up the Indian population in terms of community and analysed Indian society as a plural one of different peoples who needed special outlets in political life.[1] These 'imagined religious communities', in Romila Thapar's phrase,[2] were also seen as basically hostile to each other; and the assumption that in Ayodhya a temple had been destroyed and replaced by a mosque was of a piece with this hypothesis. That Muslim rulers in India often acted on non-religious grounds and, like all rulers everywhere, were primarily inter-ested in the maintenance of their political power, was ignored.

As Asghar Ali Engineer's article establishes, no generalizations are possible about Hindu–Muslim relations in our history. There was both conflict and amity between these communities, just as there was hostility between factions and groups within the communities. All such conflicts were limited in their impact and were not, in contrast to today, organized as confrontations between Hindus and Muslims, with repercussions en-couraged in many distant parts of the country as well. Babur himself patronized Hindu temples and individuals, and in Ayodhya itself he gave a revenue-free grant of a large piece of land to a Hindu ascetic. Mushirul Hasan outlines the dominant feature of cooperation between the Hindu and Muslim elites as well as masses in the seventeenth and eighteenth centuries. With the coming of the British, regional imbalances in economic and social development resulted in the classes who gained most from British rule being drawn predominantly from among the Hindus; and Amiya Bagchi's paper shows clearly the economic basis of the phenomenon of communalism. By the time the interior areas of India caught up with Westernization, national consciousness, particularly in Maharashtra but also in Bengal, had begun to speak increasingly in a Hindu idiom. The British, as Aditya Mukherji traces, were not slow to take advantage of the resulting increase in communal rioting. 'One hardly knows,' wrote the Secretary of State, Lord George Hamilton, 'what to wish for. Unity of ideas and action would be very dangerous politically, divergence of ideas and collision are administratively troublesome. Of the two the latter is the least risky, though it throws anxiety and responsibility upon those on the spot where the friction exists.'[3]

The policy-makers of the Raj were aware that, despite the social disharmony between the Hindus and the Muslims in India, the real rivalry

was economic and that this had been stretched, with their active connivance, to the sphere of politics and public life. As late as 1946 the
Viceroy, Lord Wavell, who could sometimes in private slip into honesty,
acknowledged this. 'Though I agree as to the contrast between the Muslim
and Hindu outlook on life and that the masses can be worked on mainly
by the appeal of religion, I think that the root of the political conflict, so
far as the leaders are concerned, lies in the fear of economic domination,
rather than difference of religion. It has been found that Hindus and
Muslims can live together without conflict where there is no fear of
economic and social domination, e.g. in the army.'[4] But whatever their
inner views, the British continued to work on the assumption that India
was a plural society divided by religion. According to the imperialist
viewpoint, 'the animosities of centuries are always smouldering beneath
the surface'.[5] The result was Partition and the formation of Pakistan on
the groundless basis that Hindus and Muslims formed two separate
nations.

In this setting the Muslims who preferred to remain in India rather than
migrate to Pakistan were, in Fernand Braudel's words about Frenchmen
in 1940, like 'dust blown by the wind from a heap of sand'.[6] The
Government of free India, which obviously rejected the two-nation
theory, had to strengthen civilized principles of national cohesion. The
logical attitude of getting rid of religion altogether was too utopian for
Indian society, where many religions were deeply entrenched. So the more
practical answer was not opposition to religion but the removal of religion
from public affairs, the separation of the State from all faiths, the insistence on religion as a private matter for the individual with no bearing on
civic rights and duties, and freedom for the profession of diverse forms
of religious worship provided they did not come into conflict with each
other. These are all elements of a modern outlook anywhere as well as of,
in the third world, the most practical approach. Only secularism of this
type, not defined in any dictionary or in accordance with Western experience but adapted to the Indian context, can be the cornerstone of an
egalitarian, forward-looking society with religious pluralism, full civil
liberties and equal opportunities. It is the only possible social cement for
a modern community and the only way of making certain that no one is
treated as a second-class citizen on the ground of religion.

These principles of secularism draw their strength from their own logic
and appropriateness and need no support from any religion, though it goes
without saying that the proclaimed aim of true religion is human fraternity.
Even in Islam, often regarded as exclusive, one finds in the Koran the

saying, 'Your religion for you and mine for me.' To the person moved by the religious impulse, the ultimate truth is one, every religion shows some traces of it and it is a matter of indifference to which religion one adheres. Only to the person exploiting religion for political ends and using it in various forms of mobilization, as in the case of fundamentalists of any variety, Hindu, Muslim or Sikh, is religion seen essentially as a divisive factor, and providing no meeting ground for followers of different faiths. But, considering that the main attack on secular objectives in free India has come from the ranks of Hindu bigotry, it is worth mentioning that the teachings of Hinduism at their best are in full accordance with such secular practices. Hinduism, unlike the Semitic religions, lacks a structure, is not linear, has no single sacred text and is not organized by a church. Even the term Hinduism, although used in the sense of a religion in the fifteenth century, came into common usage only in the nineteenth century. It is a religion without circumference, an amalgamation, under the impact of extraneous influences, of a large variety of religious beliefs with similar structures into a religious system. But while there is no Hindu religion in the sense in which that term is generally used, there is an atmosphere, a structure of feeling, which governs the different sects and lifts them to ·higher levels. This common element in the faith which binds together those who call themselves Hindus in the various parts of India is the acceptance of religion as spiritual experience, as the direct apprehension of the reality of the one supreme Universal Spirit. Devotion to truth and respect for all human beings, a deepening of inner awareness and a commitment to compassion, form the essence of the Hindu religion.

This lack of dogmatism rules out the certainty of unique revelation and leads to an acceptance of a diversity of beliefs. By its emphasis not on a specific creed but on a common quest for the truth which underlies all doctrines and denominations, Hinduism leaves no room for inter-religious misunderstandings and opens the way for religious concord. Dispensing with rule, ritual and ceremony and instead kindling the inner sense makes possible an intelligent comprehension of the deeper unity of principle among all religions and enables people to respect each other's beliefs. When Shelley wrote of 'bloody Faith the foulest birth of time' he had in mind narrow, exclusive religions seeking domination. But a religion shorn of obscurantism and one which promotes human and ethical values can have a place in a healthy human community.

- Mahatma Gandhi, the greatest Hindu of our century, described this over seventy years ago, 'Let me explain what I mean by religion. It is not the Hindu religion, which I certainly prize above all other religions, but the religion which transcends Hinduism, which changes one's very nature, which binds one indissolubly to the truth within and which even purifies. It is the permanent element in human nature which counts no cost too great in order to find full expression and which leaves the soul utterly restless until it has found itself, known its Maker and appreciated the true correspondence between the Maker and itself.'[7] It is a sad irony that those who claim to be followers of the same religion as Gandhi, should now, forsaking the majesty of the faith proclaimed for all time in the Upanishads and in the teachings of the *bhaktas*, be primarily concerned with collecting and transporting bricks in order to construct a temple on the site of a mosque which they plan to demolish. What even a few years ago would have been laughed out as a sick joke on the eccentric fringe of Indian public life has now become a pressing demand. Motivated defiance of the ground rules of historical research and analysis, hijacks and distorts the past to suit the needs of current politics and enrols it under the banner of a narrow ideology.[8] Neeladri Bhattacharya establishes the dangers of such an approach.

That such ideas are no longer a marginal aberration is in a sense testimony to the weakness in practice of secularism in India. The Hindu revivalism which followed the fact of Partition and the memories of inter-religious conflicts could not be wished away by a paper commitment to divorce religion from politics. 'All of us,' Nehru wrote sadly, 'seem to be getting infected with the refugee mentality or, worse still, the RSS mentality. That is a curious finale to our careers.'[9] But he realized that this communal feeling, if allowed to spread, would wreck India and destroy its future, and combating it became his prime task. So when, on the night of 22–23 December 1949, some rather primitive images of deities were found in the mosque at Ayodhya, obviously put together hurriedly and proclaimed to be Rama manifesting himself, Nehru immediately recognized the wider implications of this event. Because it would be a dangerous example with bad consequences, he urged the then Chief Minister of Uttar Pradesh, Govind Ballabh Pant, to interest himself personally in the matter.[10] As A.G. Noorani points out in his article, Sardar Patel, the Deputy Prime Minister, also wrote to Pant that such unilateral action, suggesting an attitude of aggression and coercion, could not be countenanced. This fact is worth stressing, because Patel is usually depicted as a supporter of Hindu chauvinism; but actually his major concern was national unity. Though Pant replied that efforts were being made to set things right in a peaceful manner, nothing happened. Concerned at this apathy in a matter of such grave importance with repercussions on all-India affairs and more especially Kashmir, at a time when a rapid increase of migration of Hindus from East Bengal was causing panic among Muslims in Calcutta and a mounting war fever in Pakistan, Nehru offered, if necessary, to go himself to Ayodhya. Pant, assuring the Prime Minister that some local officials had been replaced and stating that he was hopeful that a satisfactory solution could be found and the idols removed peacefully, dissuaded Nehru from proceeding to Ayodhya.[11] But far from a solution being found to the problem in Ayodhya, the situation in the whole province, as Nehru saw, deteriorated. 'I have felt for a long time that the whole atmosphere of the UP has been changing for the worse from the communal point of view. Indeed, the UP is becoming almost a foreign land for me. I do not fit in there. . . . All that occurred in Ayodhya in regard to the mosque and temples and the hotel in Fyzabad[12] was bad enough. But the worst feature of it was that such things should take place and be approved by some of our own people and that they should continue.'[13]

So strongly did Nehru feel on this matter of the communal disease spreading in UP and all over India that he considered at one stage leaving all else and taking up with all his strength a crusade to combat communalism. But at the time all he could do was to remind his colleagues of their old ideals and urge them to act. Finding Pant immune to his pleadings, he turned to Lal Bahadur Shastri, at that time Home Minister in UP. The matter of the idols in the mosque had by now become a major issue affecting India's whole policy and prestige; and Nehru once more reiterated his concern that conditions in Ayodhya were becoming steadily worse and spreading to Mathura and other places, with the Congress organization taking no interest and some prominent Congressmen being openly communal. 'I fear that we are heading again for some kind of disaster.'[14] But still no action followed; and indeed the multifold and intensifying consequences of official impassivity and weakness in Ayodhya are with us still. 'The fact of the matter is that for all our boasts, we have shown ourselves a backward people, totally lacking in the elements of culture as any country understands them. It is only those who lack all understanding of culture, who talk so much about it.'[15] A scathing indictment which seems to gain validity as the years pass since Nehru first made it over forty years ago. Our media today is replete with myth wearing the mask of history and myth carefully chosen, as Romila Thapar shows, to project particular obscurantist versions that help to glorify aggressive fundamentalism. The television versions of the *Ramayana* and the *Mahabharata* and, in sharp contrast, the failure to present a serious and non-partisan discussion of the Ramjanmabhumi issue, have all contributed to the heightened excitement which has led to the recent increase in communal rioting, with over a thousand Muslims killed in the last few months.

Unqualifiedly committed as Nehru was to the principles of secularism, a hesitancy on his own part in enforcing them has helped to weaken their impact. In 1948 he committed the support of the Government to a resolution of the Constituent Assembly calling for the ban of communal political parties, but did not implement the resolution because of legal difficulties. He, like Gandhi, was opposed to the banning of cow-slaughter as an unnecessary and irrational concession to Hindu feeling but permitted it to be included as one of the Directive Principles of State Policy in the Constitution, while ensuring that nothing came of it in practice. Above all, in his keenness to win the confidence of the Muslims whose feelings were still raw after the events of Partition, Nehru failed to provide equality before the law to all Indian women and to promulgate a common civil law. But there is no room in a society which declares itself to be secular for inequalities which claim religious sanction. Secularism is more than a passive attitude of religious tolerance; it is a positive concept of equality in all spheres. Religion has to be separated not only from politics but also from the law. To deny rights to Muslim women which are available to Indian women of other faiths is a violation of the provision in the Constitution that the State shall not discriminate against any citizen on grounds of religion. Indeed the Constituent Assembly had, by a resolution in 1948, refused to accept that Muslim personal law was an inseparable part of the Islamic religion and rejected attempts to exempt it from the Directive Principle regarding a uniform civil code.

All this was, of course, known to Nehru; but he felt that, at least in the early years of free India, minorities required special consideration. There might still be a few Muslims who were communal and any efforts of theirs to make mischief would have to be dealt with sternly; but more attention should be given to winning the Muslims over and making them feel at home. He was throughout, before and after 1947, of the view that the problem of minorities was basically one for the majority community to handle. The test of success was not what the Hindus thought but how the Muslims and other communities felt, just as, while minorities might turn communal out of a sense of grievance, communalism of the majority community was dangerous and, masquerading as nationalism, was in fact a form of Fascism. There could sometimes be justification for the minorities to be communal; there was none for the majority. 'Honest communalism is fear; false communalism is political reaction.'[16] That Nehru even in the thirties drew a distinction between shades of communalism and considered one of it to be legitimate, weakened the logic of his secularism and opened the door to explosive possibilities. But he was right in the general drift of his thinking that the eradication of the communal virus is a problem of social psychology. It is for the Hindus to be secular and thereby help the minorities to become secular. For it is the majority community alone that can provide the sense of security.

Whatever the innate tendencies of communities identifying themselves as Hindus, Muslims or Sikhs and the natural drift of their religions, extraneous influences have, in the years after Nehru and particularly in recent times, sought to push the majority community in the reverse direction. Successive governments, of whatever ideological complexion, have helped in this. Even the Congress when in office has not been consistent in its loyalty to Nehru's principles. In its keenness to ensure votes, it has been willing to compromise on secularism. This has sometimes brought short-term advantages, but in the long run has strengthened communal forces. These have also gained from other developments; Hindu chauvinism is an unsurprising counter to the Islamic fundamentalism that is spreading in India and various other parts of the world. Seeking to confront throw-backs to medievalism by modern, secular attitudes is a difficult endeavour; far easier to take up similar, backward-looking postures in dealing with the menace. Also, just as the Jews were denounced in Nazi Germany as a threat to the economic prosperity of the nation as a whole, so in India Muslims are today being made the scapegoats of impending decline, particularly of retail and small-scale business, in the Indian countryside. In the riots in Kota in September 1989, those killed were mostly the Muslims who had been once poor but now roused envy because they had been enriched by money from the Gulf. Tamil Nadu has been relatively free of antagonism between Hindus and Muslims; but this record was tarnished by communal rioting in Madras city in September 1990, and it is said that Marwari traders rewarded the hooligans who burnt shops owned by Muslims. In the clashes in the Bhagalpur area in October 1990, not a single Muslim weaver family was spared in the Champanagar and Nathnagar localities, famous for their silk textile production. Nor is it without significance that many of the disputed religious sites constitute valuable urban property. The craving for plunder has not departed with Mahmud of Ghazni.

Such economic greed, rivalry and exploitation draw sustenance from other sources as well. Fundamentalism is an umbrella providing shade to smuggling, drug-peddling and other dubious, anti-social activities. Indians settled abroad, clinging to obscurantist versions of their religion in an effort to salvage their identity in an alien context, have thrown their weight—and funds—on the side of reaction in their home country. The latest instance is their massive vote for L.K. Advani, the leader of the Bharatiya Janata Party (BJP), in the poll conducted by the BBC in London for selecting the Man of the Year.

All these trends have been assiduously exploited by the BJP and the Vishwa Hindu Parishad (VHP) in their campaign for political mobilization of the masses. Active in this regard especially during the last two to three years, their efforts acquired a note of urgency in recent months after the National Front Government's adoption of the report of the Mandal Commission, recommending reservation of some official jobs for the backward classes. The attention given to divisions of caste within the Hindu fold threatened to weaken the objective of pitting the Hindus as a bloc against the Muslims and led to an intensification of the mobilizing campaign. Making the Ayodhya issue a hard and easily understandable focus of their activity, calling on all devout Hindus to carry bricks from various parts of India to Ayodhya for constructing a temple, recruiting the services of sadhus and swamis, organizing a *rath-yatra* with fanfare across the long stretches of northern India with violence and bloodshed in its wake, carrying out periodic attacks on the mosque and parading through the villages of India what are claimed to be the ashes of those killed by the police—are methods of which Goebbels would have been proud. And the results are plain to see. In the general elections of 1952 the Jan Sangh secured no more than three per cent of the vote and its lone member in the Lok Sabha was Syama Prasad Mukherjee, a front-bench parliamentarian who would have done credit to any party; in the elections of 1989 the vote secured by the BJP is estimated to be anywhere between eleven and fifteen per cent, and it has in the Lok Sabha eighty-six members—which makes clear that numbers are now more important than quality. Today the Party is mounting what it hopes will be the final assault, leading to the acquisition of State power at the Centre. We are living in times which may well witness secularism in its last throes.

Secularism is more than laws, concessions and special considerations. It is a state of mind, almost an instinctive feeling, such as existed, by and large, for many centuries in India, when Hindus, Muslims, Christians, Parsis and followers of other faiths lived side by side in general harmony, whatever the religions of their rulers, adhering to their own practices but influencing each other in architecture, dress, music, food and even in their religious evolution. During the last hundred to hundred-and-fifty years, fissures, stress-cracks and structural fatigue have developed in the edifice of Indian civilization; but these can be surmounted with the impetus of democracy and the spread of education. A secular state can be strongly grounded only in a secular society, and this implies leading the people out of social backwardness into forward-looking egalitarianism. If secular attitudes are confined to a few sophisticated elements in our society, then even those few will feel, as they are beginning to do today, beleaguered, with fundamentalism spawning round them and weakening the national identity. Only by the strengthening of the human factor at all levels in India can the communalism both of fear and of reaction be overcome. Only by not living in a world of self-created myth but by facing the past with honesty, can we move beyond the tragedies which the corroding disease of communalism brings and face the future with confidence. It is the good fortune and not the curse of India that she is a land of many religions with a complex and diverse culture. That culture can now, by effort, understanding, and dedication, be expanded into a genuinely democratic culture of an educated people. Such an invigorating process, rather than the destruction of mosques and the construction of temples in their place, would be more in line with the heritage of the Indian people which always, over the centuries, flowed freely beyond its natural confines, looked for wider connections and linked the apparently separate.

Basically, it is irrelevant whether a temple had or had not existed on the site where the mosque now stands. India cannot revert to the approaches of medieval politics and set about destroying, under any circumstances, existing or erstwhile structures of worship. That such demolitions had taken place in the past offers no justification for such vandalism now. Today attention is centred on a mosque; tomorrow agitation may develop over a temple. It is established that some Buddhist and Jaina shrines were destroyed by Hindus. How far back in history does one go, correcting the past as interpreted to one's own liking?

It is pointless for religious leaders to exchange and assess what they regard as evidence, a it is to make a reference to the Supreme Court to pronounce on the validity of such data. But a correct understanding of the present confrontation could help to clear the atmosphere and facilitate the obvious solution of leaving things as they are. The essays in this volume are intended as contributions towards such an understanding.

Notes

1. Judith M. Brown, *Gandhi, Prisoner of Hope*, Oxford University Press: Delhi, 1990, p. 374.

2. Romila Thapar, 'Imagined Religious Communities? Ancient History and the Modern Search for a Hindu Identity', *Modern Asian Studies*, May 1989, pp. 209–31.

3. Lord George Hamilton to the Viceroy, Lord Elgin, Hamilton Correspondence, India Office Library, C125/2, 7 May 1897, folios 185 ff.

4. Lord Wavell to Sir A. Clow, *Transfer of Power*, vol. 8, Document 414, 7 October 1946.

5. Francis Younghusband in 1930 quoted in, G. Pandey, *The Construction of Communalism in Colonial North India*, Oxford University Press: Delhi, 1990, p. 44.

6. Fernand Braudel, *The Identity of France*, vol. 1, Collins: London, 1988, p. 24.

7. *Young India*, 12 May 1920; *Collected Works of Mahatma Gandhi*, vol. 17, Publications Division: Delhi, 1965, p.406.

8. The latest example is Koenraad Elst's *Ram Janmabhoomi vs. Babri Masjid*, Delhi, 1990. Here a Catholic practitioner of polemics fights the crusades all over again on the soil of India and the progress in rational thought and logical analysis in historical debate during the eight hundred years in between has obviously passed him by. It is difficult to take seriously an author who draws his historical evidence from newspaper reports and speaks of the centuries when there were Muslim rulers in India as 'a blood-soaked catastrophe'.

9. Nehru to Mohanlal Saxena, 10 September 1949, Nehru papers.

10. Nehru's telegram to G.B. Pant, 26 December 1949.

11. Nehru to Pant, 5 February 1950, and Pant's reply, 9 February 1950, Nehru papers.

12. A Muslim owning a hotel in Faizabad was ordered to vacate it by the local authorities and the next day some Hindus took possession of it. Later the order was withdrawn but the Muslim owner did not get back his hotel; he was allotted other premises.

13. Nehru to Pant, 17 April 1950, Nehru papers.

14. Nehru to Lal Bahadur Shastri, 9 July 1950, Nehru papers.

15. Nehru to Pant, 17 April 1950, Nehru papers.

16. 27 November 1933. *Selected Works of Jawaharlal Nehru*, first series, vol. 6, Orient Longman: Delhi, 1974, p. 164.

A Historical Overview[1]

K.N. Panikkar

During the last few years some Hindu organizations, such as the Vishwa Hindu Parishad (VHP) and the Rashtriya Swayamsevak Sangh (RSS), have claimed that the Babri Masjid of Ayodhya is located at the Ramajan-masthan, where a temple existed from the time of Maharaja Vikramaditya. The mosque, it is alleged, was built in 1528 after demolishing the temple and partially with the temple material. Referring to historical evidence to substantiate these claims, Justice Deoki Nandan, Secretary of Sri Rama Janma Bhumi Mukti Yagna Samiti, expresses this view:

> That there was an ancient temple of Maharaja Vikramaditya's time at Sri Rama Janma Bhumi *is a fact of history, which is indisputable*, although there is some controversy as to which of the Vikramadityas resurrected the place and built the magnificent temple, that it was with 84 pillars of Kasauti, a few of which still stand in the mosque-like structure at Rama Janma Bhumi and tell their own tale. That temple was desecrated and destroyed by Mir Baqi, a commander of Babar's hordes, after Babar visited to (*sic*) Ayodhya, and a mosque was sought to be raised thereat, in order to please Faqir Fazal Abbas Qalander.[2] (*emphasis mine*)

Justice Deoki Nandan is not the only one to stake a claim to history, for almost every one from the camp of the VHP, the organization spearheading the agitation for the demolition of the mosque and the construction of the temple at its site, has marshalled historical evidence to support their viewpoint.[3] In fact, the memorandum presented by the VHP to the Government of India on 6 October 1989 was largely an attempt to argue from historical evidence and hardly raised the question of faith. And it was precisely on historical grounds that the Babri Masjid Movement Coordination Committee, supported by some Muslims, sought to refute the VHP claim.[4] Evidently history and historical evidence have become crucial issues in the present controversy, although the controversy itself is decidedly political.

An inquiry into the history of Ayodhya will therefore be helpful in considering three important questions related to the dispute. First, is it possible to identify the location of Babri Masjid as the Janmasthan of Sri Rama? Second, was the Masjid constructed after demolishing an existing temple? Third, was there a popular belief either about the existence of a temple or its demolition? If so, were there attempts on the part of the Hindus of the area to reclaim the site and convert it to a temple?

Ayodhya as the Ramjanmabhumi

Whether present-day Ayodhya is the birthplace of Rama, as described by Valmiki, is not beyond doubt and uncertainty. The events of the story of Rama, originally told in the *Rama-katha* which is no longer extant, were rewritten in the form of a long epic poem, the *Ramayana*, by Valmiki. Being a poem, much of it could have been fictional, including places, characters and events.

According to tradition, Rama, the king of Ayodhya, was born in the Treta Yuga, which would make it thousands of years before the Kali Yuga—sometimes calculated to begin in 3102 BC.[5] The Ayodhya of the *Ramayana* had an advanced and relatively luxurious material life. It was an urban centre with splendid palaces and buildings and a pattern of life commensurate with developed conditions.

The description of Ayodhya in the *Ramayana* does not correspond to the archaeological evidence from this region. Two excavations were conducted in the area: one by A.K. Narain and another by B.B. Lal. Both these excavations revealed that habitation in Ayodhya begins with the early phase of the Northern Black Polished Ware culture. Lal has reported that 'the excavation revealed a fairly compact and working sequence for the antiquity of the place from its first settlement over its natural soil. This began with the use of the well-known Northern Black Polished Ware in all its shades'.[6] 'On the basis of the data available from other sites like Mathura, Shravasti, Kausambi, etc.', Lal has come to the conclusion that 'it would seem reasonable to ascribe the first occupation of the Janma Bhumi area to circa seventh century BC'.[7] The development of the area as an urban settlement came much later, certainly not earlier than the end of the sixth century or the first half of the fifth century, when several other towns emerged in the Gangetic plains.

The material conditions during the early phase of the Northern Black Polished Ware culture were fairly simple, certainly more primitive than those described in Valmiki's *Ramayana*. Since there was no settlement in the region prior to the seventh century BC and urban development had not taken place before the sixth to fifth century BC, Ayodhya as described by Valmiki could not have existed at the present day site.

The dynastic history of the post-fifth century BC is fairly well documented. Among the rulers of this period the names of Dasharatha and Rama do not figure. Therefore, if the events of the *Ramayana* are historical, they should have occurred prior to the fifth century BC. Given the archaeological evidence discussed above this is not possible either. In the event there are three possible explanations which could account for the description of Ayodhya in Valmiki's *Ramayana*. First, that the Ayodhya of Valmiki is fictional; second, that the description of Ayodhya as an urban centre was a later interpolation; and third, that the text of Valmiki belongs to a much later period.

Even after the seventh century BC Ayodhya does not seem to have had continuous occupation. After the Gupta period, of which archaeological findings are not significant at this site, there is no evidence of a settlement for many centuries. The re-occupation took place only in the eleventh century, as indicated by the floor levels of the medieval period.[8] The archaeological evidence of the region, therefore, raises serious doubts about the identity of present-day Ayodhya with the Ayodhya of Valmiki's *Ramayana*.

The literary evidence further reinforces this doubt. The major cities of Koshala, according to Buddhist sources, were Shravasti and Saketa, the latter situated on the river Saryu. Buddhist texts also refer to Ayodhya as another town located on the river Ganga, and not, as is the site of the present-day Ayodhya, on the river Saryu.[9] The association of the Buddha with Ayodhya is also on record; he had visited Ayodhya on two occasions and had preached two sermons—the *phena* and the *darukkhandha*.

Although Ayodhya was not as prominent as Saketa and Shravasti, it was not altogether insignificant, as otherwise the Andhavenhuputtas would not have attacked it.[10] But from Ayodhya they went to Dvaravati in Western India. This would suggest that Ayodhya might have been located further west than its present location. Had Saketa and Ayodhya been identical Buddhist texts would have mentioned it, as the former was an important commercial and religious centre, often visited by the Buddha.

The town of Saketa appears to have been renamed Ayodhya by a

Vikramaditya, possibly Skanda Gupta, in the late fifth century AD when he is said to have moved his residence to Saketa.[11] Thus, what may have been the fictional Ayodhya of the epic poem was identified with Saketa quite late. It is likely that in bestowing the name of Ayodhya on Saketa the Gupta king was trying to gain prestige for himself by drawing on the tradition of the Suryavamshi kings—a line to which Rama is said to have belonged. Kalidasa's identification of Saketa with Ayodhya is consistent with the possibility of Skanda Gupta taking up residence at Saketa and calling it Ayodhya.

Complementary to this is the present day local tradition about the 'rediscovery' of Ayodhya by Vikramaditya, it having been lost after the Treta Yuga which goes into mythical time. While searching for the lost Ayodhya, Vikramaditya met Prayaga, the king of *tirthas*, who knew about Ayodhya and showed him where it was. Vikramaditya marked the place but could not find it later. He then met a yogi who told him that he should let loose a cow and a calf to roam. The location of the Janmabhumi would be indicated by the flow of milk from the udders of the calf. The king followed the yogi's advice. When, at a certain point, the calf's udders began to flow, the king identified that as the site of the ancient Ayodhya.[12]

The change of name from Saketa to Ayodhya is also reflected in the account of the Chinese Buddhist pilgrims who visited India. Fa Hsien who came in the early fifth century, refers to a place Sha-ki, which has been generally identified with Saketa.[13] Hsuan Tsang who was in India in the seventh century AD describes a place called Ayodhya which was then a major centre of Buddhism with many monasteries and stupas. He refers to about three hundred monks of both the Great and Little Vehicle— namely, the Mahayana and Hinayana Buddhism—who studied in Ayodhya.[14] He also mentions that the city is said to have been the seat of government of a more or less mythical line of kings.[15]

Thus the existing archaeological and literary evidence indicate that the present-day Ayodhya was known as Saketa before the fifth century AD. The Ayodhya of Valmiki's *Ramayana*, even if it did exist, was possibly not the same as the Ayodhya that was historically identifiable later.

Ayodhya as a Religious Centre

Ayodhya has been the focal point of many religions, with various forms of religious worship flourishing concurrently. It was an important religious centre for all three religions of early India—Buddhism, Jainism and Hinduism. Among the Hindus, however, Vaishanavism and Shaivism were more popular during the early phase. Its development as a major centre of Rama worship is relatively recent.

From about the fifth century BC a fairly large Buddhist community was present in Ayodhya. Apart from several visits by the Buddha, the city is said to have had many other associations with Buddhism. Although Buddhism suffered a decline during the first millennium AD several vestiges of its early influence survived in Ayodhya as is reported by Hsuan Tsang.[16]

The Jaina tradition associates Ayodhya with the birthplace of the first and fourth Jaina Tirthankaras. One of the earliest Jaina figures found so far in excavations—a figure in grey terracotta and of the third to fourth century—is from this region. According to the Jaina canon, Ayodhya was visited by the two presumably historical founders of Jainism—Parshvanatha and Mahavira. The canon also mentions that several householders, merchants and a nobleman of Saketa were converted to Jainism by Mahavira.[17] Such associations indicate that present-day Ayodhya was also an important centre of Jaina pilgrimage.

The early places of Hindu worship in Ayodhya were either of Vaishnava or Shaiva provenance. The specific worship of Rama even as an *avatara* of Vishnu is a much later development. References to the image of Rama appear only in sixth century texts like the *Brihatsamhita* of Varahamihira.

At the present site of Ayodhya there is no evidence of the worship of Rama until the second millennium AD. Even the inscriptions from the fifth to the eighth centuries AD do not associate Ayodhya with the worship of Rama.[18] Hsuan Tsang also does not mention any place of Rama worship, even though he has recorded the existence of 'ten Deva temples' (Vaishnava temples?) in Ayodhya in the seventh century AD.[19]

Based on a detailed survey of the literary, epigraphic and archaeological sources, Hans Bakker has come to the conclusion that 'the cult in which Rama was worshipped as the supreme form and main manifestation of Vishnu did not rise into prominence before the eleventh and twelfth centuries AD'. His study also indicates that there were very few temples dedicated to Rama in the twelfth century and these were in places other than Ayodhya.[20]

The cult of Rama seems to have become popular only from the twelfth century. Yet, even in the fifteenth and sixteenth centuries Ramanandis had not settled in Ayodhya on a significant scale. It became a centre of the Rama cult, as controlled by the Ramanandi order, only from the eighteenth century.[21] Most of the Rama temples came into being only after that.

Babri Masjid: Did it Replace a Temple at the Janmasthan?

The mosque at Ayodhya, popularly known as the Babri Masjid, was constructed by Mir Baqi, a nobleman of Emperor Babur's court in 1528. The verses inscribed inside the mosque record that it was built at the command of Babur, which may or may not be true, as it was common in medieval times for the nobles to attribute all their good deeds to their masters.[22] These verses, written in Persian, read as follows:

> By the command of Emperor Babur, whose justice is an edifice reaching upto the very height of the heavens; the good hearted Mir Baqi built this alighting place of angels; *Buwad Khair Baqi* (may this goodness last forever). The year of building it was made clear likewise when I said, *Buwad Khair Baqi*. (935 A.H.)[23]

Apart from these there are three more verses inscribed on the outside of the mosque gate. They are:

> In the name of one who is the wisest of all, who is the creator of the universe, but Himself has no abode; in thanksgiving to the Prophet of all prophets in the two worlds; in celebration of the glory of Babur *qalandar* (the recluse) who has achieved great success in the world.[24]

After the battle of Panipat Babur had visited the Avadh region 'to settle the affairs of Aud',[25] although there is some doubt whether he had actually gone to Ayodhya.[26] The details of his activities during his stay in this region are not available in the *Baburnama*, as the pages covering this period are missing. Therefore, in the absence of any other contemporary accounts describing his activities during this period, the verses inscribed on the walls of the mosque form the only contemporary evidence indicating the circumstances in which the mosque was constructed. While the religious fervour of Mir Baqi is clear from these verses, particularly from the reference to the Prophet, it is important to underline the fact that there is no mention that the mosque was erected by demolishing a place of idol worship. No such reference is available in contemporary Persian chronicles also.

Given the absence of any such evidence it would be useful to refer to the attitude of Babur to other religions and places of Hindu worship. In the memoirs of Babur which contain very frank opinions on almost everything he had encountered in India, there are hardly any hostile or contemptuous references to other religious faiths. More importantly, his reign is not marked by any acts of bigotry or discriminatory treatment of his subjects on account of their religious faith. On the contrary, his general demeanour underlined his tolerance of other religions.

During his journey through different parts of the country he had come across several 'idol houses' and Hindu pilgrimage centres. He had neither tried to defile or destroy them nor interfered with the religious practices followed there: the Gur-Khattri shrine in Peshawar where Hindus offered their hair as an offering; Kachwa where a Muslim lived among Hindu yogis as their disciple and indulged in un-Islamic practices; and Gwalior where a 'lofty idol house' stood by a mosque, are examples.[27] The only exception was the destruction of Jaina idols at Urwa Valley near Gwalior, not because they were idols, but because they were 'shown naked without covering for their privates'.[28]

To a devout Muslim the construction of a mosque is an act of religious virtue; and so is the demolition of a place of idol worship. Those who undertake such religious acts receive adulatory mention in contemporary chronicles, of which examples abound in medieval India. Yet, there is no reference to the Babri Masjid in any account during the sixteenth to eighteenth centuries. A chronicler like Abdul Qadir Badauni of the sixteenth century, who wrote his books with the professed objective of demonstrating how the glory of Islam was declining during the liberal rule of Akbar, was unlikely to have remained silent about the construction of a mosque at the site of a temple of major significance, if such an event had taken place.

A medieval Persian chronicle which contains a description of Ayodhya is the *Ain-i-Akbari*, written in the seventeenth century by Abul Fazal. It refers to Ayodhya as 'one of the holiest places of antiquity' and 'the residence of Ramachandra, who in the Treta Age combined in his person both the spiritual supremacy and the kingly office'.[29] Abul Fazal does not mention the existence of a temple dedicated to a person with spiritual and temporal power and its replacement by a mosque. Nor does he record any religious strife in the area.

If Persian chronicles of this period do not refer to the destruction of a temple at Ayodhya, the texts by Hindus are also silent about it. The most significant silence is that of Goswami Tulsidas, a great devotee of Rama and author of the *Ramacharitamanas*. Judging from his description of Ayodhya, an intimate knowledge of the area cannot be doubted. Yet he does not mention the existence of a temple at the Ramajanmasthan and its destruction by Muslims. Since he was greatly concerned with the rise of the *mlecchas* he could not have overlooked it.

Tulsidas' text is not an isolated example. A eleventh century inscription of a Gahadvala ruler records his pilgrimage to Ayodhya and lists the sites at which he performed rituals and offered worship. Ramjanmabhumi is not one of them.[30] Also in a large number of Sanskrit texts of this period such as those of Lakshmidhara, Mitra Mishra, Jinaprabhasuri or the Bhushundi *Ramayana* and the Puranas, which refer to major places of pilgrimage, including Ayodhya, there is no mention of the Ramjanmabhumi. The most important pilgrimage spot at Ayodhya was the Gopratara Tirtha. It appears that the *Ayodhya Mahatmya* (fourteenth to sixteenth centuries) was the first text which demarcated the Janmasthan and indicated it as an important place of pilgrimage. Yet, even in this text, the detailed instructions to pilgrims regarding worship and offerings at the Janmasthan do not have any reference to a temple.[31]

That the Babri Masjid was constructed at the site of a temple is a relatively recent belief. It had its origin in the nineteenth century reconstruction of the history of the subcontinent by the colonial rulers. In this reconstruction the history of religious communities and their mutual antagonism held centre stage. The history of Faizabad was no exception.

The first official publication dealing with the history of the region was *A Historical Sketch of Tahsil Fyzabad, Zilla Fyzabad* by P. Carnegy in 1870. Carnegy asserted, on the basis of 'locally affirmed' information, that three temples in Ayodhya were destroyed and mosques were constructed at their sites by the Mughals, 'according to the well-known Mahomedan principle of enforcing their religion on all those whom they conquered'.[32] Carnegy's account was reproduced almost verbatim by H.R. Neville in the *Gazetteer of Faizabad* published in 1905.[33] Neither Carnegy nor Neville had anything but 'local affirmation' and their belief in the well-known 'Mahomedan principle' to support their contention. However, their opinion seems to have become an accepted fact. A.S. Beveridge most possibly relied on these accounts to assert that 'the substitution of a temple by a mosque' was done by Babur, even if there was no mention of it in the *Baburnama* which she translated into English. She suggests that Babur being a Muslim, and 'inspired by the dignity and sanctity of the ancient Hindu shrine' would have displaced 'at least in part' the temple to erect the mosque. Her logic is a good example of the colonial view of Indian history '. . . like the obedient follower of Muhammad he was in intolerance of another Faith, (thus he) would regard the substitution of a temple by a mosque as dutiful and worthy'.[34] Beveridge, like the British officials earlier, appears to base her view on the religious attitudes of the Muslims. She does not provide any evidence to support her view. It is even doubtful that she had visited Ayodhya, for she mentions that the Persian verses from the walls of the mosque were obtained through the courtesy of local officials.[35] This was an unfortunate slip, particularly by an erudite scholar like Beveridge, since her opinion has come to be accepted rather uncritically. Modern researchers tend to lean heavily on her authority and Hindu communal organizations use her authority to substantiate their viewpoint.

For instance, Hans Bakker, contrary to the evidence in the early part of his excellently researched work, accepts Beveridge's authority to assert that the 'temple was destroyed by the first Mogul prince Babar in AD 1528 and replaced by a mosque which still exists'.[36] Van der Veer, on the other hand, draws upon local belief. He not only affirms the view, but also refers to the miracles which followed the destruction of the temple, 'Mir Baqi destroyed the temple, but his efforts to build a mosque failed because each night everything that had been built during the day fell down again. This continued until Mir Baqi grew desperate and proposed to give up. Then the Faqir Khwaja dreamt that the mosque should not be built right over the *garbha* (sanctum) of the temple, but somewhat behind it. Thus the mosque was built in such a way that the *garbha* of the temple remained open to the Hindus for centuries in the form of a pit into which they could throw flowers.'[37]

Religious Conflict and Local Tradition

In all likelihood the local tradition, to which British officials and modern scholars refer, came to be accepted only in the second half of the nineteenth century. It was not unrelated to the Hindu–Muslim strife of 1855 over the Hanumangarhi temple, situated near the Babri Masjid.

At the time of the Muslim conquest, Ayodhya, according to local tradition, was 'little other than a wilderness', with very few devotees attached to Hindu shrines.[38] By the middle of the nineteenth century it had become a popular centre of Rama worship. An important factor facilitating this transformation was the liberal religious atmosphere that prevailed in Avadh during the Nawabi rule. The Nawab's attitude, however, had a political dimension. During the period of political anomie in the eighteenth century, Avadh had broken away from the Mughal empire and was struggling to consolidate its power in a region with a large Hindu population. The Nawabi rule, therefore, sought the collaboration of Hindus, particularly the Kayasthas and Rajput *zamindars* both in administra-

tion and military affairs.[39] That the Nawabs and their officials contributed
to the development of Hindu places of worship is, therefore, not surprising; it was, in fact, integral to the manner in which power was exercised
in Avadh. Not only did the Hindu officials build and support temples but
Muslim officials also patronized Hindu institutions and priests.[40]

By the middle of the nineteenth century a large number of devotees and
ascetics had congregated at Ayodhya. The main centre of this assemblage
was the temple of Hanumangarhi, over which a dispute developed into an
armed conflict between the Hindus and Muslims in 1855. The emergence
of Ayodhya as a prominent place of Hindu worship under the liberal Shia
rulers, which enraged certain orthodox sections of the Muslims, was the
context of the dispute.

The dispute over the Hanumangarhi temple has a close parallel with
the present-day dispute over the Babri Masjid. A group of orthodox Sunni
Muslims, under the leadership of Shah Gulam Hussain, claimed that the
temple of Hanumangarhi had supplanted a mosque which existed there
earlier.[41] In July 1855 Gulam Hussain led a party of his followers,
numbering about 500, to oust the Hindus from the temple. The Bairagis,
the occupants of the temple, had the support of about 8,000 people, among
whom were some large landholders and their retainers from the neighbouring countryside. In the ensuing conflict a large number of Muslims
were 'soon laid prostrate, the remainder returned and gained the Masjid
(Babri Masjid) where they were soon surrounded and cut to pieces'.
Although the Bairagis defeated the Muslims and entered the mosque, they
did not occupy it; they 'returned to the Ghurrie and other abodes'.[42]

The defeat of Gulam Hussain and his followers at the hands of the
Hindu Bairagis created considerable consternation among the Muslims
of Avadh, both Sunni and Shia. Several *fatwas* were issued against the
Hindus and the Nawab was urged to punish the 'wickedness' and
'enormities' of the infidels.[43] As further breach of peace appeared imminent, the Nawab appointed a committee of inquiry, consisting of a
Muslim, a Hindu and a representative of the British, in order to defuse the
situation. After very detailed investigations the committee came to the
conclusion that there was no masjid at the Hanumangarhi, at least in the
past twenty-five to thirty years, and most probably there never had been
one.[44] The Muslims resented this decision and Maulvi Amir Ali
Amethavi started organizing a movement to reclaim the masjid. The
Nawab toyed with the idea of constructing a mosque adjacent to the
temple to assuage the feelings of the Muslims, but this was strongly
opposed by the Hindus. A serious communal clash appeared to be brew-

ing, but was averted by the timely and decisive intervention of the British Resident.[45]

The Hanumangarhi episode of 1855 has been mistaken by many as a dispute over the Babri mosque and Ramajanmasthan. Surprisingly, Michael Fisher who has consulted the voluminous records of the British Government regarding the dispute of 1855 mistook the Hanumangarhi temple for that of the Janmasthan.[46] Many others, intentionally or unintentionally, have maintained this confusion.[47] Some of them have used this event to argue that the Hindus claimed the Babri Masjid as the Janmasthan for a long time. It is needless to emphasize that this is a misreading of the events of 1855—the dispute was about the Hanumangarhi temple and not about the Babri Masjid. [48] Summing up the dispute a British official wrote:

> . . . the cause of misunderstanding between the two sects was, that the Shah and his followers pretended that a masjid formerly existed in the immediate vicinity of Hanumangarhi and that the Byragie Fakirs have either destroyed it, or by defacing and building upon it have converted it into a part and portion of their own buildings, whilst the Byragies strenuously deny the existence of any such masjid either now or in preceding years.[49]

An important dimension of the Hanumangarhi episode is that it indicated the absence at that time of any linkage between the Babri Masjid and the Janmasthan in Hindu consciousness. Although the Bairagis captured the masjid in which the Muslims had taken shelter they did not occupy it or advance a claim to it. Instead they retreated to the Hanumangarhi almost instantaneously. It is also important that during the course of the inquiry no Hindu had mentioned the earlier existence of a temple at the site of the Masjid, even as a counter to the Muslim claims to the Hanumangarhi temple. The local tradition about the Janmasthan temple to which the British officials have referred, does not appear to be current in 1855.

The Hanumangarhi episode, however, contributed to the construction and dissemination of such a tradition. How it actually came into being is not certain, but it originated, most probably, as an attempt to checkmate the Muslim claims on the Hanumangarhi temple. The Mahant of Hanumangarhi was quick to realize the implication of the proceedings initiated by Gulam Hussain and Amir Ali. The proposal of the Nawab to build a mosque adjoining the temple was quite alarming to him.[50] He apprehended that the decision of the Government need not necessarily go in favour of the Hindus if the agitation were to be renewed in future. A counter-claim on the areas controlled by the Muslims could be an effective move to foil the designs of orthodox Muslims to gain possession of the temple. The demand for the Janmasthan thus originated as a defensive ploy.

Soon after the Revolt of 1857 the Mahant took over a part of the Babri Masjid compound and constructed a *chabutra* (raised platform). This attempt of the Mahant was opposed by the local Muslims. On 30 November 1858 Maulvi Muhammad Asghar, *khatib* and *muazzin* of Babri Masjid, submitted a petition to the magistrate complaining that the Bairagis had built a *chabutra* close to the mosque and that they had written 'Rama, Rama' on the walls of the mosque. Similar complaints were made in 1860, 1877, 1883 and 1884.[51] In 1885 the Mahant filed a suit to gain legal title to the land and for permission to construct a temple on the *chabutra*. His suit and appeals were dismissed. His claim for the proprietorship of the land in the compound of the masjid was also dismissed by the judicial commissioner.[52] Yet the idea that the masjid was constructed at a holy place of the Hindus and that it was a disputed area was firmly established.[53]

A local tradition which has developed rather recently is now sought to be made into a matter of national faith. It is argued that the site of the Babri Masjid being the Janmabhumi of Rama is a matter of faith.[54] Just as the Christians believe that Jesus Christ was the Son of God and the Muslims believe that Mohammad was the Prophet of Allah, the Hindus believe that Rama was the *avatara* of Vishnu. These are matters of faith. But not so the birth of Mohammad at Mecca or of Rama at Ayodhya. They are questions of fact. The known history of Ayodhya does not indicate that what is claimed as the Janmasthan was in fact the birthplace of Rama or that a temple existed at the site of the Babri Mosque.

Notes

1. In preparing this essay I have drawn upon the notes provided by my colleagues at the Centre for Historical Studies: Romila Thapar, Harbans Mukhia, Muzaffar Alam and Neeladri Bhattacharya. I am thankful to them for their help. I would also like to thank my other colleagues at the Centre who had earlier published a pamphlet entitled, *The Political Abuse of History: Babri Masjid–Rama Janma Bhumi Dispute* from which I have borrowed facts and arguments.

2. Justice Deoki Nandan, *Sri Rama Janma Bhumi: A Historical and Legal*

Perspective, Lucknow, n.d., p. 2.

3. See, for instance, S.P. Gupta, 'Ram Janmabhumi Controversy: What History and Archaeology Say', *Organiser*, Republic Day Issue, 1990; 'Sri Rama Janmabhoomi or Babri Masjid', *Organiser*, 29 March 1987; Dr Harish Narain, 'Muslim Testimony', *Indian Express*, 26 Feb 1990.

4. Asghar Ali Engineer (ed.), *Babri Masjid–Ramjanma Bhoomi Controversy*, Delhi, 1990, pp. 218–29.

5. According to Aihole inscription. *Epigraphia Indica*, vol. VI, 1900–1, New Delhi, 1981, p. 1ff.

6. *Indian Archaeology—A Review*, 1976–77, p. 52.

7. ibid.

8. ibid., p. 53. S.P. Gupta claims in newspaper articles that he was present when a part of the site referred to as the Ramjanmabhumi was being excavated. He maintains that he saw the pillar-bases of foundation pillars, which would have been part of the architecture of the temple and would date to approximately the eleventh century AD. It is curious, however, that such important evidence, if it actually existed, is not mentioned in the excavation reports published by the director of the excavation, Prof. B.B. Lal, in *Indian Archaeology —A Review*. The excavator states that floor levels of the medieval period were found but makes no reference to pillar-bases. It is unlikely that he would have omitted such important evidence.

As for the pillars incorporated into the mosque, they do not in themselves indicate the presence of a temple of Rama. There is no certainty either that they belong to the site itself and were not brought there from the neighbourhood. There were, as reported by British officials in the nineteenth century, similar pillars lying scattered in the region.

9. B.C. Law, *Geography of Early Buddhism*, London, 1932, pp. 5 and 23; G.P. Malalasekera, *Dictionary of Pali Proper Names*, vol. I, London, 1960, p. 165.

10. *Ghata Jataka*, no. 454, book 10, 82, vol. IV, p. 53.

11. S.R. Goyal, *A History of Imperial Guptas*, Allahabad, 1967, pp. 211 and 215.

12. Peter Van Der Veer, *Gods on Earth*, London, 1988, p. 20.

13. J. Legge, *The Travels of Fa Hien*, Oxford, 1886, p. 54.

14. Hans Bakker, *Ayodhya*, Grasingen, 1986, p. 38.

15. T. Walters, *On Yuan Chwang's Travels in India*, London, 1904, p. 354.

16. Hans Bakker, op. cit., p. 38.

17. ibid.

18. *Epigraphia Indica*, vol.2, p.344; vol.15, pp. 115 and 142–44; vol. I, p. 15, refers to an Ayodhya which, it has been suggested, was a village in Uttara Kashi.

19. Hans Bakker, op.cit., p. 42.

20. ibid., pp. 64–65.

21. Peter Van Der Veer, op.cit., p. 11.

22. There is no other contemporary evidence to suggest that Babur had ordered the construction of the mosque. While *farmans* exist for the

construction of other buildings by Babur, for this mosque no *farman* was issued.

23. A.S. Beveridge (trans.), *Baburnama*,1922, Reprint, Delhi, 1970, II, pp. LXXVII.

24. A.S. Beveridge, who has appended these verses to her translation states as follows, 'Thanks to the kind response made by the Deputy Commissioner of Fyzabad to my husband's inquiry about two inscriptions mentioned by several gazetteers as still existing on "Babur's mosque" in Oudh, I am able to quote copies of both.' *Baburnama,* p. 656, p.n.1.

25. *Baburnama*, p. 602.

26. For this argument see Sushil Srivastava, 'Ayodhya Controversy: Where Lies the Truth', Asghar Ali Engineer, op.cit., pp. 29–33.

27. *Baburnama,* pp. 230, 394 and 613. Also see Mohibbul Hasan, *Babar: Founder of the Mughal Empire in India*, Delhi, 1985, pp. 190–91.

28. *Baburnama*, pp. 611–12.

29. Abul Fazal, *Ain-i-Akbari*, Ii. Translated into English by H.S. Jarrett, Reprint, Delhi, 1978, p. 182.

30. Hans Bakker, op.cit., p. 51.

31. ibid., pp. 125–29. It has been argued that pillar-bases found in the excavations at Ayodhya are proof of the existence of a temple. This question needs to be looked at more closely. In a recent article in the RSS magazine, *Manthan*, the Director of the Ramayana Archaeology project, Prof. B.B. Lal, has made the following statement:

> In the Janmabhumi area, the uppermost levels of a trench that lay immediately to the south of the Babri Masjid brought to light a series of brick-built bases which evidently carried pillars thereon. In the construction of the Babri Masjid a few stone pillars had been used, which may have come from this preceding structure. However in order to confirm this and to obtain a full plan and other details of this earlier structure, it would be necessary to carry out further excavation in the area.

This statement differs from his official reports on his excavations of this site published in the journal of the Archaeological Survey of India (*Indian Archaeology–A Review*, 1976–77, 1979–80) and his many papers on the archaeology of Ayodhya, in which he nowhere mentions such pillar-bases and in fact says that nothing of significance was found at the Janmabhumi site at Ayodhya from the Gupta period upto the medieval floor levels. Was the evidence regarding pillar-bases deliberately concealed at that time or has it now been thought up to suit the theories of the RSS?

The above statement is curious because it contradicts itself. If the pillar-bases were found at the uppermost level they should be quite recent. How then could they have been the bases for a pre-sixteenth century temple? Professor Lal does not seem to want to commit himself to any date for the so-called pillar-bases. Nor does he tell us why he regards them as pillar-bases. It is unlikely that brick-built pillar-bases would be used for supporting heavy stone columns. It would have been constructionally more logical to use stone pillar-bases. The present bases, if that is what they are, could equally well have been the bases of brick arches or some other brick structure, possibly a hall or rooms adjoining the site of the mosque. The use of brick in the medieval period was fairly common. Even if pillar-bases were to be found indicating the existence of a structure preceding the mosque, a co-relation between that structure and the pillars in the mosque is not necessarily established nor need the preceding structure necessarily be regarded as a temple.

It is interesting that Martin writing about the Janmabhumi and the Babri Masjid at Ayodhya in 1838 has this to say:

> It is possible that these pillars have belonged to a temple built by Vikrama; but I think the existence of such temples doubtful; and, if they did not exist, it is probable that the pillars were taken from the ruins of the palace. They are only six feet high. There is a Sivalinga called Nageshwara, which is called on by all the pilgrims to witness their faith, when they have performed the usual ceremonies; and this is supposed to be the oldest image of this place.

Montgomery Martin, *History, Antiquities, Topography and Statistics of Eastern India*, vols. I–III, London, 1838, vol. II, pp. 336–37.

32. P. Carnegy, *A Historical Sketch of Tahsil Fyzabad Zillah Fyzabad*, Lucknow, 1870, p. 21.

33. H.R. Neville, *Fyzabad—A Gazetteer*, Allahabad, 1905, pp. 173–74.

34. *Baburnama*, Appendix, LXXVII.

35. ibid.

36. Hans Bakker, op.cit., p. 44.

37. Peter Van Der Veer, op.cit., p. 21.

38. P. Carnegy, op.cit., p. 21.

39. Muzaffar Alam, *The Crisis of Empire in Mughal North India: Awadh and the Punjab*, Delhi, 1986, pp. 212–42; Michael H. Fisher, *A Clash of Cultures: Awadh, The British, and the Mughals*, Delhi, 1987.

40. ibid.

41. J.R.I. Cole, *Roots of North Indian Shiism in Iran and Iraq*, Delhi, 1989, p. 244.

42. *Foreign Political Consultation*, no. 34, 28 December 1855.

43. Michael H. Fisher, op.cit., pp. 229–30.

44. *Foreign Political Consultation*, no. 356, 28 December 1855.

45. J.R.I. Cole, op.cit., pp. 244–49.

46. Michael H. Fisher, op.cit., p. 227.

47. Justice Deoki Nandan, op.cit., p. 3; Rajendra Prasad Jaina, op.cit. A good account of the incident is available in G.D. Bhatnagar, *Awadh Under Wajid Ali Shah*, Varanasi, 1968, pp. 117–40.

48. Apart from the British records the details of this event are available in Urdu and Persian accounts which also make it clear that the dispute was over the Hanumangarhi temple and not about the Babri Masjid. See Kamal-ud-din Haider, *Qaisar-ut-Tawarikh*, vol. II, Lucknow, 1879; and Saiyed Ilahi Baksh al-Husaini, *Kurshid-i-Jahan Nama*, Persian, Ms. Buhar 102,

National Library, Calcutta.

49. *Foreign Political Consultation,* no. 356, 28 Dec. 1955.

50. *Foreign Political Consultation,* no. 360, 28 Dec. 1955.

51. 'Papers Relating to the Dispute About the Ramchabootra', *Records of the Faizabad Collectorate* (copies), Institute of Objective Studies, Jamia Nagar.

52. S.K. Tripathi, 'One Hundred Years of Litigation', Asghar Ali Engineer (ed.), op.cit., pp. 17–19.

53. Joseph Tieffenthaler who toured Ayodhya between 1766 and 1771 has stated that the Emperor Aurangzeb destroyed the fortress called the Ramakota, and built at the same place a Mohammedan temple with three domes. Others say that it has been built by Babur. Tieffenthaler has obviously confused the mosque built by Aurangzeb at the east of the Svargadvara with the Babri mosque. In this context it is necessary to make a distinction between the Janmasthan and Janmabhumi (location of birth and place of birth). For Tieffenthaler's account see Abhas Kumar Chatterjee, 'Ram Janmabhumi: More Evidence', *Indian Express*, 26 March 1990.

54. 'In religion, it is a matter of faith and not of proof.... So by faith alone Christians embrace Jesus Christ to be the Son of God, by faith and faith alone Muslims believe Muhammad to be the Prophet of Allah, and by faith and faith alone Hindus believe Ramjanmabhumi in Ayodhya to be the birthplace of Lord Rama,' K.S. Lal, 'Ramjanmabhumi—Some Issues', *Organiser*, October 1989.

How the British Saw the Issue

Sushil Srivastava

The city of Ayodhya stands on the right bank of the river Ghagra, or Saryu, as it is called within the sacred precincts, on latitude 26° 48' north and longitude 82° 13' east, at a distance of about ten kilometres from the city of Faizabad. According to the traditions of the orthodox Hindus, it was founded for additional security not on the transitory earth but on the chariot wheel of the Great Creator himself.[1]

Ayodhya is pre-eminently a city of temples but all the places of worship there are not connected with the Hindu religion. In fact, till the close of the nineteenth century there were six Jaina temples, some mosques and tombs and several Hindu temples in the city.[2] A. Cunningham, Archaeological Surveyor to the Government of India, was convinced that some important Buddhist traces were hidden under the great mounds in Ayodhya.[3] The city had always had a cosmopolitan attitude towards religion and culture. Remnants of Buddhism, Jainism, Brahminism–Hinduism and Islam can still be found in Ayodhya. It is certain that in this city several religions have grown and prospered either at different or simultaneous periods of time in the past.

It is therefore surprising that some British officials insist on referring to Ayodhya as the Hindu city.[4] Montgomery Martin, who was assigned the task of compiling historical and topographical data on eastern India by the English East India Company, observed that Ayodhya was a Hindu city and the adjacent Faizabad was a Muhammadan city.[5] He published his report in 1838. Martin provides us information regarding several cities and districts adjoining Gorakhpur, but he does not distinguish the other cities by the nomenclature 'Hindu' and 'Muhammadan'. He describes the cities of Prayag (Allahabad), Kasi (Varanasi), Haridwar (Hardwar), Dadri or Dardara Kshatra and the district of Benares, but does not call them Hindu cities.[6]

The attempt to classify Ayodhya in religious terms could not have been made according to the religious distribution of the local population. In both Ayodhya and Faizabad, the Hindus were in majority. In 1869, when the First Census Report was compiled, it was found that in Ayodhya the Hindus constituted 66.4 per cent of the total population and in Faizabad they numbered a little over sixty per cent of the total population.[7] It must be added that in both cities there was a complete absence of the Wahabi Muslims, and the Shia Muslims were more in number than the Sunni Muslims. In Faizabad the Shias were 67.4 per cent of the total number of Muslims and in Ayodhya they were 64.7 per cent of the Muslim population. British officials apparently justified the demarcation of the cities on the basis of religion because of local political developments. Patrick Carnegy wrote that when the seat of government was shifted by Nawab Safdarjang from Ayodhya to Faizabad in AD 1740 Ayodhya started growing as a Hindu city.[8] He argued that in the absence of the Muslim court from Ayodhya, Hindu elements now had the freedom to involve themselves in religious activities. However, Carnegy and other British officers did not extend this theory beyond Ayodhya. In AD 1775 Nawab Asaf-ud-daulah shifted the capital of his kingdom from Faizabad to Lucknow but this did not enable Faizabad to grow as a Hindu city. In 1877 W.C. Benet gave another justification for classifying Ayodhya as a Hindu city. He wrote:

> About a hundred and fifty years ago there was a revival. Whether a national feeling was aroused by the tyranny of Aurangzeb, or by the success of the Marathas, or by the translation into popular language of the *Ramayana*, somehow or other Ayodhya became again esteemed as a holy place; it grew in favour each year, and now in all India, perhaps except the Jaggannath festival and that at Hardwar, there is none to equal the Ramnaumi celebration at Ayodhya.[9]

British observers of Ayodhya in the nineteenth century generally agree that the Hindu revival of Ayodhya was a phenomenon of modern times.[10] P. Carnegy writes that in AD 1720 when Nawab Saadat Khan was appointed the Mughal Viceroy in Avadh, Hindu activity in the city gained ground. It seems he intended to differentiate the attitudes of the Shia and the Sunni Muslim governors towards their Hindu subjects. He probably wanted to justify the establishment of the Ramanandi *akharas* (sects) after that time.[11] He added that when the second Nawab Safdarjang shifted the seat of government from Ayodhya to Faizabad, Raja Naval Rai, a minister at the court of the Nawab, encouraged the construction of Hindu temples in Ayodhya.[12]

Raja Naval Rai was a Hindu Kayastha and was said to have been a staunch devotee of Shri Rama. Local traditions relate that Raja Naval Rai supported and extended Vaishnava activity in Ayodhya. However, it is clear from a reading of the *Tarikh Farah Baksh* that in number the Vaishnava Hindus were very small in comparison to the Shaiva Hindus in Ayodhya. By 1869 the Vaishnavas were only forty-four per cent of the total Hindu population in Ayodhya.[13] We can assume that their number must have been less in the beginning of the nineteenth century. Raja Naval Rai is credited with having constructed some temples along the Svargadwar. It is said that because of his efforts several temples and settlements of sadhus and people learned in the Shastras came up. Carnegy provides us a list of 209 such institutions and temples in Ayodhya in 1870.[14]

The British, who have written the history of the province of Avadh, and with it the city of Ayodhya, unanimously agree that in the absence of reliable historical evidence it is difficult to relate with certainty the developments in the city until the tenth century AD. The developments in Ayodhya after the advent of the Turks are inferred from the general contemporary account of developments in North India. H.C. Irwin, lamenting the dearth of evidence, wrote:

> It is a somewhat humiliating confession, but it is probably a true one, that of the history of Oudh, from the time of Syed Salar's expedition to the appointment of Saadat Khan as Subahdar of the province in AD 1720, a period of nearly seven hundred years, we have next to no real information. Written Hindu records there are almost none, and from Muhammadan chronicles little can be gleaned beyond such unfruitful items as this governor was suspended by that, or that the infidels of such a place revolted, and were put down with great slaughter. Local Hindu traditions there are in abundance, but it seems almost impossible to connect them with any degree of certainty with such facts as are to be gathered from the Muhammadan historians.[16]

The British writers on Ayodhya begin by recounting the state of affairs in Ayodhya after the advent of the Turks in Avadh. On the basis of *Mirat-i-Masudi* they accept that Syed Salar Masud led an expedition into Avadh in AD 1030. He was successful in controlling the area and was stationed in Bahraich, a place north of Ayodhya. After him Turkish influence in the area waned but rose again in the twelfth century. In AD 1194 an expedition was led by Shahab-ud-din Ghori and Avadh was conquered. Avadh became a province of the Sultanate in Delhi and Nasir-ud-din Mahmud was appointed its governor. Between AD 1226 and 1720, the province of Avadh with its capital in Ayodhya (except for a few years) remained an important part of the empire in Delhi. After AD 1720 the history of Ayodhya has been inferred from the memoirs of Mohammad Faiz Baksh.[17]

Official British writing on Ayodhya asserts that before the annexation of the kingdom of Avadh on 13 February 1856, an incident of great importance took place in Ayodhya. W.H. Sleeman, who was assigned the task of preparing a report on the state of affairs in Avadh, wrote that Hindus and Muslims of Ayodhya fought against each other and the troops of the Nawab did not interfere.[18] This prompted him to comment that in Avadh during the period of the Nawabs there was no security to life and the law and order machinery had completely collapsed. Sleeman dates this incident as having occurred in 1853. He submitted his report in 1855. However, both Carnegy and Benet wrote that the great Hindu–Muslim conflict in Ayodhya took place in 1855. Benet writes:

> In 1855, when a great rupture took place between the Hindus and Muhammadans, the former occupied the Hanuman Garhi in force, while the Musalmans took possession of the Janamasthan. The Muhammadans on that occasion actually charged up the steps of the Hanuman Garhi, but were driven back with considerable loss. The Hindus then followed up this success, and at the third attempt took the Janamasthan, at the gate of which seventy-five Muhammadans were buried in the martyrs' grave (Ganj-i-Shahidan).[19]

At another place in the *Gazetteer*, Benet refers again to the same incident. 'The last occasion, and almost the only one in modern times, when the Hindus ventured to shed the blood of their Moslem masters in a religious war, was in defence of Hanuman,'[20] wrote Carnegy and Benet before 1880. In 1905, H.R. Neville also reported the incident. He observed that 'the desecration of the sacred spots of the Hindus by the Muslim rulers caused great bitterness between Hindus and Musalmans'. He added, 'On many occasions the feeling led to bloodshed and in 1855 an open fight occurred, the Musalmans occupied the Janamasthan in force and thence making a desperate assault on the Hanuman Garhi. They charged up the steps of the temple, but were driven back with considerable loss. The Hindus then made a counter attack and stormed the Janamasthan, at the gate of which seventy-five Musalmans were buried, the spot being known as the Ganj Shahidan or the martyrs' resting place.'[21]

These accounts of the British officials, describing the religious conflict in Ayodhya before the annexation of Avadh, reflect the changing attitude of the British towards the religious issue. Sleeman gives us the correct year of the beginning of the conflict. Sleeman's basic intention was to highlight the collapse of the law and order machinery in Avadh during the rule of the Nawabs. British officers who wrote after the annexation were apparently more concerned to show that the Hindus entered the conflict to defend their places of worship. They do not relate the happenings between 1853 and 1858. In fact, Benet is determined to show that the reaction of the Hindus was in the defence of their god Hanuman. The British writers had not adopted an impartial position in the recounting of the events in Ayodhya. They insisted on calling the Babri Masjid the Janmasthan.

The actual facts regarding the religious conflict in Ayodhya in the pre-annexation days were made public in 1902.[22] Between 1865 and 1900 some Indians published their views on the Babri Masjid issue and some of them even recounted the events of the years 1853 and 1855.[23] For instance, the account of the events provided by H.J. Boas which was confirmed by Rai Mahadeo Bali of Rampur in Pargana Daryabad.[24] The incident occurred in 1853 and the cause of the occurrence was one of the numerous disputes that have sprung up from time to time between the Hindu priests and the Muslims of Ayodhya 'with regard to the ground on which formerly stood the Janamasthan temple'. It was said that the temple had been destroyed by Babur and replaced by a mosque. The ground had become peculiarly sacred to the Hindus and therefore was seized by the Bairagis (Hindu ascetics) and others. This action became 'a fertile source of friction'. The account goes on to relate that one of the Mahants (priests) was expelled by his brethren, and in revenge, he proceeded to Lucknow and became a Muslim. He spread the news that the Hindus had destroyed the mosque. The Mahant came in contact with Maulvi Amir Ali, a resident of Amethi and a well-known fakir.

Maulvi Amir Ali was a descendant of the famous Sufi saint, Sheikh Bandagi Mian.[25] The saint was stationed in Amethi and his fame had reached the Mughal emperor Akbar.[26] He had visited the saint in Amethi while on his way from Ayodhya. Akbar was quite impressed by Bandagi Mian and had granted him a few rent-free villages.

Maulvi Amir Ali was in Lucknow when the ousted Mahant was spreading the tale that the mosque in Ayodhya had been destroyed. Amir Ali had not been able to seek an audience with Nawab Wajid Ali Shah[27] and it is probable that he exploited the news of the destruction of the mosque for his advantage. In Lucknow, he immediately proclaimed a *jehad* (holy war) in the city. Nawab Wajid Ali Shah was disturbed to hear about the *jehad* to liberate the mosque. He immediately sent orders to Faizabad to enquire into the matter but the mosque was not released by the Bairagis.[28]

The Maulvi was adamant on continuing the war and therefore returned to his native place, Amethi. Here he amassed a large and well-armed force of Muslims. When the Nawab heard of this development, he ordered Badrir-ud-daulah of Amethi to summon the Maulvi to Lucknow. In the meantime the Nawab asked the people not to use force in the religious conflict and ordered that the mosque in question be restored.[29] Maulvi Amir Ali was not impressed by the actions of the Nawab and therefore decided to march with his force to Bansa, a village about three miles to the north of Safdarjung in the district of Bara Banki. In Bansa several more men joined Amir Ali. This time a large number of people from the lower castes among the Hindus and Muslims also joined the forces of the Maulvi.[30]

Nawab Wajid Ali Shah was quite disturbed by the turn of events. He realized the futility of his orders and, therefore, approached the British Resident in Lucknow to help resolve the situation in Ayodhya. Nawab Wajid Ali Shah now had adopted the right course to resolve the crisis, for the *mahal* of Haveli Avadh, which included Ayodhya, had been put under the care of the British Resident by the terms of the agreement of 1816.[31] (In the Treaty of 1816 between the Bahu Begam and the British Resident in the Kingdom of Avadh, the territories of Haveli Avadh were placed under the direct administration of the Resident, therefore it was necessary to ask for the Resident's interference in any law and order problem that arose in the area of Ayodhya.)

It is clear that when Nawab Wajid Ali Shah realized the implications of the agreement he 'left it to the Resident to put a stop to the movement of the Moulvi in any way he (the Resident) could'.[32] But the British Resident, on instructions from his superiors in Calcutta, refused to take any action and allowed the situation to take its course.

The Nawab was concerned about these developments and decided to intervene directly. He ordered the Nazim (the administrative and revenue official of the State) of Faizabad to despatch a strong force to stop the

Maulvi. The Nasim went to Bansa and met Amir Ali who said that he would give up the march if the mosque at Hanumangarhi was restored to the Muslims. Maulvi Amir Ali stayed in Bansa for a month, and when he heard that nothing had been done regarding the restoration of the Hanumangarhi mosque he marched ahead to Daryabad and remained there for twenty days. Nawab Wajid Ali Shah immediately ordered four *muftis* (divisions) to move to Daryabad 'to preach obedience to the Maulvi and his forces'.[33] As a result of this action the contingent of Maulvi Amir Ali was reduced by half. The remainder, however, stood by their leader and persisted in their intention of marching to Ayodhya and destroying the Hanumangarhi.

The Nawab had despatched his soldiers under the command of Colonel Barlow, who commanded the First Regiment of the Avadh Irregular Infantry.[34] Colonel Barlow was ordered to arrest the progress of the Maulvi and his forces. In this mission the Colonel was assisted by Rai Abhairam Bali of Rampur. Colonel Barlow and his forces met the Maulvi's army at Shujagunj, a large market on the old high road, and a hamlet of Phugauli, close to Hayatnagar. The insurgent force was said to have numbered about 2,000 men and the Nawab's troops consisted of one regiment and two guns. On coming up with the rebels, Colonel Barlow gave orders to fire and the Maulvi's forces started retreating. The encounter was said to have been a desperate one, and fierce hand-to-hand combat took place for three hours. The day was decided by flanking movements on the part of Colonel Barlow; the rebels were surrounded by Sher Bahadur Singh of Kamiar, Thakur Singh and the sepoys of Rai Abhairam Bali. The insurgents broke and fled, but not before a large number of them were killed. Their estimated loss was between 120 to 700 men, while the First Infantry was almost destroyed. Maulvi Amir Ali was killed in the act of prayer and his head was sent to the Nawab in Lucknow.[35] It is presumed that the defeat of the Maulvi was completed by 1855.[36]

For several people in Rudauli, a place in Bara Banki district, the death of the Maulvi apparently meant that he had attained martyrdom. His headless body was buried at Rahimgunj in Rudauli, and from 1856 an annual fair was held there. It started on 27(Safar) February and lasted for three days.[37] However, by 1905 the memory of the Maulvi probably faded and the fair came to an end.[38]

Thereafter, an attempt was made to resolve the religious situation in Ayodhya.[39] The elders of both the communities worked out a compromise by which the Hindus were to offer prayers at the *chabutra* outside the mosque in the east, and the Muslims were to pray inside the Babri Masjid. Benet observed, 'It is said that up to that time (before the Revolt of 1857) the Hindus and the Muhammadans alike used to worship in the mosque–temple.'[40] The situation changed after 1859. The Government contended that as the question of the Babri Masjid could lead to an escalation of conflict between the Hindus and the Muslims, it was necessary to adopt preventive measures. As such a fence was erected to physically separate the places of worship of the Hindus and the Muslims. In the new set-up the Hindus were to make their offerings at the raised platform outside the mosque in the east. The Hindus would enter from the east gate and were not allowed access into the mosque. The Muslims were to pray inside the mosque and their entry was to be from the north gate. The Muslims were not to enter from the east.[41]

The attempt of the Government to separate the places of worship of the Hindus and Muslims by the erection of a fence did not have any basis. During and after the Revolt of 1857 the controversial issue of the Babri Masjid was not raised by either community. However, the attitude of the British observers regarding the erection of the fence assumes a stricter tone with the passage of time.[42]

British writing on the Babri Masjid–Ramjanmabhumi issue in the nineteenth century is not above suspicion. In writing about the controversy in Ayodhya they have made no distinction between local myths and historical evidence and have utilized local myths as dependable sources. This is clear from their attitude towards the rediscovery of Ayodhya by Vikramaditya of Ujjain in the fourth century AD. Montgomery Martin was the first British observer who related the myth of Vikrama,[43] but he was convinced that the story was myth and no more. Yet in 1860, Sir H.M. Elliot wrote confidently that Vikramaditya, also known as Bikramajit, came to Ayodhya and erected temples in 360 places rendered sacred by their association with Rama.[44] After Elliot everyone came to consider the rediscovery of Ayodhya a historical fact. However, Benet expressed surprise at the erection of 360 temples and observed in 1877 that at that time there were only forty-two such temples in Ayodhya.[45] In 1905 Neville saw only eighty-three temples dedicated to Rama within the limits of Ayodhya.[46] Most of the British writers of the nineteenth century observed that all the 360 temples were destroyed by Muslim zealots and new temples were raised after the period of Aurangzeb on the ruins of the old temples.[47] They do not mention anything about the old fort that had been constructed in Ayodhya in the thirteenth century.

The English traveller William Finch (1608–11), wrote that there was a castle of a Muslim ruler in Ayodhya. He observed, 'citie of ancient note, and seate of a Potan king, now much ruined; the castle built foure hundred yeers agoe'.[48] It is clear that the buildings erected in AD 1200 had fallen into ruin by the seventeenth century. It is probable that several temples had been raised on such ruins after the rise of the Ramanandi sects.

The Ramanandi sects were said to have been in conflict with the Shaiva Sanyasins throughout the eighteenth century. Gradually the Bairagis gained the upper hand and occupied several places of Shaiva worship in Ayodhya. The Bairagis also received royal patronage and their influence, along with their temples, grew in numbers. It is clear that the ministers of the Nawabs of Oudh helped in extending the activity of the religious orders to which they belonged. Raja Naval Rai, a devotee of Rama, encouraged the construction of temples whose chief deity was Rama. Similarly, Kesari Singh helped in the construction of Jaina temples dedicated to the Tirthankars.[49] We are also informed by British writers that, after the suppression of the Revolt of 1857, Hindu activity in Ayodhya was allowed to grow. It is reported that during the Revolt, British life and property in Ayodhya and Faizabad were endangered and some landlords offered help to the British and 'a similar offer was made by the Mahants of the Hanuman Garhi'.[50] It is therefore certain that after the successful suppression of the Revolt, all those who had helped the British were to be suitably rewarded. All land in Ayodhya was *nazul* (government land) and therefore it was easy for the Government to distribute land as reward for services rendered during the Revolt. The Bairagis received land in Ayodhya and its adjoining areas.[51] Land belonging to Muslim institutions was confiscated. The former royal gardens Hayat Baksh and Farhat Baksh passed into Hindu hands. The former was assigned to Pandit Uma Datta by the British Government and the latter was partly owned by the Raja of Jaipur and partly by the Digambara sect.[52]

It is quite clear that before and after the Revolt of 1857 the British Government encouraged Hindu activity. But it cannot be overlooked that Hindu revivalism had started spreading in Ayodhya much before the arrival of the British in Avadh. British writers accept that the emergence of Ayodhya as an important religious place among the Hindus was a modern phenomenon.[53] We can agree that the rendering of the *Ramayana* in the local dialect in the form of *Ramacharitamanas* helped in projecting Rama as the most popular *avatara* of Vishnu and a deity in North India. As such sects associated with the *bhakti* of Rama emerged and Ayodhya naturally became the main centre of their activity. In the early part of the eighteenth century the Shaiva Sanyasins controlled several places of

Hindu worship in Ayodhya. But gradually a struggle ensued between the Sanyasins and the Vaishnava Bairagis for the several places of worship. This is evident from contemporary writings on Faizabad and Ayodhya.[54] However, the Bairagis continued to gain in strength because of royal patronage. The Shia Nawabs and their ministers were more inclined to support the Bairagis. As such the domination of the Vaishnavas became complete by the end of the eighteenth century.[55]

From all this it is apparent that the clash in Ayodhya was between Bairagis and Sanyasins rather than Hindus and Muslims. The first bloody conflict between Hindus and Muslims occurred between 1853 and 1856. It seems probable that in the nineteenth century the idea started developing in Avadh that Babur had destroyed the Ramjanmabhumi temple and erected a mosque in its place. In 1838, Montgomery Martin wrote that the people of Ayodhya maintained that a mosque had been raised by Babur.[56] Martin added that as in other parts of North India, in Ayodhya too, Aurangzeb was blamed for the destruction of several Hindu temples. However, it was Babur's mosque that attracted Martin's attention most. He wrote that in the construction of the mosque, carved black stone-pillars had been used and as they were un-Islamic they confirm the destruction of temples by Muslim zealots.[57] However, Martin felt that the Babri Masjid had not been built from the debris of the temple said to have been erected by Vikrama of Ujjain.[58]

The story of Babur and his mosque started gaining significance in the nineteenth century. In 1819, John Leyden translated the memoirs of Babur and he wrote that Babur had encamped near Ayodhya on 28 March 1528.[59] In 1826 Erskine remarked that he had found a document that confirmed that Babur had remained in Ayodhya for a fortnight and was involved in building activities.[60] The remarks by these two scholars confirmed the local myth that Babur had destroyed the Ramjanmabhumi temple during his stay in Ayodhya. In 1866, H.M. Elliot asserted that Babur came to Ayodhya and destroyed the famous temple. He added that the mosque was constructed about the time of his expedition to Bihar.[61] It was on the basis of these writings that the idea gained popularity. Most of the British officials and scholars who tried to put together a history of Ayodhya highlighted the desecration of the temple commemorating the birthplace of Rama.[62] This idea became so strongly entrenched in the psyche of the British officials and the local people that it was difficult to dislodge it. In 1923, A.S. Beveridge published her translation of the memoirs of Babur. She said that Babur was encamped seventy-two miles north of Ayodhya on 28 March 1528, but she did not revise the theory that

Babur destroyed the famous Ramjanmabhumi temple.[63] However, her translation does not include the issue of the desecration of the temple and the construction of a mosque in the main body of the book.

The treatment of the issue of the Babri Masjid and the Ramjanmabhumi temple becomes questionable when we realize that no claims had ever been raised regarding the two ruined mosques in Ayodhya. These mosques are said to have been constructed by Aurangzeb. However, we do not have any evidence to support the fact of Aurangzeb's visit to Ayodhya. The local stories relate that two important temples had been destroyed by Aurangzeb and the mosques were raised on their ruins. The two temples are said to have been extremely important. One was the Svargadwar temple, the temple commemorating the occasion when Rama left for heaven; the other is called the Treta-ke-Thakur, or the temple where Rama organized a sacrificial *yagya*. Both the temples naturally signify important events in the life of Rama. But no Hindu seems to be concerned about them. These mosques, also known as the mosques of Naurang Shah, have been mentioned by Martin and it seems from his account that in 1838 the two buildings had not been reduced to ruins.[64] After the Revolt of 1857 Naurang Shah's mosques were in ruins.[65] At one time claims about one of these ruins were strengthened when the rumour was circulated that an inscription had been found near the mosque at the Treta-ke-Thakur. It was said that the inscription indicated that a temple had been raised there by Raja Jai Chand. It is surprising that the inscription is not to be found anywhere today. The only person who claimed to have seen it was unable to say where he saw it. A. Fuhrer reported in 1898 that there was a fragment of the said inscription but he was also unable to say where he saw it.[66] However, despite such claims over the mosque no one seems concerned either to preserve the ruins or to claim the site of the ruins.

It is quite evident that no temple–mosque controversy was known in Ayodhya till the nineteenth century. Local stories were put into circulation and claims were raised over the places of worship in Ayodhya. The British played a significant role in strengthening the claim by providing the local stories with a historical basis. The British in Faizabad and Ayodhya had come to stay after AD 1816. The developments in Ayodhya were an extension of whatever was happening in the adjoining district of Benares, where a great riot had occurred in 1809. By then the British had been in the area for over twenty-five years. It is therefore certain that the attempt of the British writers to provide a historical basis to the circulating local myths, fostered the Babri Masjid—Ramjanmabhumi issue in Ayodhya.

The British administrators and scholars did so with a purpose. Most of the British civil servants and observers of British–Indian affairs perceived India and Indian history according to the views of James Stuart Mill that were included in his book, *The History of British India*. Mill saw Indian society as divided into two strict compartments of Hindus and Muslims. He was convinced that the two were diametrically opposed to each other and peaceful co-existence was impossible between the two. The Muslims had lived in India as rulers and as such had oppressed and persecuted the Hindus. Mill saw both Hindus and Muslims as obsessed with religion, and while the Hindus were subservient by nature, Islam made the Muslims intolerant. According to him, Islam and Hinduism were opposed to each other because while the Hindus worshipped idols the Muslims were idol-breakers. Mill rationalized that British rule was a boon for the Hindus because it liberated them from the intolerant rule of the Muslims. He made the point indirectly that the British Empire was better than the earlier Mughal Empire. British officials and writers influenced by Mill saw themselves as the liberators of the Hindu spirit. For them the justification of the British Empire necessarily meant the undermining of everything that had anything to do with the Mughal Empire.

In the context of Ayodhya the same attitude of the British was evident. It was this influence that led them to suppose that Ayodhya was a Hindu city. Their conviction that the two religious communities could not live in peace made them separate physically the places of worship of the Hindus and Muslims. The British continued to extend their support to the local Hindus not only by providing a historical basis to the circulating beliefs but also by helping them to strengthen their claims. In 1902, the District Magistrate of Faizabad formed a local committee to mark the religious places of only the Hindus. Hindu claims over the Babri Masjid were strengthened by the erection of a marker in front of the mosque.[67] This stone marker read 'No. 1—Ramjanambhoomi'.

The annexation of the kingdom of Avadh and the Revolt of 1857 seem to have decided the stand of the British in the religious controversy raging in Ayodhya. In the pre-annexation period the British demonstrated a neutrality in religious issues that arose in states not ruled by the East India Company; however, they never forgot to point out the ineffectiveness of the rule of the Indian princes. Martin, the first British officer who gave a detailed account of Ayodhya, refused to accept the circulating local myths as facts of history. He expressed his doubts without reservations towards the local beliefs. Although he was critical of the Islamic intolerance for other religions, he expressed his appreciation of the rule of the 'Muhammadans' in India. Comparing Muslim rule with the preceding Hindu rule and the succeeding British rule, he wrote that Muslim rule alone preserved the social fabric in India. [68] In the post-annexation years British officer and scholars clearly adopted a biased stand towards the Hindus on the Babri Masjid–Ramjanmabhumi issue in Ayodhya. They began by providing a historical basis to the circulating local myths. Elliot went to the extent of asserting that Chandragupta Vikramaditya had raised 360 temples venerating Rama in Ayodhya. Carnegy and others with him concluded on the basis of the local stories that Babur had come to Ayodhya and had brought down the Rama temple. The British attempt at mythifying history was deliberate. They wanted to project the view to the people that the earlier Mughal Empire was oppressive and intolerant towards religion.

Notes

1. W.C. Benet (ed.), *Gazetteer of the Province of Oudh*, 3 volumes, vol. II, Lucknow, 1877, p. 2.

2. H.R. Neville, *Fyzabad: A Gazetteer Being Volume XLIII of the District Gazetteer of the United Provinces of Agra and Oudh*, Allahabad, 1905, p.173.

3. A. Cunningham, *Report of the Archaeological Survey of Northern India*, vol. I, Allahabad, 1865, p. 293.

4. Several British officials had published their observation on the city of Ayodhya in the nineteenth century. The majority of such works started appearing after the annexation of the Kingdom of Avadh in February 1856. Before the annexation of the kingdom some British officials and other private persons wrote about the general state of affairs in Avadh but among them only two mentioned anything about Ayodhya. These were Montgomery Martin who was commissioned by the East India Company to compile historical and topographical statistics of eastern India. His observations were published as *The History, Antiquities, Topography, and Statistics of Eastern India*, 6 volumes, London, 1838. The other was a report on the state of affairs in Avadh compiled by Colonel W.H. Sleeman, the British Resident in Lucknow. His report was published as *Journey Through the Kingdom of Oude*, 2 volumes, London, 1856. All the British writers tend to refer to Ayodhya as the 'Hindu' city.

5. Montgomery Martin, op. cit., vol. III, Bhagulpoor, Gorakhpoor, p. 305.

6. ibid., pp. 291–345.

7. W.C. Benet, op. cit., vol. II, p.453. The distribution of the population as given in the Census Report of 1869 was as follows:

City	Muslims		
	Shias	Sunnis	Wahabis
Ayodhya	1,630	889	—
Faizabad	9,868	4,752	—

City	Hindus				
	Shaiva	Shakti	Vaishnava	Nanak Shahi	Other Sects
Ayodhya	975	1,100	2,222	100	602
Faizabad	7,000	7,620	3,655	3,655	—

8. P. Carnegy, *Historical Sketch of Fyzabad Tahsil Including the Former Capitals of Ayodhya and Fyzabad*, Lucknow, 1870.

9. W.C. Benet, op. cit., vol. II, p. 452.

10. ibid. Also see P. Carnegy, op. cit.; and H.C. Irwin, *The Garden of India*, London, 1880, pp. 62–70.

11. Carnegy was probably not aware of the developments in Rama *bhakti*. The Ramanandi sect started developing in the late seventeenth century. In Ayodhya also their activity started after this time. However, in Ayodhya these sects came into conflict to the Shaiva and Shakti strongholds in the city. (See *Srimaharajacaritra* of Raghunathaprasada, pp. 42ff.) The distribution of population among Hindus in 1869 clearly indicates the rising domination of the Vaishnavas. In 1869 the Shaivas numbered 975, the Shaktis were 1,100 and the Vaishnavas were 2,222.

12. P. Carnegy, op. cit., p. 9.

13. W.C. Benet, op. cit., p. 453.

14. P. Carnegy, op. cit., Appendices I–XI.

15. W.W. Hunter, *The Imperial Gazetteer of India*, vol. III, London, 1851, p. 232.

16. H.C. Irwin, *The Garden of India*, London, 1880, p. 75.

17. Mohammad Faiz Baksh had been commissioned by Darab Ali Khan, an officer attached to the Bahu Begam, to compile the history of the Kingdom of Avadh. He completed writing the history in 1818 and gave it the title *Tarikh Farah Baksh*. The work is in two parts: the first part deals with the history of Delhi and Faizabad, and the second part is devoted entirely to the history of Faizabad. This work has been translated by W. Hoey, *Memoirs of Delhi and Faizabad*, Allahabad, 1881.

18. W.H. Sleeman, *Journey Through the Kingdom of Oude*, vol. I, p. 145.

19. Benet, op. cit., vol. II, p. 7.

20. ibid., p. 452.

21. Neville, *District Gazetteer of Fyzabad*, p. 174.

22. Thomas Catania, 'An Episode in Oude History', *Pioneer*, 20 June 1902.

23. We have reference to the events of 1853–85 in some of the written works by Indians. We have taken into account the work of Raja Durga

Parshad, *Bostan-i-Avadh*. Originally printed at Queen Press, Sandhila, 1888; but later reprinted in 1892 at Ahmadi Press, Lucknow. We have also taken into account the work of Kamal-ud-din Haider, *Swainhat-i-Salatin-i-Avadh*, Lucknow, 1889. In both these works it is held that the idea had become popular that Hanumangarhi had been raised on the foundations of a mosque said to have been constructed by Aurangzeb. The Muslims therefore charged the steps of the Hanumangarhi and occupied it but soon they were driven out and a fight ensued for the possession of the spot of the Babri Masjid.

24. There appears to be a discrepancy with regard to the year of occurrence of the event and the cause of conflict. British officials writing on this conflict between the Hindus and Muslims generally contend that the event occurred just before the annexation. See Benet, op. cit., vol.II, p.7 and p.452; and Neville, *District Gazetteer of Fyzabad*, p. 174. The conflict occurred in 1853 because Sleeman records it. Some of the British officers hold the opinion that Maulvi Amir Ali raised the banner of revolt in 1856. In case 1856 be taken as the year of occurrence then the event must have taken place either in January or in February 1856, i.e. before the annexation of Avadh on 13 February 1856. The British officers also contend that the conflict arose with regard to the Hanumangarhi. However, their account cannot be taken as true. We have from Sleeman's account that a religious conflict arose in Ayodhya. He was in Faizabad in 1853. As such we can take the account of H.J. Boas as authentic. This account was confirmed by Rai Mahadeo Bali of Rampur in Pargana Daryabad. The same account has also been confirmed by Neville's *District Gazetteer of the United Provinces of Agra and Oudh, Bara Banki, being vol. XLVIII*, Allahabad, 1904, p. 168.

25. Benet, op. cit., vol. III, p. 43.

26. *Pioneer,* 20 June 1902.

27. Benet, op. cit., vol. III, p. 43.

28. Neville, *District Gazetteer of Bara Banki*, op. cit., p. 169.

29. ibid., p. 169.

30. *Pioneer,* 20 June 1902.

31. Bahu Begam, the wife of Nawab Shuja-ud-daulah and the mother of Nawab Asaf-ud-daulah, refused to leave Faizabad when Nawab Azaf-ud-daulah transferred the capital to Lucknow. She was disappointed with her son, Asaf-ud-daulah, and was suspicious of his designs on her wealth. She had been provided for by her husband and had been granted several *mahals*, the profits of which she could use to maintain herself. She was afraid that after her death the Nawabs would neither care for her husband's mausoleum nor for her servants. As such, to secure everything dear to her, she entered into an agreement with the British. The agreement was drawn up in 1816. In return for assurances from the British Resident that after her death the mausoleum would be cared for and her servants would receive pension, she transferred her possessions and her wealth to the British Resident. As such after 1816, although the *mahal* of Haveli Avadh was a part of the kingdom, these areas were under the control of the Resident. The Resident was to look after revenue and police affairs. See, Mohammad Faiz Baksh's *Tarik Farah*

Baksh; C.U. Aitchison's *Collection of Treaties, Engagements and Sunnads*, Calcutta, 1909; and Benet, op. cit., vol., II, pp. 12–13.

32. Neville, *District Gazetteer of Bara Banki*, op. cit., p. 170.

33. ibid.

34. H.J. Boas in his account says that Colonel Barlow was made the officer-in-charge to crush the rebels. Neville also calls the officer Barlow (Neville, *District Gazetteer of Bara Banki*, p. 170). Benet writes that the officer was Colonel Boileau (Benet, op. cit., vol. II, p. 274).

35. Neville, *District Gazetteer of Bara Banki*, p. 170.

36. It would seem that the death of the Maulvi took place in 1855 because the compromise between the Hindus and Muslims had been worked out in Ayodhya before the annexation.

37. Benet, op. cit., vol.II, p. 274.

38. Neville, *District Gazetteer of Bara Banki*, p. 170. Neville writes that some years back an annual fair was held in the memory of the Maulvi. Neville's gazetteer was published in 1904.

39. Neville, *District Gazetteer of Fyzabad*, p.174.

40. Benet, op. cit., vol. II, p.7.

41. ibid., also see Neville, *District Gazetteer of Fyzabad*, p. 174.

42. Changing British attitudes towards the issue of the Babri Masjid–Ramjanmabhumi dispute can be discerned from the nature of their writings. In 1877 Benet wrote, 'Since British rule, a railing has been put up to prevent disputes, within which, in the mosque the Muhammadans pray while outside the fence the Hindus have raised a platform on which they make their offerings.' (Benet, op. cit., vol. II, p. 7.) Neville relates the same thing in 1905, 'Since the mutiny an outer enclosure has been put up in front of the mosque and the Hindus who are forbidden access to the inner yards, make their offerings on a platform which they have raised in the outer one.' Neville, *District Gazetteer of Fyzabad*, p. 174. Neville's writing clearly indicates the helpless state of the Hindus by pointing to a strict demarcation whereby Hindus are not allowed to enter the mosque.

43. Montgomery Martin, op. cit., vol. III, p. 333. He writes, 'The people of Ayodhya imagine that, after the death of Vrihadbala, their city was deserted, and continued so until the time of Vikrama of Ujjain, who came in search of the holy city, erected a fort called Ramgar, cut down the forest by which the ruins were covered, and erected 360 temples on the places sanctified by the actions of Rama, of his wife Sita, of his brother Lakshmana, and of his general Mahavira.'

44. H.M. Elliot, *History of India as Told by its Own Historians*, vol. I, London, 1866.

45. Benet, op. cit., vol. II, p.4.

46. Neville, *District Gazetteer of Fyzabad*, p. 177.

47. Benet, op. cit.; P. Carnegy, op. cit.; A. Cunningham, op. cit.; A. Fuhrer, *Report of the Archaeological Survey of India* (new series), vol. II, Allahabad, 1891, pp. 295–300; H.R. Neville, *District Gazetteer of Fyzabad*. All these observers blame the Muslim rulers for having destroyed the temples of Ayodhya.

48. William Foster (ed.), *Early Travels in India*, London, 1921, p. 176. This has the record of the travels of William Finch who came to India during the years 1608 to 1611. Finch writes that during that period it was believed that the city enclosed the ruins of the fort of Rama. He adds about Ayodhya, 'The Indians acknowledge for the great God, saying that he tooke flesh upon him to see the *tamasha* of the world.' However, Finch wrote that the religious places of the Brahmins were limited to the bathing ghats on the banks of the river.

49. Benet, op.cit., vol. II, p. 9.

50. Neville, *District Gazetteer of Fyzabad*, p. 163.

51. ibid., pp. 61–64.

52. ibid., p. 175.

53. Nearly all British writers on Ayodhya believe that long before the penetration of the Islamic forces in Ayodhya the place was covered by a thick jungle. At that time Ayodhya, at best, was known as a famous hunting ground. They are therefore surprised at the emergence of Ayodhya as an important centre of Hindu pilgrimage. Benet writes, 'It may, however, be remarked here that Hindu revival at Ayodhya is one of the most remarkable things in modern India.' Benet, op. cit., vol. II, p. 452.

54. Mohamed Faiz Baksh's *Tarikh Farah Baksh* relates that after the signing of the treaty of 1765 the influence of the Mughals in Ayodhya started declining. The Mewati soldiers who represented the Mughals were withdrawn. The absence of the Mewatis provided freedom of movement to the spear-wielding Sanyasins. The Sanyasins were well known for disturbing the peace of Ayodhya and after 1765 the law and order situation in Ayodhya deteriorated. Raghunathaprasada wrote that in the eighteenth century in Ayodhya, the Bairagis and the Sanyasins were involved in a fight for domination in the area. He describes an incident, 'At that time. . . when the occasions of Rama's birth came people went to Kosalapur and assembled there—who can describe the enormous crowd? At that place there was unlimited (number of) strong warriors in Sanyasins garb, carrying weapons with matted hair and ashes smeared on every limb—an unlimited army of soldiers taking pleasure in battle. Fighting with the Bairagis broke out. This fight was of no avail (to the Bairagis), owing to lack of strategy. . . They made a mistake of going towards them; the Bairagi garb became a source of misery. All people dressed in the Bairagi garb fled—through fear of them Sanyasins. Avadhpur was abandoned. Wherever they happened to find people in Bairagi garb there they struck fear into them. Through fear of them everyone was frightened, and wherever they could they took shelter in a secret place and hid themselves. They changed their dress and hid their sectarian markings. No one showed his proper identity.'

55. In the nineteenth century the domination of the Vaisnavas in Ayodhya had become complete. All festivals and fairs connected with the life of Rama attracted Hindus, irrespective of the sects to which they belonged, to Ayodhya. The Hindus of the Shaiva and Shakti sects came together to celebrate occasions associated with Rama. The place had emerged as the main point of congregation for the Hindus in the nineteenth century. Benet writes, 'Ayodhya, as is related in the account of this town, is the great centre

of the hero worship which has selected the ancient king Ram Chandar as the object of its adoration. At the Ramnaumi festival 5,00,000 people assemble in honour of that potent monarch and innumerable shrines have been erected to Rama Chandra, his brother Bharat, his wife, Sita and his ally in the great Dekkan war, Hanoman the monkey. This saint worship at the same time does not seem to interfere with the more spiritual theology which concerns itself with the most unearthly beings—Vishnu, Mahadeo, and Bhawani or Debi.' Benet, op. cit., vol. II, p. 451.

56. Montgomery Martin, op.cit., vol. III, p.335.

57. ibid., p. 336.

58. ibid., p. 337.

59. John Leyden, *Memoirs of Zehir-ed-din Muhammad Baber, Emperor of Hindustan,* London, 1819. It is quite clear that Leyden had no idea of the geography of the area around Ayodhya and Faizabad. Babur writes in his 'memoirs' (folio 338-A) that on 28 March 1528 he was stationed 7 or 8 *kurohs* above Aud—this clearly means north of Aud. Leyden confused Aud with Ayodhya and fixed the ferry port of Serwa (in the south of Ayodhya) as the place where Babur encamped on 28 March 1528.

60. William Erskine, *A History of India under the Two First Sovereigns of the House of Taimur, Baber and Humayun,* 2 volumes, London, 1854. Erskine claims to have come across a page in the memoirs of Babur in 1826 which according to him related the activities of Babur in Ayodhya. It read, 'After spending several days pleasantly in that place where there are gardens, running waters, well-designed buildings, trees particularly mango trees and various kind of coloured plumage, I ordered the march towards Ghazipur.'

Beveridge, commenting on this page of the manuscript, wrote that she found it in the memoirs (p. 420) and in Erskine's own codex of the *Waqiat-i-Babri* (f-371) where, however, several circumstances isolated it from the context. She wrote that this particular place can be distinctly disassociated from Abdur-rahim's text. She adds that Babur did not march to Ghazipur in 935 A.H. (See A.S. Beveridge, *Baburnama*. p. 680.)

61. H.M. Elliot, *History of India as Told by Her Historians,* Calcutta, 1872, vol. IV, p. 283. Elliot agreed with the earlier translations of the memoirs of Babur and was convinced that the Mughal Emperor was stationed south of Ayodhya. He, like Leyden and Erskine, made the mistake of reading *daal* for *'wao'*.

62. See the writings of Benet, Carnegy, Cunningham, Irwin, Furher a. d Neville.

63. A.S. Beveridge, *Baburnama* (Memoirs of Baber), 1921, p. 602. Beveridge stayed in Faizabad for two months while translating the memoirs. She acquainted herself with the local geography and therefore was able to point to the spot where Babur had encamped on 28 March 1526. While in Faizabad she heard several local stories and was led to believe that Babur had destroyed the famous temple of Rama. She seemed to have been so impressed with the local stories that while translating the inscriptions she drew the conclusion that as the Muslims believed that it was the birthplace

of Rama therefore they were convinced that the angels descended there. However, she does not put her ideas on this issue in the main body of the translation of the memoirs. This is contained in the appendix.

64. Montgomery Martin, op. cit., vol. III, p. 334.

65. P. Carnegy, op. cit.; W.C. Benet, op. cit., vol. II, p. 6.

66. Only A. Fuhrer records the discovery of the fragmentary inscriptions. He writes, 'A fragmentary inscription of Jaya Chandra of Kanauj dated 1241 and recording the erection of a temple of Vishnu was rescued from the ruins of Aurangzeb's mosque, known as Treta-ke-Thakur, and is now in the Fyzabad Museum.' Fuhrer, op. cit., vol. II, p. 297. This inscription cannot be traced anywhere. However, we do have a copper-plate grant which recorded the grant made by Jai Chand in AD 1187. He gave away Komali to Alenga of the Bhardwaj line. The copper-plate grant records Vishnu and Lachhmi as the gods. It is difficult to support Fuhrer's interpretation.

Regarding the temples destroyed by the Mughal rulers in Ayodhya, Benet writes, 'It is locally affirmed that at the time of Muhammadan conquest there were three important Hindu shrines, with but few devotees attached, at Ayodhya, which was then little other than wilderness. These were the Janamasthan, the Swargaddwar Mandir also known as Ram Darbar, Treta-ke-Thakur.

'On the first of these the Emperor Babur built the mosque, which still bears his name AD 1528. On the second Aurangzeb did the same AD 1658 to 1707; and on the third that sovereign or his predecessors built a mosque, according to the well-known principles of enforcing their religion on all those whom they conquered.

'The Janamasthan marks the place where Rama Chandar was born. The Swargaddwar is the gate through which he passed into paradise, possibly the spot where he was burned. The Treta-ke-Thakur was famous as the place where Rama performed a great sacrifice, and which he commemorated by setting up there images of himself and Sita.

'The two other old mosques to which allusion has been made (known by the common people by the name of Naurang Shah by whom they mean Aurangzeb) are now mere picturesque ruins. Nothing had been done by the Hindus to restore the old *mandir* of Ram Darbar. The Treta-ke-Thakur was reproduced near the old ruin by the Raja of Kulu, whose estate is said to be in the Panjab, more than two centuries ago; and it was improved upon afterwards by Aholya Bai, Marathin, who also built the adjoining *ghat*, AD 1784. She was the widow of Jaswant Rao Holkar of Indore, from which family Rs 231 are still received annually at the shrine.' Benet, op. cit., vol. II, pp.6–7. However, he does not mention anywhere about the fragmentary inscription that is mentioned by Fuhrer.

67. H.R. Neville, *District Gazetteer of Fyzabad*, p. 176. 'In 1902 a local committee was formed with the object of commemorating the coronation of His Imperial Majesty King Edward VII, and a sum of over Rs 1,000 was collected and expended on the erection of stone pillars marking the sacred spots in Ayodhya and its neighbourhood. This work has been carried out and no fewer than 145 such stones have been erected; their ostensible

purpose being to preserve the memory of the various holy spots and to serve as a guide to pilgrims and others interested in the place.' This committee marked only the Hindu places of worship and one Sikh gurdwara in Ayodhya.

68. Montgomery Martin, op. cit., vol. III, p. 344. 'It must be observed, notwithstanding the ferocity usually attributed to the Muhammedan conquerors of India, that scarcely any family of note among the native chiefs, who possessed the country before the conquest, had become extinct, or been deprived of its lands during the long period which followed under Muhammedan control. But that, during the Hindu government, each change had been followed by the complete destruction or banishment of the family that was subdued. Although many of the chiefs pretend to be descended of the family of the sun, none of these allege, that their ancestors have retained uninterrupted possession; on the contrary they all admit, that their ancestors had retired to the west, from which they again returned, after an interval of many ages. . . . It is also to be observed, and I think to be much regretted, that the operations of our systems of finance and law have done more in twelve years to impoverish and degrade the native chiefs, who succeeded the impure tribes, than the whole course of the Muhammedan government.'

Legal Aspects to the Issue

A.G. Noorani

The strength and quality of a Constitution which establishes a democratic order governed by the rule of law are put to the test when popular passions are aroused to stifle the rights which the Constitution guarantees or violate the norms on which it rests. The quality of the country's political process is also tested on such occasions. It must seek to resolve such issues expeditiously when they arise before they put the legal and constitutional system under strain. Failing that, of course, the law must be allowed to take its course and the rights must prevail.

On neither count can India derive much satisfaction. It is four decades now since a mosque was forcibly occupied and converted into a temple and the country's legal system has completely failed to redress the wrong. This is an understatement. The record reveals some graver lapses than those of mere omission. That the Babri Masjid at Ayodhya, in the Faizabad district of Uttar Pradesh, was converted into a Ramjanmabhumi Mandir on the night of 22–23 December 1949 is an outrage in itself. That this was, and yet remains, part of a movement which seeks likewise to occupy and convert the mosques at Mathura (adjoining the Krishna Janmasthan) and Varanasi (at Kashi Vishwanath Mandir) makes it sinister.

Even that is not all. The movement is aimed at avenging perceived historical wrongs by converting India's secular, democratic system into a Hindu State.

Justice Deoki Nandan Agarwal, a former judge of the Allahabad High Court and one of the leading figures in the movement, has expounded its outlook in a booklet. (*Sri Rama Janma Bhumi*, Sri Rama Janma Bhumi Mukti Yagna Samiti, Lucknow) It is also reproduced substantially in the periodical *Parlance*. (January–February 1990, Calcutta, pp. 6–18.) He wrote:

> Maryada Purushottam Bhagwan Sri Rama, Bhagwan Sri Krishna and Shiva Shanker Mahadeva are the three deities worshipped by the Hindus all over the world. They sym-

bolize the rule of Dharma and suppression of Adharma among the mankind. They are the epitomes of our national aspiration of establishing Rama Rajya, which Mahatma Gandhi gave to us during our struggle for freedom from the British yoke. The three places where the three first manifested themselves, namely, Sri Rama Janma Bhumi at Ayodhya, Sri Krishna Janmasthan at Mathura, and the Gyanvapi at Varanasi, are all of them situated within Uttar Pradesh, the very heartland of Bharatvarsha; and all the three received the special attention of Muslim vandalism.

And with the attainment of independence from foreign rule, it became the bounden duty of every citizen of India that is Bharat, to remove the mosque-like structures raised by Muslim marauders after destroying and desecrating ancient Hindu temples situated there, and to restore them to their pristine glory, as the continued existence of such mosque-like structures is galling to the Hindu psyche and a matter of National shame.

Agarwal professes to offer 'a legal and historical perspective'. He adds in the same breath, 'That there was an ancient temple of Maharaja Vikramaditya's time at Sri Rama Janma Bhumi is a fact of history, which is indisputable, although there is some controversy as to which of the Vikramadityas resurrected the place and built the magnificent temple. . . . '

There are, in fact, at least two other places in Ayodhya besides the mosque proper which are claimed as the 'exact spots' where Sri Rama was born. There is a Rama *chabutra* outside the mosque, but within its compound, which has been worshipped as the Ram Janmasthan since the mid-nineteenth century. It is a raised platform, 17x21 feet in area, about a hundred paces away from the mosque proper. A railing was constructed to separate the *chabutra* from the masjid. Till 22 December 1949, the Hindus worshipped at the *chabutra* and the Muslims in the mosque. There is, besides, a most impressive Ram Janmasthan Mandir which is close to the Babri Masjid. Between the two lies the famous Sita-ki-Rasoi, itself claimed by some to be Sri Rama's birthplace.

Altogether different from these is the Hanumangarhi Mandir constructed by Mansoor Ali, the Nawab of Avadh. About 200 yards from the mosque is Kaushalya Bhawan and 500 yards away from it is the Dasharatha Bhawan. In a sense, the whole of Ayodhya is Ramjanmabhumi; but, not surprisingly, none can identify with certainty the birthplace as, among others, Satyapal Dang, the Communist Party of India leader, discovered on a visit to Ayodhya on 3 October 1989. ('Ayodhya Visit—an Experience', *New Age*, 15 October 1989; *vide* also D.R. Goyal's impressions, 'At Peace with Themselves', *Indian Post*, 12 October 1989.) The historian, Prof. R.S. Sharma, said in an interview with *Janashakti* of Patna, 'I have been there (in Ayodhya). There are at least 15–16 mandirs, the pujaris of which claim that their temple is the real birthplace of Rama.' ('Dr Ram Sharan Sharma on Ram Janam Bhoomi', *New Age*, 8 October 1989.)

These facts must be appreciated in the historical context. In the entire country there is no temple at all built before the seventeenth century with Sri Rama as the presiding deity. The oldest one is at Allahabad and the second oldest is the Ram Janmasthan Mandir at Ayodhya, to the north of the Babri Masjid.

The whole issue brings to mind Macaulay's words in the context of the seizing of Silesia by Frederick the Great on the plea that it had belonged to Germany two centuries earlier. Khushwant Singh quoted the following excerpt in his column in the *Hindustan Times* of 16 December 1989:

> Is it not perfectly clear that, if antiquated claims are to be set up against recent treaties and long possession, the world can never be at peace for a day? The laws of all nations have wisely established a time of limitation, after which titles, however illegitimate in their origin, cannot be questioned. It is felt by everybody, that to eject a person from his estate on the ground of some injustice committed in the time of the Tudors would produce all the evils which result from arbitrary confiscation, and would make all property insecure. It concerns the Commonwealth—so runs the legal maxim—that there be an end of litigation. And surely this maxim is at least equally applicable to the great commonwealth of states; for in that commonwealth litigation means the devastation of provinces, the suspension of trade and industry, sieges like those of Badajoz and St Sebastian, pitched feuds like those of Eylau and Borodino. We hold that the transfer of Norway from Denmark to Sweden was an unjustifiable proceeding; but would the King of Denmark be therefore justified in landing, without any new provocation, in Norway, and

commencing military operation there? The King of Holland thinks, no doubt, that he was unjustly deprived of the Belgian provinces. Grant that it were so. Would he, therefore, be justified in marching with an army on Brussels? The case against Frederick was still stronger, inasmuch as the injustice of which he complained had been committed more than a century before. Nor must it be forgotten that he owed the highest personal obligations to the House of Austria. It may be doubted whether his life had not been preserved by the intercession of the prince whose daughter he was about to plunder.

Two features of the controversy are highly significant. One is the relative indifference of the local populace (*vide*, Dang and Goyal). Sanjay Suri, a correspondent with the *Indian Express*, reported that 'the disputed place is not believed even by pandits to be the birthspot of the legendary God Ram. The pandits, who have not timed the birth within thousands of years, have pinpointed the "Janam Sthan" as Ram *chabutra*. This *chabutra*, marked by a platform under a tree, is outside the disputed area. The Janam Sthan is not claimed by Muslims'. (*Indian Express*, 11 February 1987.)

Ayodhya has *become* important. The Kartika Purnima attracts lakhs of people for performing the ceremonies. 'Now those coming to Ayodhya for such occasions *also* visit the Ramjanmabhumi which attracted least attention before the Vishwa Hindu Parishad in cooperation with the Ram Janmabhoomi Mukti Yagya Samiti launched the liberation movement.' (*Indian Express*, 13 May 1990.)

The other feature is not the mere fact of the arousal of passions by the movement launched by the Vishwa Hindu Parishad (VHP) and the Samiti. It is their profound disdain for evidence itself and, as a logical consequence, a total rejection of the relevance of the legal processes to a resolution of this issue. Alone among the political parties, the Bharatiya Janata Party (BJP) shares this outlook with the VHP and the Samiti.

In his reply to Prof. Hiren Mukherji's letter of 5 June 1989, Atal Behari Vajpayee wrote, 'It is not possible to pinpoint the exact spot where Ram was born. But it is known that Ram, the King of Ayodhya, whom vast masses of Hindus regard as the incarnation of God, was born in that historical city and a temple dedicated to him had been in existence since long. This temple was built and rebuilt over the ages.' (*Organiser*, 24 September 1989.) He, for one, was prepared to delink Ayodhya from

Mathura and Varanasi because 'we cannot go on fighting against history as such'. But he refused to apply this salutary principle to Ayodhya. Uncertainty about 'the exact spot where Ram was born' did not deter him from joining the demand for legalizing the takeover of the mosque. Assertion was readily substituted for argument.

On 6 April 1989, Vajpayee asserted in Bombay that the issue could not be solved by the courts. The Muslims should be persuaded to give up their claim to the mosque. It should be handed over to the Hindus unconditionally. He rejected the proposal to declare the mosque a national monument, saying it belonged to the Hindus as a part of their cultural heritage. (*Indian Post*, 7 April 1989.) The speech is most instructive for an understanding of the stakes involved. Vajpayee is reputed to be a 'moderate', and not without reason either. He said that the need of the hour was to revive the Hindu nationalist spirit to fight fissiparous tendencies. 'Being secular does not mean that *we* disown our religion.' Yet, even a person of his high intelligence could see no contradiction between asking the Muslims to deliver the historic mosque to the Hindus, while rejecting the proposal to declare it a national monument on the one hand and asserting, on the other, that Hinduism was a geo-cultural concept. *Ergo*, all those who are on this side of the Sindhu river are Hindus.

As against such mumbo-jumbo and arrogant disdain for evidence and for the legal process is the stark reality that what is at issue is the forcible conversion of the house of worship of one religious denomination into one of another religious denomination. An incident of this kind anywhere in the world would arouse shock and revulsion. That these reactions have been voiced in India testifies to its vitality and its innate sanity and decency, the frailties of the constitutional system and the political process notwithstanding.

At stake is nothing less than religious freedom. The United Nations General Assembly adopted without a vote on 25 November 1981, a Declaration on the Elimination of All Forms of Intolerance and Discrimination Based on Religion or Belief (Resolution 36/55). Article I (1) says that 'every one shall have the right to freedom of thought, conscience and religion. . . .' Para 3 refers to 'limitations as are prescribed by law and are necessary to protect public safety, order, health or, morals or the fundamental rights and freedoms of others'.

Article VI is important. It spells out the contents of the right. It says, 'In accordance with Article I, and subject to the provisions of paragraph 3 of Article I, the right to freedom of thought, conscience, religion, or belief shall include, *inter alia*, the following freedoms: (a) to worship or assemble in connection with a religion or belief, and to establish and maintain places for these purposes. . .' Denial of the right to 'maintain' a house of worship of a religious denomination is as much a denial of religious freedom as a refusal of the right to establish it in the first instance.

Article VII enjoins the states to accord the rights embodied in the Declaration; it says there should be recognition in 'national legislation in such a manner that everyone shall be able to avail themselves of such rights and freedoms in practice'.

The General Assembly has since been reminding the states of these international legal obligations. The last such, Resolution (44/131), also adopted without a vote on 15 December 1989, recalled the Declaration as well as the Universal Declaration of Human Rights and the International Covenant on Civil and Political Rights.

India ratified the Covenant on 10 April 1979 and is obligated to report to the Human Rights Committee established by the Covenant (Article 28) on its observance of the rights mentioned in the Covenant; including, of course, Article 18 which guarantees religious freedom.

But then this ethos is no different from that which inspired the founding fathers of the Indian Constitution. Part III of the Constitution embodies the Fundamental Rights. They are judicially enforceable. Let alone executive action, any law which 'takes away or abridges' the rights shall be void. Article 25 embodies the guarantee of 'freedom of conscience and the right freely to profess, practice and propagate religion'. Article 26 is pertinent. It reads thus, 'Subject to public order, morality and health, every religious denomination or any section thereof shall have the right: (a) to establish and maintain institutions for religious and charitable purposes; (b) to manage its own affairs in matters of religion; (c) to own and acquire movable and immovable property; and (d) to administer such property in accordance with law.'

If this be the law, domestic and international rejection of the legal processes and of the relevance of objective evidence itself, as distinct from one's own religious beliefs, is a tacit assertion of validity of brute force of the majority in defiance of the law and of the values of civilized society. History does not support the claims of the VHP, the Samiti and the BJP. There is no evidence at all on any of the three propositions asserted by these groups. There is no evidence, historical or archaeological, that: (a) the site on which the Babri Masjid was constructed in 1528 by Baqi Bag Tashkandi, known as Mir Baqi who was appointed Governor of Avadh by Babur, was the birthplace of Sri Rama; (b) that on this site a temple was built in honour of Sri Rama; and (c) that this temple was demolished and a mosque was built thereon in 1528.

In fact, the claim to the mosque itself is recent. *Originally only the* chabutra *was claimed* . This becomes all too clear from the records to the litigation a century ago. The proceedings are very relevant to the present controversy.

On 29 January 1885, Raghubar Das, who claimed to be the Mahant of the Janam Asthan Ayodhya, filed a civil suit against the Secretary of State for India in Council for 'a decree for awarding permission to construct a temple over the Chabutra Janam Asthan situated in Ayodhya and restraining the defendant from prohibiting or obstructing the plaintiff in the construction of the temple'. The dimensions of the *chabutra* were specified.

Para 2 of the plaint read thus, 'The Chabutra of Janam Asthan is 21 feet towards East and West and 17 feet towards North and South, and therein Charan Punya lies and there also a small temple over it, which is worshipped.' If in his view the sanctum sanctorum of the temple lay in the mosque, the Mahant would surely have claimed it or at least mentioned it. No reference was made to the mosque.

This was a suit filed by a Mahant who surely knew tradition. It was this Janam Asthan, the *chabutra* he so precisely defined, which he described as 'an old and sacred place of worship of Hindus and the Plaintiff is the Mahant of the place of worship'.

The Deputy Commissioner of Faizabad had prohibited the construction of the temple 'on account of the objections raised by some Muslims' in March–April 1883. The suit was keenly contested. The plaintiff, the Government pleader, one Mohammed Asghar and his pleader were fully heard. The Mahant argued that 'if a temple is constructed no harm is done to any one and *the worship which is done at present will continue in the same manner in future also'* . That was at the *chabutra*.

The Sub Judge of Faizabad, Pandit Hari Kishan Singh, however, dismissed the suit by a judgment dated 24 December 1885. The parties had adduced extensive documentary evidence. The plaintiff had cited the *Gazetteer of Oudh*, vol. 7 of which much is made today. Oral evidence was recorded and 'an inquiry on the spot was made in the presence of the parties' and their pleaders.

The Judge found that the plaintiff was, indeed, in possession of the *chabutra* and collected the offerings made there, 'In 1855 after the fight amongst Hindus and Muslims, a boundary wall was constructed to avoid future disputes, so that the Muslims should worship inside that wall and the Hindus should worship outside that wall, hence the *chabutra* and the land which situate (*sic*) outside the boundary wall, belong to Hindus and the Plaintiff.'

He explained why he declined to decree the suit, 'This place is not like other places where the owner has got the right to construct any building he likes. On perusal of the plan it can be found the situation is as such. The prayer for permission to construct the temple is (*sic*) at such a place where there is only one passage for the temple as well as for the mosque. The place where the Hindus worship is in their possession from of old and their ownership cannot be questioned and around it there is the wall of the mosque and the world Allah is inscribed on it. If a temple is constructed on the *chabutra* at such a place then there will be sound of bells of the temple and *sankh* when both Hindus and Muslims pass from the same way and if permission is given to Hindus for constructing a temple then one day or the other a criminal case will be started and thousands of people will be killed.' A century later the prophecy came true, albeit for other reasons.

The plaintiff appealed to the District Court. The judgement of the District Judge, Col. F.E.A. Chamier, in Civil Appeal No. 27 of 1885 dated 18 March 1886 is as instructive. He had read the *Gazetteer of Oudh*, as had Pandit Hari Kishan; but was more impressed. The errors in the *Gazetteer* and in English writings on Babur and Ayodhya have been fully exposed by now; most notably by Sushil Srivastava of the Department of Medieval and Modern History, University of Allahabad in *Probe India* (January 1988) and in his article in this volume. (See also the letter by Indrajit Datta and nine others in *The Statesman*, 22 October 1989.)

The District Judge remarked, 'I visited the land in dispute yesterday in the presence of all parties. I found that the masjid built by the Emperor Babur stands on the border of the town of Ayodhya, that is to say to the west and south it is clear of habitations. It is most unfortunate that a masjid should have been built on land specially held sacred by the Hindus, but as that event occurred 356 years ago it is too late now to remedy the grievance, all that can be done is to maintain the parties in *status quo*. In such a case as the present one any innovation could cause more harm and derangement of order than benefit.'

He added, '*This* chabutra *is said to indicate the birthplace of Ram Chandra*. In front of the gateway is the entry to the masonry platform of the masjid. A wall pierced here and there with railways divides the platform of the masjid from the enclosure on which stands the chabutra.' (*italics mine*)

The Judge noted, 'The true object of the suit was disclosed by B. Kuccu

Mal (the plaintiff's pleader) yesterday when we were standing near the Masjid—namely that the British Government as no respecter of persons was asked through its courts to remedy an injustice committed by a Mohammedan Emperor.' Even so, the claim was to the *chabutra*, not the mosque. The appeal was dismissed on the ground that 'there is no "injuria", nothing which would give a right of action to the plaintiff' (*vide*, *Muslim India*, March 1986, pp. 105–8 for the texts.)

The Mahant appealed, once again, on 25 May 1886 to the highest court in the province. He contended that the District Judge was wrong in cancelling the findings of the Sub Judge, 'declaring the right of property to rest in the plaintiff', and that the District Judge was wrong in stating that the Masjid was built by Emperor Babur.

The Judicial Commissioner, W. Young, also dismissed the appeal by his judgement dated 1 November 1886 and observed:

> This spot is situated within the precinct of the grounds surrounding a mosque erected some 350 years ago owing to the bigotry and tyranny of the emperor who purposely chose this holy spot, according to Hindu legend, as the site of his mosque. The Hindus seem to have got very limited rights of access to certain spots within the precinct adjoining the mosque and they have for a series of years been persistently trying to increase those rights and to erect buildings on two spots in the enclosure namely: (1) Sita-ki-Rasoi (kitchen of Sita) and (2) Ram-Chander-ki-Janmabhoomi (birthplace of Lord Rama). The executive authorities have persistently refused these encroachments and absolutely forbid any alteration of the status quo.

The Judicial Commissioner added:

> I think this is a very wise and proper procedure on their part and I am further of the opinion that the civil courts have properly dismissed the plaintiff's claim. The pleas on appeals to this court are wholly unsupported by facts in the case or by any argument that appears to be weighty. I see no reason to interfere with the order modifying the wording of the part of the judgement of the Court of first instance. There is nothing whatever on the record to show that the plaintiff is in any sense the proprietor of the land in question. This appeal is dismissed with costs of all courts.

In a thoroughly documented article entitled 'The Ayodhya Controversy: One Hundred Years of Litigation', published in the *Indian Express* on 30 March 1986, from which the Judicial Commissioner's remarks are reproduced, S.K. Tripathi wrote, 'Nothing significant is reported to have occurred between 1886 and 1934. The Babri Masjid suffered damage during communal riots in 1934 which were triggered off by the slaughter of a cow in the village of Shahjahanpur near Ayodhya on 27 March that year. According to available documents, Hindus demolished the domes, one of which had a large hole. However, the mosque was rebuilt and reconditioned at the cost of the government through a Muslim contractor.'

An inquiry was conducted in 1936 by the then Commissioner of Waqfs under the UP Muslims Waqfs Act, and it was held that the Babri Masjid was built by Babur who was a Sunni Muslim. The report was published in the official gazette dated 20 February 1944. This was found in the 1945 litigation between the Shia Central Board of Waqfs and the Sunni Central Board of Waqfs in the court of the Civil Judge, Faizabad. The Civil Judge, S.A. Ahsan, in his judgement dated 23 March 1946, held that the mosque was founded by Babur Shah and that evidence showed that the mosque has been used by the members of both sects.

The mosque and its appurtenant land, a graveyard known as Ganj-e-Shaheedan Qabrastan, were registered as Waqf no. 26 Faizabad with the UP Sunni Central Board of Waqfs under the Act of 1936. The Shias contended that Mir Baqi was a Shia and the Mutawalliship devolved on his descendants. However, both sects prayed in the mosque. The last Imam of Babri Masjid (Maulana Haji Abdul Gaffar), who led the last *namaz* on 22 December 1949 is a Sunni. He is ninety-three years old now. The Civil Judge, S.A. Ahsan, delivered the Judgement in suit no.29 of 1945 on 23 March 1946, not 30 March, while the Report of the Commissioner was gazetted on 26 February and not on 20 February as Tripathi wrote. (*Muslim India*, 1986, p.112; *Parlance*, p.14.) These proceedings are relevant. They show that Muslims exercised their rights in respect of the mosque till partition; their two sects litigated over it openly; and, there was no challenge to Muslims' rights in any legal proceedings by Hindus.

This situation was altered forcibly in the changed communal climate in the wake of the Partition. What exactly happened on 22–23 December 1949? The RSS journal, *Organiser*, of 29 March 1987 will have us believe that 'on the historic morning of 23 December 1949 the idols of Sri Ramachandra and Sita Devi miraculously appeared in the Janmasthan. As the Hindu devotees rejoiced over the miracle and thronged in their thousands', the Government proclaimed the premises a disputed area and locked the gates.

It is a patently absurd explanation. The truth about the take-over of the mosque is too shocking to be admitted. Justice Deoki Nandan Agarwal has also to take cover under this 'miracle'. (*Parlance*, 1986, p.10.)

In truth, the 'miracle' was the climax to a nine-day, non-stop recitation of the *Ramacharitamanas* just outside the mosque organized by the Akhil Bharatiya Ramayana Mahasabha. There was one man who had the moral courage to speak up against the outrage and continues still to denounce it—Akshay Brahmachari (see his interview in *Sunday Mail*, 2 July 1989). He was then Secretary of the Faizabad District Congress. He wrote to Lal Bahadur Shastri, then a Minister in the UP Government, and went on hunger strike twice in 1950.

Akshay Brahmachari's memorandum to Shastri is a truly historic document. He wrote:

> In November 1949, I was told that the Muslim graves near the Babri Mosque were being dug out *en masse*. I personally went and saw that it was actually so. . . .
>
> In front of the Babri Masjid, where the graves were dug out, there was a nine-day continuous reading from the Ramayana, and for many more days there was public feasting and all that. Mass meetings were held. Loudspeakers fitted in tongas and cars kept on screaming day in and day out calling upon the people to come for Darshan in the Mosque where Yajna was taking place, as the place of Ram's birth was being reclaimed. People began coming in thousands also from outside the town in cars sent by the organisers of the show. Inflammatory speeches were made and it was openly announced that the Babri Mosque had to be converted into a Sri Ram Temple. Mahatma Gandhi, Congress and Congressmen were openly abused. . . .
>
> Thus communal poison was spread in an organised manner and the attitude of the officials gave the idea to the people that either the Government wanted all that to happen, or they had completely given in to the communalists. On the 23rd morning the District Magistrate told me at about 9 a.m. that the image of Rama Chandraji was implanted in the Babri Masjid the preceding night, and that he had learnt of the incident at 6 a.m. from Sri Bhai Lal

and that he had gone to see it. . . .

I went to the Babri Mosque with the District Magistrate at about 12 noon. The image was kept there. Some people had gathered near the Mosque. At that moment the Mosque could have been easily saved and the image removed, but the District Magistrate did not think it proper. From that very morning loudspeakers started announcing the appearance of Bhagwan, exhorting all Hindus to come to Darshan. I pointed out this hectic propaganda to the District Magistrate both in Faizabad and Ayodhya while going with him to Ayodhya in his car. Tension went on increasing. Notices and handbills continued to be distributed. Thousands of people started pouring in for Darshan into the city in cars and public carriers sent out from Faizabad. In the Babri Mosque itself, even after the Government took possession of it under Section 145 IPC, Hindu worship remaining unchecked, only the Muslims could not say their namaz there. . . .

There is terror in the hearts of the Muslims of Faizabad, and most of them have sent their families away to relations living elsewhere. And some of them have left with all their belongings for good. I tried to draw the attention of the Government to all this but failed. It has been recently reported that pressure is being brought upon Ayodhya Muslims to declare that the Babri Mosque was in fact a Hindu temple. They are threatened with dire consequences if they will not do so. Muslims shopkeepers are being forced to vacate their shops. The boycott of Muslim shops is openly encouraged. . . .

I do not view this question as one of saving the Mosque or Muslims. I view it as saving the great ideals of the Congress and Mahatma for which we have been struggling all these days. If we do not resist these reactionary ideas with all the forces at our command, the ideals of the Congress will become extinct and reactionary forces will sweep the country.

(*Muslim India*, June 1988, pp. 252–54.)

The background has been recorded in two reports by the Waqf inspector Muhammad Ibrahim dated 10 and 23 December 1949 respectively to the

Secretary of the Waqf Board. Interestingly, these two reports figure among the thirteen 'legal/historical documents' submitted by the VHP to former Union Home Minister Buta Singh on 6 October 1988.(*Muslim India*, July 1989, pp. 305–6.) It must be assumed, therefore, that their contents are accepted. They certainly ring true.

The first report complained that 'any Muslim going towards the Masjid is accosted and called names, etc. . . . People there told me that there is a danger to the Masjid from the Hindus. . . .' The second report recorded the inspector's impressions on 22 December 1949 the last day before the take-over of the mosque. It is relied on by the VHP presumably because at one place it complained that *namaz* (prayers) and *azan* (the call for prayers) were not being said. But it did record that the Friday prayers were being said and '*Subhe* (dawn) *namaz* is also done (*sic*). Then it is locked.' He recorded also that 'the keys of the lock of the masjid are with the Muslims'.

The abnormalities are all faithfully recorded. 'When the *namazies* (worshippers) leave, from the surrounding houses shoes and stones are hurled towards the *namazies*. Muslims out of fear do not utter a word. Lohia also visited Ayodhya after Raghodas and gave a lecture. . . don't harm the graves. . . The Bairagis said Masjid is Janmabhoomi and so give it to us. . . I spent the night in Ayodhya and the Bairagis are forcibly taking possession of the Masjid. . . '

Both these witnesses are fully corroborated by two incontrovertible and uncontroverted documents—a radio message sent at 10.30 a.m. on 23 December 1949 by the District Magistrate K.K. Nayar to the Chief Minister Pandit Govind Ballabh Pant, the Chief Secretary and the Home Secretary. It read thus, 'A few Hindus entered Babri Masjid at night when the Masjid was deserted and installed a deity there. DM and SP and force at spot. Situation under control. Police picket of 15 persons was on duty at night but did not apparently act.'

This message was based on police constable Mata Prasad's report to the Ayodhya police station earlier. Here is a translation of the FIR lodged by Sub Inspector Ram Dube, police station Ayodhya, on 23 December 1949, as certified by the office of the city magistrate on 11 February 1986:

According to Mata Prasad (paper no.7), when I reached to (*sic*) Janam Bhumi around 8 o'clock in the morning, I came to know that a group of 50–60 persons had entered Babri Mosque after breaking the compound gate lock of the mosque or through jumping across the walls (of the compound) with a stair and established therein, an idol of Shri Bhagwan and painted Sita Ram, etc., on the outer and inner walls with *geru* (red loam). Hans Raj on duty asked them to defer but they did not. These persons have already entered the mosque before the available PAC (Provincial Armed Corps) guards could be commanded. Officials of the district administration came at the site and involved themselves in necessary arrangements. Afterwards, a crowd of 5–6 thousand persons gathered around and while chanting bhajans and raising religious slogans tried to enter the mosque but were deferred and nothing untoward happened thereon because of proper arrangements. Ram Das, Ram Shakti Das and 50–60 unidentified others entered the mosque surreptitiously and spoiled its sanctity. Government servants on duty and several others are witness to it. Therefore it is written and filed.

The acts constituting offences under Sections 295 and 297 of the Penal Code read thus:

295. Injuring or defiling place of worship with intent to insult the religion of any class. Whoever destroys, damages, or defiles any place of worship, or any object held sacred by any class of persons with the intention of thereby insulting the religion of any class of persons or with the knowledge that any class of persons is likely to consider such destruction, damage or defilement as an insult to their religion, shall be punished with imprisonment of either description for a term which may extend to two years, or with fine, or with both.

297. Trespassing on burial places, etc. Whoever, with the intention of wounding the feelings of any person, or of insulting the religion of any person, or with the knowledge that the feelings of any person are likely to be wounded, or that the religion of any person is likely to be insulted thereby,

commits any trespass in any place of worship or on any place of sculpture or any place set apart for the performance of funeral rites or as a depository for the remains of the dead, or offers any indignity to any human

> corpse, or causes disturbance to any persons assembled
> for the performance of funeral ceremonies,
> shall be punished with imprisonment of either descrip-
> tion for a term which may extend to one year, or with
> fine, or with both.

To this day the spoiled sanctity has not been rectified. It is a standing blot on our legal and political system, a mockery of secularism, a contempt for elementary minority rights and, indeed, the rule of law. In the *Statesman* of 26 October 1986, Chandan Mitra quoted a Faizabad official as saying, 'obviously the guard had been bribed heavily'. It is by such sordid means that a house of worship was taken over. (*vide, Muslim India,* June 1986, p. 248 for the text of the FIR; and Tripathi, op. cit., for the text of the radio message.)

S.K. Tripathi reported that 'the then Prime Minister, Jawaharlal Nehru, was furious and ordered the then Chief Minister, Govind Ballabh Pant, to undo the harm done. The Deputy Prime Minister, Vallabhbhai Patel, wrote to Pant that any unilateral action based on an attitude of aggression or coersion could not be countenanced; and Pant replied that efforts were continuing to set things right in a peaceful manner.'(see note 1 at the end of this essay.) The Chief Secretary, Bhagwan Sahay, and the Inspector General of Police, V.N. Lahiri, had been sending frantic messages to Faizabad for the removal of the idols. However, Nayar was not prepared to carry out their instructions because of fear of 'bloodshed and manslaughter'.

Nayar wrote two detailed letters to Chief Secretary Bhagwan Sahay in quick succession. In his letter dated 27 December 1949, Nayar, after explaining the pros and cons of removing the idols, concluded, 'I would, if the Government decided to remove the idols at any cost, request that I be relieved and replaced by an officer who may be able to see in that solution a merit which I cannot discern. For my part I cannot in my discretion, which is the only legal sanction behind my action in this matter, essay to enforce such a solution as I am fully aware of the widespread suffering which it will entail to many innocent lives.' Nayar was removed eventually. He later served a term as a Jan Sangh MP and his portrait was placed in the mosque after the take-over. (Satyapal Dang, *New Age,* 15 October 1989.)

The law is not inadequate to deal with such situations. The criminal law provides a summary remedy against forcible dispossession leaving the claimant free to prove title in a regular civil suit against the party originally in possession. But possession is first speedily restored to the dispossessed.

The Code of Criminal Procedure 1898, then in force, contained an entire chapter on 'disputes as to immovable property'. So does Code of Criminal Procedure 1973, with substantially similar provisions.

Section 145 of the Code of 1898 reads:

(1) Whenever a District Magistrate, Sub-Divisional Magistrate or Magistrate of the first class is satisfied from a police-report or other information that a dispute likely to cause a breach of the peace exists concerning any land or water or the boundaries thereof, within the local limits of his jurisdiction, he shall make an order in writing, stating the grounds of his being so satisfied, and requiring the parties concerned in such dispute to attend his Court in person or by pleader, within a time to be fixed by such Magistrate, and to put in written statements of their respective claims *as respects the fact of actual possession of the subject of dispute*, and further requiring them to put in such documents, or to adduce, by putting in affidavits, the evidence of such persons, as they rely upon in support of such claims.

(2) For the purposes of this section the expression 'land or water' includes buildings, markets, fisheries, crops or other produce of land, and the rents or profits of any such property.

(3) A copy of the order shall be served in manner provided by this Code for the service of a summons upon such person or persons as the Magistrate may direct, and at least one copy shall be published by being affixed to some conspicuous place at or near the subject of dispute.

(4) The Magistrate shall then, *without reference to the merits or the claims of any of such parties to a right to possess the subject of dispute*, peruse the statements, documents and affidavits, if any, so put in, hear the parties and conclude the inquiry, as far as may be practicable, within a period of two months from the date of appearance of the parties before him, if possible, *decide the question whether any and which of the parties was at the date of the order before mentioned in such possession of the said subject.*

Provided that the Magistrate may, if he so thinks fit, summon and examine any person whose affidavit has been put in as the facts contained therein:

Provided further that, if it appears to the Magistrate that any party has within two months next before the date of such order been *forcibly and wrongfully dispossessed*, he may treat the party so dispossessed as if he had been in possession at such date.

Provided also that, if the Magistrate considers the case one of emergency, he may at any time attach the subject of dispute, *pending his decision under this section.*

(5) Nothing in this section shall preclude any party so required to attend, or any other person interested, from showing that no such dispute as aforesaid exists or has existed; and in such case the Magistrate shall cancel his said order, and all further proceedings thereon shall be stayed, but, subject to such cancellation, the order of the Magistrate under sub-section (1) shall be final.

(6) If the Magistrate decides that one of the parties was or should under the second proviso to sub-section (4) be treated as being in such possession of the said subject he shall issue an order declaring such party to be entitled to possession thereof until evicted therefrom in due course of law, and forbidding all disturbance of such possession until such eviction and when he proceeds under the second proviso to sub-section (4), may restore to possession the party forcibly and wrongfully dispossessed.

Sub-sections (7) to (10) are not relevant.

This section was, however, invoked and perverted to *sanctify the dispossession.* Markanday Singh, Magistrate, first class, and Additional City Magistrate Faizabad-cum-Ayodhya after being 'fully satisfied from information received from police sources and from other credible sources that a dispute between Hindus and Muslims of Ayodhya over the question of rights of proprietorship and worship in the building claimed variously as Babri Masjid and Janmabhoomi Mandir, Mohalla Ram Kot, within the local limits of my jurisdiction, is likely to lead to a breach of the peace', ordered the attachment of the 'said buildings' under Section 145 of the Criminal Procedure Code (CrPC) and appointed Priya Dutt Ram, Chairman, Municipal Board, Faizabad-cum-Ayodhya, as receiver to arrange for the care of the property in dispute on 29 December 1949. The Receiver took charge of the disputed property on 5 January 1950 and submitted a scheme as was desired in the Additional City magistrate's order. (Tripathi, *Indian Express,* 30 March 1986.)

The crucial issue of dispossession was deliberately ignored. 'A dispute' existed which was likely to 'lead to a breach of the peace'. The property was attached. The party in possession which was dispossessed on 22–23 December 1949 was completely excluded. Muslims were forbidden to enter the mosque. The organized mobs which took over the mosque acquired access to it. In 1986 the limitations on access were removed.

Contrast this with the Order of the Sub-Divisional Magistrate, Parliament Street, New Delhi, A.G. Cutting, of 7 February 1972 in The State vs. Sadiq Ali and Others. and S.D. Sharma & Others under Section 145. He ordered restoration of possession of 7, Jantar Mantar Road (Congress House) in New Delhi to Congress(O). Not because it was the 'real' Congress, but because it had been forcibly dispossessed by Congress (R) on 13 November 1971. That order was also made under Section 145 of the CrPC. A similar order should have been made in the Babri Masjid case in 1949. The contrast is glaring. As Magistrate Cutting said, the Congress (O)'s men 'were dispossessed. They are therefore entitled to be put back into possession until they are evicted from the said premises by an order of a competent court' (in a regular civil suit on title).

In the Ayodhya case, the Receiver's scheme, predictably, said 'the most important item of management is the maintenance of Bhog and Puja in the condition in which it was carried on when I took over charge'. There were to be at least three *pujaris* who 'should be allowed free access' to the installed idols. (*Muslim India,* May 1987, see p. 208 for the text of the scheme.) Under the scheme Muslims were altogether forbidden to pray in the mosque, Hindus were permitted to offer puja and have darshan of the idols from a side gate and make offerings through four pujaris employed by the Receiver who was appointed by the Magistrate.

Next, a civil suit no. 2 of 1950, was filed on 16 January 1950, by Gopal Singh Visharad in the Court of the Civil Judge, Faizabad, praying for a declaration that he was entitled 'to worship and visit without obstruction or disturbance, Shri Bhagwan Ram Chandra and others installed at Asthan Janmabhoomi', and a perpetual injunction restraining the defendants from removing these idols. Amongst eight defendants were five Muslims, the State of Utter Pradesh, the Deputy Commissioner and the Superintendent of Police of Faizabad.

The Civil Judge, N.N. Chadha, granted an interim injunction as prayed for on 16 January 1950. The District Magistrate, Faizabad, thereupon instructed the District Government Counsel to move for modification of the order on the ground that the site in dispute is claimed both by Hindus and Muslims and unrestricted admission of the public has been allowed and that if the public is freely allowed for puja and darshan, *it would amount to allowing one party the exercise of rights which are in dispute*. Accordingly, an application was moved and the order dated 16 January 1950 was modified on 19 January 1950 as follows, 'The parties are hereby restrained by means of the temporary injunction to refrain from removing the idols in question from the site in dispute and from interfering with the puja, etc., *as at present carried on*. The order dated 16 January 1950 stands modified accordingly.'

The interim injunction was later confirmed by the Civil Judge in his order dated 3 March 1951 with the observation, 'The undisputed fact remains that *on the date of this suit the idols of Shri Bhagwan Ram Chandra and others did exist on the site* and that worship was being performed by the Hindus including the plaintiff, though under some restrictions put by the executive authorities.' (Tripathi, op. cit.) That the 'undisputed fact' of the presence of the idols was created by force and sheer justice required restoration of the *status quo ante* evidently did not weigh with the judge even in a civil proceeding where both title and possession are relevant. (*vide, Muslim India*, March 1986, pp. 108–9 for the text of the judgment of 3 March 1951.) 'There are several other mosques in the mohalla in question,' the Judge said as if there were no other temples there as well. Thus, for the second time the forcible dispossession of 22–23 December 1949, recorded in two official documents, was sanctified in a judicial pronouncement marked by pathetically tortuous reasoning. The High Court confirmed this order on 26 April 1955.

The Deputy Commissioner of Faizabad, J.N. Ugra, filed a written statement in the Court on 24 April 1950. *It is of cardinal importance not least because it was filed 'on behalf of Defendant No. 6, the State of Uttar Pradesh'*. Paras 14,15 and 16 are relevant. 'The property in suit is known as Babri Masjid and it has been *for a long period in use as a mosque* for the purpose of worship of the Muslims. *It has not been in use as a temple* of Shri Ram Chandraji.'

In para 15 he stated that, 'On the night of December 12, 1949 the idols of Shri Ram Chandraji were surreptitiously and wrongly put inside it.'

Para 16 added, 'That as a result of the said *wrongful* act a situation imperilling public peace and tranquillity was created and the public authorities had to intervene in order to prevent breach of peace and tranquillity.'

This statement was filed in another civil suit no. 25 of 1950 by Shri Param Hans Ram Chandra Dass vs. Zahoor Ahmad and Others. Apparently a similar statement had been filed in the earlier suit no. 2 of 1950 as well. (*Muslim India,* March 1986, p. 112.)

Ugra's authoritative statement totally belies the BJP President L.K. Advani's assertion on 19 September 1989 that no prayers were said in the mosque since 1936.

Two more civil suits were filed in addition to suit nos. 2 and 25 of 1950. One was by Nirmohi Akhara in 1959 for the discharge of the Receiver appointed under Section 145 and delivery of possession of the mosque to them. (Suit no. 26 of 1959, Nirmohi Akhara vs. Babu Priya Dutta Ram and others.)

On 18 December 1961 the first civil suit by Muslims was filed—suit no. 12 of 1961 Sunni Cental Waqf Board vs. Gopal Singh Visharad & Others. The first relief sought in suit no. 12 of 1961 was for a 'declaration that the property indicated by letters ABCD is a mosque commonly known as Babri Masjid and the land shown in the sketch map by the letters EFGH is a public Muslim graveyard commonly known as "Ganjshahidan".' The second relief sought was for delivery of possession of the mosque and graveyard in suit by removal of the idols and other articles which the Hindus had placed in the mosque as objects of their worship. This suit came to be treated as the leading suit.

The VHP owed its existence to the Rashtriya Swayamsevak Sangh (RSS) Chief M.S. Golwalkar and Swami Chinmayananda's deliberations in Bombay on 19 August 1964, though its first session was held at the 1966 Kumbh Mela in Allahabad. (*Indian Post* quoted in *Muslim India,* April 1990, p. 164.)

Agarwal recalls:

> At its session held at Vigyan Bhavan, New Delhi, on 7 and 8 April 1984 the Dharma Sansad of the Vishwa Hindu Parishad gave a call for the removal of the three mosque-like structures raised by Muslim marauders after destroying the ancient Hindu temples at Sri Rama Janma Bhumi, Ayodhya, and Sri Krishna Janmasthan, Mathura and of Kashi Vishwanath at Gyanvapi, Varanasi. *The so-called Babari Masjid at Ayodhya was taken up first.* Sri Rama Janma Bhumi Mukti Yagna Samiti was formed with Sri Dau Dayal Khanna as its convenor and Gorak-

shapeethadishwar Mahant Sri Aveda Nathji as its President. In order to create national awareness and arouse public opinion in support of the cause of liberation of Sri Ram Janma Bhumi, the Vishwa Hindu Parishad organised a Ratha-yatra of Sri Rama Janakji Virajman on a motorised chariot, which started from Sitamarhi in Bihar on 25 September 1984. The Ratha passed through important towns of Bihar and reached Ayodhya on 6 October 1984.

(*Parlance*, Jan–Feb 1990, p. 16.)

Indira Gandhi's assassination led to the suspension of the *rath-yatra*. But it was revived from twenty-five places on 23 October 1985. The VHP spearheaded the move. The ninth of March 1986 was fixed as D-day. Its leaders met Chief Minister Vir Bahadur Singh and the District Magistrate, I.K. Pandey. Neerja Chowdhury reported the disclosure in *The Statesman* (20 April 1986) by 'a senior Vishwa Hindu Parishad leader' that 'Rajiv Gandhi had indicated in no uncertain terms that all the gates of the edifice must open to the devotees' before Shivratri on 8 March 1986.

Agarwal himself admits that, 'On December 19, 1985 Sri Veer Bahadur Singh, the Chief Minister of Uttar Pradesh visited Ayodhya on the occasion of the Ramayana Mela sponsored by government agencies. A few of us headed by our President Justice Shiva Nath Katju, had assembled at Ayodhya.' They met V.B. Singh. (*Parlance*, pp. 16–17.)

A twenty-eight-year-old local lawyer Umesh Chandra Pandey filed an application on 25 January 1986 in the court of the *munsif* seeking removal of the restrictions on the puja. It was an application in the civil cases to which he was not party and he did not implead the Muslims who were parties to the suit either. The *munsif* declined, judiciously enough, to pass orders since the file in the main case of 1961 was in the High Court and orders could be made only in that suit. An appeal was filed on 31 January and heard on 1 February 1986. An application by Mohammed Hashim, who came to know of the proceedings for being impleaded, was rejected. K.M. Pandey, the District Judge of Faizabad, recorded the statements of the District Magistrate and the Superintendent of Police on the issue of law and order and in forty minutes ordered the opening of the locks. He observed, 'It is clear that it is not necessary to keep the locks at the gates for the purpose of maintaining law and order or the safety of the idols. This appears to be an unnecessary irritant to the applicant and other members of the community.'

Having refused to hear the Muslims altogether, the Judge said, 'After having heard the parties it is clear that the members of the other community, namely, the Muslims, are not going to be affected by any stretch of imagination if the locks of the gates were opened and the idols inside the premises are allowed to be seen and worshipped by the pilgrims and devotees. It is undisputed that the premises are presently in the court's possession and that for the last 35 years Hindus have had an unrestricted right of worship as a result of the court's order of 1950 and 1951. If the Hindus are offering prayers and worshipping the idols, though in a restricted way for the last 35 years, then the heavens are not going to fall if the locks of the gates are removed. The district magistrate has stated before me today that the members of the Muslim community are not allowed to offer any prayers at the disputed site. They are not allowed to go there.'

The Order was palpably bad in law. The *munsif's* order could not be appealed. Pandey was not party to suit no. 2 of 1950 in which he made the application nor did he apply to be impleaded as party either. The plaintiff in the suit, Gopal Singh Visharad, had died years earlier and his suit had abated since no one else had been substituted as plaintiff in his place. All the four suits had been consolidated and suit no. 21 of 1961 was made the leading case. Yet, Muslims were not heard because in District Judge K.M. Pandey's opinion, since Muslims were 'not allowed to go there. . . there is no occasion for law and order problem arising as a result of the removal of locks. *It is absolutely an affair inside the premises.*' He meant inside the community, evidently. *(vide, Muslim India,* March 1986, pp. 110–11 for the text.)

On 3 February 1986 Mohammed Hashim applied for quashing of the Order before the Lucknow Bench of the High Court in writ petition 746 of 1986. The Court ordered the same day that 'until further orders of the Court the nature of the property in dispute *as existing today* shall not be changed'.

The Sunni Central Waqf Board also filed writ petition no. 3106 of 1986 on 12 May 1986 against the District Judge's Order of 1 February 1986. On 11 December 1987 the State of Uttar Pradesh applied to the Allahabad High Court that the hearing of the two writ petitions be deferred and the four civil suits be withdrawn from the Court of Munsif Sadar, Faizabad and tried by the High Court. *The curious thing is that to this day the State itself has not filed any written statement declaring its stand.* Sheer honesty required it to do so promptly and to reaffirm its earlier statement made through J.N. Ugra. No less curious is the stand of the VHP. It has profited by successive interim orders of the courts endorsing the altered status quo in 1949 and 1986. It, nonetheless, refuses to go to trial on the merits of its claim.

Some idea of the contours of the litigation and the hurdles it will have to surmount is afforded by the issues framed in the case by the special bench of the Allahabad High Court on 26 May 1990.

Counsel for the All India Hindu Mahasabha had proposed the framing of eight issues including the question of revaluation. But the court, after going through the same, filed only one which asked whether the suit was liable to be dismissed with special costs.

Some other issues are as follows:

Whether the building described is a mosque as claimed by the plaintiff. If so, whether it was built by Babar as alleged by the plaintiff or by Meer Baqi as alleged by defendant no. 13;

Whether the plaintiff (issue no. 10) or the Hindus in general (issue no. 4) have perfected their right of adverse possession as alleged by them respectively;

Whether the plaintiff had no right to maintain the present suit since no valid notification under section 5(1) of the Muslim Waqf Act (No. XIII of 1936) was ever made in respect of the property in the dispute;

Whether the suit is barred by limitation as it was filed after the commencement of the UP Muslim Waqf Act, 1960;

Whether the present suit is a representative suit, the plaintiffs representing the Muslims and the defendants representing the interest of Hindus;

Whether the idols of worship were placed inside the building in the night intervening 22/23 December, 1949, as alleged in the plaint or had they been in existence there since before, in either case its effect;

Whether the pillars inside and outside the building in question contain images of Hindu gods and goddesses and so the building in question could not have the character of a mosque under the tenets of Islam;

Whether the waqf in question cannot be a Sunni waqf as the building was not allegedly constructed by a Sunni Mohammedan but was allegedly constructed by Meer Baqi who was allegedly a Shia Muslim and the alleged Mutawallis were allegedly Shia Mohammedan; if so its effects.

The court had earlier ordered the execution of the survey by the commissioner to be appointed by the registrar-secretary of the board of revenue not below the rank of a PCS officer having knowledge of surveys. Photography, video recording and carbon-dating was also directed to be performed by the director, archaeological department, UP.

(*The Times of India*, 27 May 1990.)

Manoj Mitta, a Lucknow correspondent of the *Times of India* reported in the issue of 25 June 1990, on the unique course which the litigation had taken. He doubted whether it would lead to a solution of the tangle. He wrote:

Several of the 43 issues framed by the court on May 25 pertain neither to law nor any verifiable fact. Rather, those issues fall in the grey areas of history, mythology and religion.

Here is a sample: 'Is the property in suit the site of Janam Bhumi of Sri Ram Chandraji?

'Whether the building and the graveyard stand dedicated to almighty God, as alleged by the plaintiffs (Sunni Wakf board)?

'Have the Muslims been in possession of the property in suit from 1528 AD continuously, openly and to the knowledge of the defendants and Hindus in general? If so, its effect?

'Whether the building has been used by the members of the Muslim community for offering prayers from times (*sic*) immemorial? If so, its effect?

'Have the Hindus been worshipping the place in dispute as Sri Ram Janam Bhoomi or Janamasthan and have been visiting it as a sacred place of pilgrimage as or right since times (*sic*) immemorial? If so, its effect?

'Whether any portion of the property in suit was used as a place of worship by the Hindus immediately prior to the construction of the building in question?

'Whether the building has been constructed on the site of an alleged Hindu temple after demolishing the same? If so, its effect?

'Whether even after the construction of the building deities of Bhagwan Sri Ram Virajman and the Asthan Sri Ram Janambhoomi continued to exist on the property. . . and the said places continued to be visited by devotees for purposes of worship? If so, whether the property in dispute continued to vest in the said deities?'

The judges—Justice S.C. Mathur, Justice Brijesh Kumar and Justice S.H.A. Raza—had to frame such intractable issues because of the constraints of the judicial process. Before the trial begins, the judges have to frame the issues on the basis of the written statement filed by all the parties to the suit.

But, while framing the issues, the judges do have some discretion to reject points which are extraneous to the dispute. And, in the Ayodhya case, the judges used their discretion to reject some contentions which would have had absurd political ramifications.

For instance, one of the parties, the Hindu Mahasabha, had proposed the following issue, 'Whether the division of India was unauthorised and unconstitutional and whether the UP Wakf Act was adopted by any lawfully constituted government of India?' The judges, while declining to frame that issue, noted in their order that it was 'political' and, therefore, 'beyond the purview of courts'.

But, as the issues enlisted earlier show, they had framed some that are purely matters of faith. The nature of the four suits that had been consolidated from the Faizabad district courts and placed before this special bench of the high court had apparently made such issues unavoidable. . . .

When the special bench had been set up, the VHP had no option but to stand by the various Hindu parties embroiled in the suit. In a bid to redeem its position, the VHP had suggested in vain to the special bench to drop altogether one 'unprovable' issue framed in the district court.

The issue was whether the disputed site was really the birthplace of Ram. The high court's order dated May 25 records: 'Learned counsel, Sri (V.K.S.) Chaudhary has objected to the above issue. According to him, this issue is not based on the pleading of any of the defendants. We are unable to agree with the submission of the learned counsel as the pleading is contained in paragraph 27 of the written statement filed on behalf of defendants 3 and 4 (Nirmohi Akhara and another Hindu party). Accordingly, the issue is retained.'

But Chaudhary subsequently turned the tables on the votaries of Babri Masjid by getting the High Court to frame issues concerning Islamic scriptures as well. Some of these altogether new issues, which form part of the 43 framed last month are:

'If a portion of the disputed site was used as a place of worship by the Hindus immediately prior to the construction of the building in question, whether no mosque could come into existence in view of the Islamic tenets at the place in disputes?

'Whether the building in question cannot be a mosque under the Islamic laws in view of the admitted position that it does not have minarets?

'Whether the building in question cannot legally be a mosque as it is admittedly surrounded by a graveyard on three sides?

'Whether the pillars inside and outside the building in the question contain images of Hindu gods and goddesses? If the finding is in the affirmative, whether on that account the building in question cannot have the character of mosque under the tenets of Islam?'

These and other contentious issues framed in the Ayodhya case have never been decided before in judicial history. It remains to be seen how the bitter claimants of the Ayodhya property will produce evidence for or against such issues. More importantly, how will the special bench pronounce a reasoned verdict on them?

The first step taken was in December 1949, to oust Muslims from the Babri Masjid and convert it into a mandir with limited rights of access to the lay public. The next step had been taken in February 1986, to remove the restrictions. The last step contemplated is the demolition of the mosque and the construction of a temple on its site.

It is not exactly a matter for celebration that India's political system was just barely able to halt the last step. Satyapal Dang exposed a pact between the VHP and the Union Home Minister, Buta Singh, on 27 September 1989 which would have enabled the VHP to initiate its plans of constructing the temple on the site of the mosque.

Quoting a report in the *Navbharat Times* of 29 September 1989, he said, 'According to the agreement the government would allow Ram Shila Pooja functions to go on all over the country, the VHP would take to Ayodhya a limited number of Ram Shilas on November 9.' The foundation stone of the new temple would be laid some distance away from the mosque. But 'there is no undertaking that the Babri Masjid would not be sought to be demolished subsequently'. (*New Age*, 15 October 1989.)

On 18 October 1990 the Government of India published the text of the VHP–Buta Singh accord which, to a certain extent, confirmed the press reports. The Shilas procession *was* allowed on condition of good behaviour. However, *unknown to the public and to its own followers, the VHP had agreed to abide by the Court's order of 14 August 1989*. The agreement is set out in full (in note 2 at the end of this essay.)

Under the VHP's ground plan, as revealed by its Secretary General, Ashok Singhal, 'The sanctum sanctorum or the *garbha griha* of the proposed temple will remain at the same place where at present worship is being made of the idol.' (*Organiser*, 27 September 1989.) That is, right inside the sanctum sanctorum of the mosque. Interestingly, while Muslim leaders were banned from entering Ayodhya, the VHP leaders stayed there for months.

The Buta Singh–VHP pact came shortly after the Lucknow Bench of the Allahabad High Court passed an order on 14 August 1989 accepting the application by the UP Government's standing counsel, R.N. Trivedi, to restrain all 'parties, groups and persons represented by them from interfering in any manner with the site in dispute, to disturb the status quo, and further to organise or extend threats of interference by organising any activity which may bring about confrontation between two major rival communities, which is bound to threaten public peace and public order'. The application referred specifically to the Shila Puja. Earlier, on 12 July the bench had summoned all the five pending cases relating to the dispute for trial by a full bench of the High Court. The fifth case (suit no. 236 of 1989) was filed by Agarwal with Sri Ram as plaintiff no. 1.

Mohan Sahay reported in the *Statesman* of 26 October 1989:

> Highly placed sources claim that the green signal was given by Mr Buta Singh to the secretary-general of the VHP, Mr Ashok Singhal, at a meeting in Lucknow on 27

September. The home minister had instructed all the officials concerned to make efforts so that the Ram Shila bricks were transported to and the Shilanyas completed without hindrance. *This is acknowledged in the house journal of Shree Ram Shila Pujan Samiti quoting Mr Ashok Singhal.*

After Buta Singh's approval on 27 September 1989, the Shila Puja began three days later. The Lucknow correspondent of the *Indian Express* reported (3 October 1989) that the VHP leaders 'bluntly told the Home Minister that the sanctum sanctorum of their temple would be the same place where the idol of Lord Rama is presently placed and worshipped. The size of the proposed temple would be over 34,000 square feet besides appurternances. It would be 270 feet long, 126 feet wide and 132 feet high. It is so designed as to absorb the disputed structure standing on an area of about 6,000 feet. The foundation for the Singhdwar would be laid about 270 feet away from the *garbha griha* which would be retained as a sanctum sanctorum of the new temple'.

The judiciary could have prevented the Shilanyas. But once again the judiciary proved ineffective and for palpably wrong reasons.

On 27 October 1989, the Manan Ekta Edyan petitioned to the Supreme Court to ban the Ram Shila Pooja processions and also the Shilanyas on 9 November. The Court refused. One of the judges, Justice B.C. Ray, asked counsel in the course of the hearing, 'Is it your proposition that all religious processions in the country should be banned?' (*Hindustan Times*, 28 October 1989.) V.M. Tarkunde's counsel for the petitioners pointed out that the object of the procession was to construct a Ramjanmabhumi temple which in itself was a provocation.

The Fundamental Rights to freedom of speech and expression and to freedom of assembly embodied in Article 19(1) of the Constitution are subject to 'reasonable restrictions' under clause (2) *inter alia* in the interests of public order. What is more, clause (2) of Article 25 explicitly says that the right to religious freedom guaranteed by Article 25 (1), will not prevent the State from regulating any secular activity associated with the practice of religion. The Court simply directed the authorities to take action 'against those spreading communal rancour'.

On 3 November 1989 the Bihar Government did what the UP Government did not. It banned all religious processions. (*The Telegraph*, 4 November 1989.)

A sad feature of the whole episode since 1949 has been the failure of the judiciary to provide reliefs which the law empowers and the people expect it to provide. Hopes for judicial redress were not exactly raised when the Special Bench of the Allahabad High Court at Lucknow, trying the Babri Masjid case, remarked in its order of 7 November 1989, 'It is doubtful that some of the questions involved in the suit are soluble by judicial process.' (*The Hindu*, 8 November 1990.)

Addressing a seminar in New Delhi on 10 November on 'The Constitution and Growing Communalism', a former judge of the Supreme Court, V.R. Krishna Iyer, angrily remarked, 'The judiciary will be described as the villain of the piece.' In his view it lacked the guts to face the issue. (*The Times of India*, 11 November 1989.)

The Shilanyas was eventually held at Ayodhya. On 9 November 1989 the plinth for a massive fifty-five crore rupees temple was dug 192 feet away from the mosque. The next day the foundation of the temple was laid. (*The Telegraph*, 10 and 11 November 1989.)

This was in clear breach of the High Court's stay order and of the rules. They required the Collector's permission for any construction on state-owned land. Most of the land around the Mosque belongs to the State. (P.K. Roy, *Frontline*, 28 October 1989.)

Only a day earlier, on 7 November, the Allahabad High Court had, on the request of the State, issued a clarificatory order which said that 'the order of injunction dated 14 August 1989 was in respect of the *entire* property mentioned in the suit, *including plot no. 586*, in so far included within the boundary described by letters E, F, G, H, in the site plan'. The site plan is part of the court record in the plaint of the suit 12 of 1961 filed by the Sunni Central Board of Waqfs, UP and others.

But on 8 November Buta Singh told the Lok Sabha that 'the site of the Shilanyas is clearly outside the limits of EFGH in the site plan. This position was explained by the Advocate General of UP at a meeting in Lucknow earlier that day'. (See *India Today*, 15 December 1989, p. 159, for a sketch map of the site.) The Shilanyas was held on the disputed plot no. 586.

On 28 December 1989, after assumption of office at the Centre by the National Front, Home Minister Mufti Mohammed Sayeed said in the Lok Sabha, in answer to starred question no. 79, that 'the State Government has identified the concerned plot as Nazul Plot No. 586'. In its view, based on legal advice and that of the District Magistrate, 'the whole of it cannot fall within the limits spelled out by the Lucknow Bench of the Allahabad High court in its clarificatory order dated November 7, 1989'.

On 11 November the VHP leaders took everyone by surprise by

declaring that the construction of the temple was being deferred and would be decided at a meeting of Hindu leaders in Allahabad on 27 and 28 January 1990. By then the National Front Government had come to power. Its election manifesto said that 'the controversy can be settled through negotiations, based on mutual understanding. The National Front feels that the Babri Masjid should not be demolished. At the same time, the Hindu sentiments to have a temple dedicated to Lord Rama should be respected'.

On 15 February 1990 the National Front Government constituted 'a Committee which will talk with various groups to find an amicable solution to this issue'. It consisted of Madhu Dandavate, George Fernandes and Mukhtar Anis. Neither the Committee's deliberations nor the VHP's deferrals need detain us.

What is more to the point is that the Government's electoral pledge records a clear national consensus which is not shared by the BJP–RSS–VHP combine alone.

Several formulae have been suggested. The most remarkable feature of all the solutions proposed is their implicit acceptance of the fundamental principle that the Babri Masjid be declared a national, protected monument under the Ancient Monuments and Archaeological Sites and Remains Act, 1958, just like those built by other rulers of India. Under Section 4 (1) of the Act, 'where the central government is of the opinion that any ancient monument. . . is of national importance, it may, by notification in the Official Gazette, give two months notice of its intention to declare such monuments. . . to be of national importance'. Objections are heard and the site is purchased or agreement entered into with the owner. The monument acquires a nationally protected character under the law of the land.

A devout Hindu like the late Kamlapati Tripathi had no hesitation in proposing, in a letter to the Prime Minister dated 24 March 1989, that the 'Babri Masjid–Ram Janmabhoomi complex may be declared a national monument'. This would be a fitting, tangible expression of the ideal of communal harmony and the co-existence of diverse faiths. (*Muslim India*, July 1989, p. 209.) Bombay justly boasts a traffic island which has housed a temple, a church and a mosque. In this spirit the basic principle can be amplified by building on the *chabutra* a magnificent temple in honour of Shri Ramachandraji.

Karan Singh's solution, proposed on 15 January 1987, is along the same lines: 'It is not befitting that at this sacred place Sri Ram should be worshipped in an unsuitable setting. What is needed is the construction of a new temple at the Janmabhoomi which would be a really fitting tribute to Lord Rama. *There seems to be no controversy regarding the chabutra where in fact worship has been carried on for many years.* I suggest that a National Committee be formed to draw up plans for the construction of a magnificent temple on the site, where really beautiful statues of Sri Rama, Sita and Lakhman can be installed and which can become a focus of worship and devotion for the Hindus of the world.' Karan Singh offered to make, 'a token donation of a lakh of rupees on behalf of the Dharmarath Trust'. (*Muslim India*, February 1987, p. 63.)

In a public appeal to the Prime Minister on 10 May 1986, S. Shahabuddin, then a Member of Parliament, also proposed a solution 'based on the separate existence of the two structures known as Babri Masjid and Ram Chabutra, separated by a wall. Ram Chabutra marks the Janmasthan of Shri Ramachandraji'. He suggested, 'First, let the *status quo ante* be restored in the Babri Masjid as on 22 December 1949. Second, let a magnificent temple dedicated to Shri Ramachandraji be built on Ram Chabutra. Thirdly, let the Babri Masjid be notified as a Protected National Monument of historic importance and taken under the care of the central government.' (*Muslim India,* June 1986, p. 249.)

Indeed, in 1891 a noted writer on the monuments and antiquities of the region, A. Fuhrer, classified the Babri mosque as a monument in the possession of private persons but which should be protected. A bill, broadly on these lines, was moved in the Rajya Sabha last year by a member of the Communist Party of India (CPI) to declare the whole Babri Masjid–Ram Janmabhumi complex a national monument under the Act. This was in keeping with the CPI National Council's Resolution of 1 April 1987. In 1989 a large number of public figures issued a call for a settlement on these lines. Among them were Rajni Kothari, Ram Vilas Paswan, and George Fernandes. (*Muslim India*, March 1989, p. 110.) According to the Press Trust of India (PTI), the conversion of the complex into a national monument was also suggested at a meeting of the leaders of recognized political parties in Parliament with Buta Singh on 29 March 1989. Satya Prakash Malaviya of the Janata Dal endorsed the suggestion on 27 May 1989 and so did the Bharat Kisan Union (BKU) leader Mahendra Singh Tikait on 12 December 1988—restore the mosque, he said, and allow the Hindus to renovate the ancient temple there.

The solitary note of dissent from this truly national consensus is struck by the BJP. Atal Behari Vajpayee's proposal on 1 October 1989 to relocate the mosque is preposterous and the BJP, the RSS and the VHP's pronouncements are nothing if not arrogant.

The judicial process is rejected in terms which reflect a contempt for evidence and a dangerous recourse to demagogy. If the BJP president, L.K. Advani says that 'the controversy is about accepting *rashtra purush* Ram against a foreign invader Babur' (*The Telegraph*, 17 May 1990) the VHP leader Ashok Singhal asserts that 'the Constitution does not rest powers in the Court to question the divine factor of the people'. (*The Telegraph*, 6 October 1989.) The RSS leader Rajendra Singh wrote to the then Prime Minister Rajiv Gandhi on 12 April 1987, 'All Hindus are convinced it is the Ram Janmabhoomi and they do not need the proofs from *Baburnamas* and your white-washing historians.' (*Muslim India*, June 1987, p. 249.)

The RSS chief Babasaheb Deoras said, 'This is not a case on which the judiciary can pass a judgement. What type of evidence are the Hindus expected to produce? That Rama was born and that his birthplace is Ayodhya?' (*Organiser*, 12 March 1989.)

The BJP National Executive's resolution at Palanpur on 11 June 1989 said, 'The BJP holds that the nature of this controversy is such that it just cannot be sorted out by a court of law.' Having ruled out adjudication it went on to propose that the sentiments of the people must be respected, and Ram Janmasthan handed over *to the Hindus* if possible through a negotiated settlement or also by legislation. 'Litigation certainly is no answer.' But nor is legislation, for the statute will be patently unconstitutional. A law or a notification under the Act which declares the mosque a *national* monument will be perfectly justified. But one which hands it to a *particular community* will be discriminatory and will violate of the Fundamental Rights. It will be a legislative verdict on a civil suit, moreover, and bad on that ground as well.

Against this background the existence of a consensus in support of a compromise is a priceless asset. It achieves that remarkable feat of reconciliation of morality with expediency and of sentiment with reality. Vajpayee once came a little closer to it. In a speech at Bombay on 15 February 1987, he urged the Muslims to give up their claim to the Babri mosque and hand it over the Hindus as a gesture of goodwill and respect for their sentiments while the Hindus should reciprocate by allowing the present structure of the masjid to stand as it is while constructing a temple adjoining it befitting Ramjanmabhumi. (*Indian Express,* 16 February 1987.)

He said it represented his personal view. Sadly, his plea of respect for feelings was unevenly balanced. As the *Hindustan Times* of 13 April 1987 pointed out, 'Vajpayee is silent on whether the mosque should be used for prayers and without this assurance it is difficult to see even enlightened

Muslim leaders accepting his proposal.' Evidently, the only concession which Vajpayee was prepared to make, with self-conscious magnanimity, was not to demolish a mosque built in 1528 in which Muslims prayed for four centuries. The newspaper cited an apt parallel—the agreement signed on 8 October 1968 by the Shahi Idgah Trust and Shri Krishna Asthar Sewa Sangh on the Mathura temple–mosque controversy. Under it the mosque and the temple co-exist side by side.(See note 3 at the end of this essay.)

The core of the matter surely is: Who is entitled to the ownership and possession of the premises known as Babri Masjid by law? The proceedings which followed the attack by the mob in December 1949 were in the nature of summary proceedings under the CrPC and not a regular civil suit for title. Precisely such a suit on title is now pending before the special bench of the Allahabad High Court at Lucknow. Even L.K. Advani has affirmed repeatedly that matters of title are justiciable and courts of law can decide them. It is therefore misleading to say that issues of faith are before the Lucknow bench of the High Court.

Under the Civil Procedure Code it says the civil courts can only decide issues of a civil nature. As we have seen, such a case involving title is before the Lucknow bench of the Allahabad High Court and it alone has the right and jurisdiction to decide it. Neither the Executive nor the Commission of Enquiry suggested by Rajiv Gandhi can usurp that Court's authority.

Under the national consensus, instead of relinquishing the mosque to the Hindus, the Muslims as a community should give it to the nation at large under the law of the land as a historic monument worthy of national protection. Such a compromise solution will be a truly national achievement. Only the VHP and the BJP reject this consensus. On 9 January 1950, Sardar Patel characterized the surreptitious planting of the idols in the Babri Masjid as a 'unilateral action based on an attitude of aggression or coercion'. It is unlikely that he would have regarded the BJP President L.K. Advani's attempt to resolve the issue by use of force through his *rath-yatra* other than 'an attitude of aggression or coercion'.

Notes

NOTE 1

New Delhi
9 January 1950

My dear Pantji,

The Prime Minister has already sent to you a telegram expressing his concern over the developments in Ayodhya. I spoke to you about it in Lucknow. I feel that the controversy has been raised at a most inopportune time both from the point of view of the country at large and of your own province in particular. The wider communal issues have only been recently resolved to the mutual satisfaction of the various communities. So far as Muslims are concerned, they are just settling down to their new loyalties. We can reasonably say that the first shock of partition and the resultant uncertainties are just beginning to be over and that it is unlikely that there would be any transfer of loyalties on a mass scale. In your own province, the communal problem has always been a difficult one. I think it has been one of the outstanding achievements of your administration that, despite many upsetting factors, communal relations have generally improved very considerably since 1946. We have our own difficulties in the UP organisationally and administratively as a result of group formations. It would be most unfortunate if we allowed any group advantage to be made on this issue. On all these grounds, therefore, I feel that the issue is one which should be resolved amicably in a spirit of mutual toleration and goodwill between the two communities. I realise there is a great deal of sentiment behind the move which has taken place. At the same time, such matters can only be resolved peacefully if we take the willing consent of the Muslim community with us. There can be no question of resolving such disputes by force. In that case, the forces of law and order will have to maintain peace at all costs. If, therefore, peaceful and persuasive methods are to be followed, *any unilateral action based on an attitude of aggression or coercion cannot be countenanced.* I am therefore quite convinced that the matter should not be made such a live issue and that the present inopportune controversies should be resolved by peaceful (methods) and accomplished facts should not be allowed to stand in the way of an amicable settlement. I hope your efforts in this direction will meet with success.

Yours sincerely,
Vallabhbhai Patel

The Hon'ble Pandit G.B. Pant
Premier of United Provinces
Lucknow

Lucknow
13 *January 1950*

My dear Sardar Sahib,

I do not know how to thank you for all the trouble you took in coming over to Lucknow almost immediately after your return from Bombay in response to my request without any previous notice. I was reluctant to approach you, especially because of the strain which you had already undergone in the course of your recent trip to Bombay. But I felt somewhat worried over the situation as I sensed it. Whenever in difficulty I look up to you. You are always so kind and generous and an unfailing source of strength and light in moments of gloom and depression. When I recall all that had happened here in your presence I feel deeply mortified. It may have given you an idea of the agony that I have to undergo almost from day to day. There has been hardly any improvement since. We are, however, discharging our duties as best as we can.

The Selection Committee has completed its labours and the following candidates (see enclosure) will I trust be finally and formally elected today. The list has, I am told, on the whole been well received. Many have, however, been disappointed and some have not been able to suppress their feelings. I have received a letter from Shri Kala Venkata Rao which indicates that he was not quite happy over the selection of three erstwhile members of the Provincial Legislature. The reasons were in each case quite adequate and convincing, but they have probably not been brought to his notice. I shall be writing to him in this connection shortly. The executive committee of our party has asked some of the signatories who have made wild allegations against the Government and some of its members in their letter to the President to explain their position. They were present at the meeting at my house that day but did not in spite of my enquiry state any facts. Even at our meeting yesterday they were not able to do so. They have been given further time. Their replies will be reaching today or tomorrow. That letter seems to have been signed also by a Deputy Minister. If it were a purely local or provincial affair it would not have been very difficult to tackle, but because of other currents and forces the difficulties are considerably aggravated. I need not say more as I expect to be in Delhi soon after your return from Calcutta. I wonder if you will be able to find any rest there. I only hope and pray that your frail health will be able to stand all this strain; still great care has to be taken and I trust that Behn (Maniben) will do the needful and regulate things in the desired manner.

I have to thank you for your letter about the Ayodhya affair. It will be of great help to us. *Efforts to set matters right* in a peaceful manner are still continuing and there is a reasonable chance of success, but things are still in a fluid state and it will be hazardous to say more at this stage.

With best regards,

Yours sincerely,
G.B. Pant

The Hon'ble Sardar Vallabhbhai Patel
Deputy Prime Minister
Government of India
New Delhi

*

NOTE 2

The following is the text of the agreement reached on 27 September 1989 at a meeting held in Lucknow convened by the Chief Minister of Uttar Pradesh with representatives of the VHP in which the Union Home Minister was also present. The agreement was signed by Shri Ashok Singhal, Shri Dau Dyal Khanna, Mahant Avaidnath and Shri Nrityagopal Das.

A meeting was held in Lucknow by the Chief Minister of Uttar Pradesh on 27 September 1989 with the representatives of Vishwa Hindu Parishad (VHP) during which the Union Home Minister was also present.

In this meeting all aspects of the situation arising in the wake of VHP's programme to perform Shila Poojan in different parts of the country and carry the 'sanctified' bricks to Ayodhya for laying the foundation-stone of Rama Temple on 9 November 1989, were discussed.

Formulations

As a result of these discussions, the following were agreed:

a) The VHP will give prior intimation to the concerned District authorities of the Shila Procession route and agree to change in routes in case the District authorities so desire in public interest.

b) The VHP and its followers would not raise any provocative slogans which may endanger communal harmony.

c) As far as possible the 'sanctified' bricks will be carried in trucks on the routes determined before-hand in consultation with the concerned District authorities.

d) Senior and responsible VHP functionaries would take the responsibility of guiding the procession and will extend full cooperation to the District authorities.

e) The spot in Ayodhya where the sanctified bricks will be collected, will be decided in consultation with the District authorities.

f) *The VHP undertakes to abide by the directive of the Lucknow Bench of Allahabad High Court given on 14.8.1989 to the effect that the Parties to the Suits shall maintain the status quo and shall not change the nature of the property in question and ensure that the peace and communal harmony are maintained.*

Following representatives of VHP will cooperate/coordinate with UP Government.

1. Sh.Dau Dyal Khanna
2. Sh.Dixit, Ex-DGP (UP)
3. Sh.Onkar Bhave
4. Sh.Suresh Gupta, Ex-Vice-Chancellor
5. Sh.Mahesh Narain Singh, Ayodhya

Signed
Sh. Ashok Singhal
Sh. Mahant Avaidnath
Sh. Nrityagopal Das
Sh. Dan Dyal Khanna

(*Statesman*, 18 October 1990)

THE DISPUTED SHRINE AT AYODHYA

The above is a sketch of the disputed shrine at Ayodhya. The dispute is over the shaded area. The idols are placed under the central dome which was kept locked in the past. Pujaris and other visitors used the gate to the right. Ram Chabutra is a platform under a tree in the outer enclosure. To the right of the main entrance is a tin shed the pujaris use as an office. Sita Ki Rasoi is a small platform to the right. Singhdwar is not in use. The chabutra on the left is raised space. There are several little idols in the outer enclosure where devotees make offerings. The main entrance faces east.

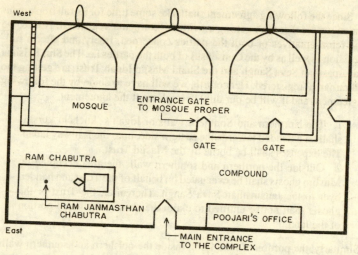

A rough sketch of the mosque and the Ram Chabutra in its compound. The idols were placed on 22–23 December 1949 under the central dome of the mosque.

NOTE 3

Translation of the Agreement between the Shahi Idgah Trust and Sri Krishna Janmasthan Seva Sangh, Mathura.

We, Shri Deodhar Shastri, U.P. Manstri Authorised by the Shri Krishna Janamasthan Seva Sangh, Mathura, *As First Party* and Shri Shah Mir Malih and Shri Abdul Ghaffar, Advocate, the Representative of the Shahi Masjid, Idgah Trust, Mathura, *As the Second Party.*

Under the Trust's Resolution No. 2 Dated 8.10.1968.

In order to settle the longstanding disputes between the Shri Krishna Janamasthan Sangh and the Shahi Masjid Idgah Trust and the so-called Ghosi tenants and licencees of the second party, we, under the suggestion of the members of both Hindu and Muslim communities, have reached an agreement, henceforth, to settle our bilateral disputes and avoid cases against each other.

The following agreement agreed to by the Second Party i.e. Shahi Masjid Idgah Trust has the permission of the Uttar Pradesh Central Wakf Board *vide* their express letter no. 2876, 43 CIR dated 9.9.1968 and Shri Shah Mir Malih and Shri Abdul Ghaffar, Advocate have been authorised to get the Agreement implemented. Under their resolution No.2 in the meeting of 8.10.1968.

Similarly the first Party i.e. the Shri Krishna Janamasthan Seva Sangh has also accepted the agreement at its meeting of 25.8.1968 and authorised Shri Deodhar Shastri to get the Agreement implemented.

Since the following agreement shall take some time for its full implementation we are therefore getting a written 'Ikrarnama' registered. Hence, we the representatives of both the parties concerned, freely and after a full-decision as well as by the Consensus of both the parties i.e. The Shri Krishna Janamasthan Seva Sangh and the Shahi Masjid Idgah Trust, are getting the 'Ikrarnama' registered. Henceforth, we will have to abide by the following agreement and it will be our duty to implement the agreement.

1. The Northern and Southern walls of Idgah's 'kuchchi kurshi' shall be extended towards the eastern side, upto the Railway ladan. The expenses shall be borne by the Masjid Trust.

2. Outside the northern and southern walls the area occupied by Muslim ghosis shall be evacuated on behalf of the Trust and handed over to the Janamsthan Seva Sangh. Thereafter, the Trust or the ghosis shall not be entitled to claim the above-mentioned portion of the land.

Similarly, the portion of land lying inside the northern and southern walls shall be the Trust's property. Hence there shall be no claim on this land on the part of the Seva Sangh.

3. In the west-northern corner of Idgah kuchchi kursi a portion of land is occupied by the Seva Sangh (shown in the map ABCD). The Trust shall acquire the kuchchi kursi and it shall become the Trust's property.

4. The controversial debris of the stairs on the southern side, for which there are cases filed in the court, shall be cleared by the Trust by 15 October, 1968. Thereafter the portion shall be the Seva Sangh's property.

5. The houses built by Muslim ghosis out of the northern and southern walls under settlement with the Trust shall be evacuated on behalf of the Trust and handed over to the Seva Sangh. Only after the completion of evacuation, the Trust shall be entitled to get the walls constructed.

The Trust, moreover, shall not open doors, windows, pinjars etc. nor any water outlets (drains) in the proposed wall, towards the Seva Sangh. The Seva Sangh too shall not do any such thing against the Idgah.

6. The outlets (parnalas) of Idgah flowing already westward of the Janamasthan shall be removed and turned towards Idgah by piping. The expenses shall be borne by the Seva Sangh. During the laying of the pipe, a representative of the Janamasthan shall be present.

7. A portion of the railway land in front of Idgah's northern and southern walls which is going to be acquired by the Janamasthan Seva Sangh, after acquiring the land, the Janamasthan Seva Sangh shall transfer that portion to the Trust which falls inside the north and south walls of the Idgah.

8. The portion of land in front of kuchchi kurshi towards the Eastern side (shown in the map EFGHIJKL) and in the west-northern corner

(shown in the map ABCD) which is left by the Seva Sangh in favour of the Trust is shown in oblique line in the map.

9. The cases against each other shall be withdrawn according to the above agreement.

10. Both the parties shall have the right to appeal to the court for having the agreement implemented if either party deviate from the agreement.

Hence this agreement reached in writing by the consent of both the parties.

Date of writing: 12 October 1968

Boundary of Masjid Idgah Shahi
East—Railway line
West—Chabutra Janamasthan
North—Ground Janamasthan
South—Ground Janamasthan
      banke katra, Keshaw—deve Mathura ton

Writer: Navnit Lal Sharma Shastri
Deodhar Shastri
Signature: Abdul Ghaffar: In English
Signature: Md. Shah Mir Malih

NOTE 4

Relevant extracts from the Ancient Monuments and Archaelogical Sites and Remains Act 1958, (Act 24 of 1985)

Suggestions have been made that to resolve the Ayodhya Controversy, the Babri Masjid complex may be declared a Protected Monument. Extracts from Act 24 of 1958 under which an ancient monument can be so declared follow:

Section 2 (a): Ancient monuments mean any structure, erection or monument. . . which is of historical, archaeological or artistic interest and which has been in existence for not less than 100 years. . .

2 (j): 'Protected monuments' mean an ancient monument which is declared to be of national importance by or under this Act. . . .

Section 4 (1): *Where the Central Government is of the opinion that any ancient monument. . . is of national importance, it may, by notification in the Official Gazette, give two months' notice of its intention to declare such ancient monument. . . to be of national importance.*

4(2): Any person interested in such ancient monument. . . may, within two months, after the issue of the notification, object to the declaration. . .

4(3): On the expiry of the said period of 2 months, the Central Government, may, after considering the objections, if any, received by it, declare by notification in the Official Gazette, the ancient monument. . . to be of national importance.

Section 5(1): **The Director General may, with the sanction of the Central Government, purchase or take a lease of or accept a gift or bequest of any protected monument.**

5(6): *Nothing in this section shall affect the use of any protected monument for customary religious observances.*

Section 6(1): The Collector, when so directed by the Central Government, shall propose to the owner of a protected monument to enter into an agreement with the Central Government within a specified period for the maintenance of the monument.

Section 13: *If the Central Government apprehends that a protected monument is in danger of being destroyed, injured, misused, or allowed to fall into decay, it may acquire the protected monument under the provision of the Land Acquisition Act, 1894, as if the maintenance of the protected monument were the public purpose within the meaning of that Act.*

Section 16(1): *A protected monument* maintained by the Central Government under this Act *which is a place of worship or shrine shall not be used for any purpose inconsistent with its character.*

16(2): Where the Central Government has acquired a protected monument under Section 13 or where the Director-General has purchased. . . under Section 5 and *such monument or any part thereof is used for religious purpose or observances by any community, the Collector shall make due provision for the protection of such monument or part thereof from pollution or desecration—*(a) *by prohibiting the entry therein, except in accordance with the conditions prescribed. . . of any person not entitled so to enter by the religious usages of the community by which the monument or part thereof is used;* or (b) *by taking such other action as he may think necessary. . . .*

Competing Symbols and Shared Codes: Inter-Community Relations in Modern India

Mushirul Hasan

I shall tell the truth, O Brahmin, but take it not as an offence:
The idols in thy temple have decayed.
Thou hast learnt from these images to bear ill-will to thine own people.
And God has taught the (Muslim) preacher the ways of strife.
My heart was sick: I turned away both from the temple and the Ka'abah,
From the sermons of the preacher and from thy fairy tales, O Brahmin
To thee images of stone embody the divine—
For me, every particle of my country's dust is a deity.
Come, let us remove all that causes estrangement
Let us reconcile those that have turned away from each other, remove all
signs of division.
Desolation has reigned for long in the habitation of my heart—
Come, let us build a new temple in our land.
Let our holy places be higher than any on the earth,
Let us raise its pinnacle till it touches the lapel of the sky;
Let us awake every morning to sing the sweetest songs;
And give all worshippers the wine of love to drink.
There is power, there is peace in the songs of devotees—
The salvation of all dwellers on the earth is love.[1]

Mohammad Iqbal

The controversy over the Babri Masjid–Ramjanmabhumi issue has not just aroused deep religious passions but has raised the fundamental issue of how best to allow competing religious symbols to co-exist in a society committed to the secular ideal. Admittedly, the pressing need is to resolve conflicting claims over the mosque at Ayodhya. But, in the long run, all concerned citizens will need to marshal their intellectual resources so as to evolve a mechanism and, at the same time, define social codes for resolving controversies of this nature. Otherwise, the initiative, as always, will rest with those who manipulate both political institutions and processes to create and widen arenas of conflict.

It is not surprising that the flare-up, centred around the mosque in

Ayodhya, should cause such deep concern. After all, no other issue since India's independence has generated such violent passions, led to such widespread riots[2] (see table), gripped the people with panic, fear and anger, and threatened to destroy the democratic, secular consensus envisaged by the architects of the Indian Constitution. Sentiments have been polarized to such an extent that two successive governments have fallen in the course of just a year, with the Bharatiya Janata Party (BJP) succeeding in placing the mandir issue on the national agenda.[3] As the *Times of India* commented on 17 October 1989, 'Jettisoning once and for all its mumbo-jumbo about Gandhian values, the BJP, under Mr L.K. Advani's spirited leadership, has gone on the offensive with a strategy clearly designed to polarise life in the country along antagonistic religious lines.'

State	No. of Places	No. of Deaths
Andhra Pradesh	4	27
Assam	1	7
Bihar	8	19
New Delhi	–	8
Gujarat	26	99
Karnataka	22	88
Kerala	2	3
Madhya Pradesh	5	21
Maharashtra	3	4
Rajasthan	13	52
Tamil Nadu	1	6
Tripura	1	–
Uttar Pradesh	28	227
West Bengal	2	6
Total	116	567

Communal Riots from 1 September to 20 November 1990

This is not all. For the first time, religious zealots, bolstered by politically articulate groups, found both a cause and an opportunity to create a bond of fraternal unity among their divided and stratified constituency. In the Shilanyas ceremonies, the Vishwa Hindu Parishad (VHP), backed by the BJP and the Rashtriya Swayamsevak Sangh (RSS), found a unifying symbol and a cementing bond which had, for centuries, eluded Hindu reformers and preachers.[4] Through flamboyant demonstrations of religious worship and through mindless retaliatory acts, these groups have clearly succeeded in stoking the fires of communal unrest.

On the other side of the spectrum, members of the Babri Masjid Action Committee (BMAC), acquired much political legitimacy and support. Some of its members, having tasted success over the Shah Bano case, began to make strident claims on behalf of their community. They reached out to the Muslim population, aired their long-standing grievances and extracted concessions from political parties on the eve of the 1989 general elections and their aftermath. Given their capacity to mobilize Muslim opinion, especially in Uttar Pradesh and Bihar, it was neither possible nor expedient to ignore the powerful Imam of the Shahi Jama Masjid in Delhi or the renowned head of the prestigious Nadwat-al-ulama, a theological seminary at Lucknow. They represented a Muslim consensus which had been achieved only once in the history of Indian Islam, i.e., during the Khilafat movement in the early 1920s.

Many contemporary aspects of the Babri Masjid–Ramjanmabhumi dispute remain shrouded in mystery. For example, why was a district judge in Ayodhya allowed to disturb the *status quo* and pass a verdict which brought alive an issue that was dormant for nearly four decades after independence? To court the so-called Hindu constituency? Or, to mollify enraged feelings over the Government's 'surrender' over the Shah Bano case? Even if these explanations are seemingly valid, it is still not clear why the VHP and their allies enjoyed the freedom to make political capital out of the judgement and launch a massive countrywide agitation which, in an extremely surcharged atmosphere, could only exacerbate tensions among the rival contestants? It would appear that the ruling party, already riven with dissensions over the handling of the Shilanyas ceremonies, slowly but steadily lost the initiative to the VHP and was unable to keep its leaders on a tight leash. Soon, the concern was not just confined to Rama's birthplace in Ayodhya. Amid the chanting of Vedic hymns and the ringing of temple bells, a general clamour was raised fo: 'recovering' other mosques, such as the ones in Varanasi and Mathura. Today, such demands are being unabashedly voiced on public platforms and expressed in ominous terms.[5] They are contested with equal vigour and fervour by the hot-headed members of the BMAC and their vociferous supporters.

It is not uncommon to find scapegoats in history—to place the blame on the medieval Sultans of Delhi who defiled and destroyed temples—and to attribute Muslim intransigence to the policies of the British Government and its successor, the Congress party.[6] It is pointed out that the colonial rulers courted the Muslims by granting them privileges and special concessions in order to create their separate and distinct identity in Indian politics. It is also argued that the Congress fared no better: it succumbed to the pressures of the Muslim League in agreeing to the partition of the country. After independence, the Congress leadership continued to placate the Muslims and pandered to their 'separatist' sentiments for electoral reasons. In this way, secularism has merely served the interests of the minorities, especially the Muslims. The Hindus, on the other hand, have been at the receiving end. While their co-religionists in neighbouring Pakistan and Bangladesh have been relegated to the status of second-class citizens, Indian Muslims have received more than their due share. They have been allowed to retain their personal law, conduct their proselytizing activities and preach and practise their religion without inhibition.[7] This was the essence of the BJP's advertisements published in the national newspapers from 30 October to 1 November 1991.

Such generalized and simplistic formulations are backed by perspectives which dwell on the separateness and inherently contradictory nature of the Hindu and Muslim traditions and their estrangement both in colonial and pre-colonial days. Thus the contest over the Babri Masjid–Ramjanmabhumi issue is seen as part of a recurring theme of conflict and tension in Indian history.

This is not the place to refute such ill-conceived theories. My main aim is to highlight certain broad aspects of Hindu–Muslim relations during the last decade of the nineteenth and the early decades of the twentieth centuries. In the final section, the focus of analysis is shifted from the national and provincial arenas to Faizabad/Ayodhya—a district with a long and chequered history. The attempt is to outline the broad contours of local politics and to see if political linkages and socio-economic relations were able to transcend religious cleavages. The Babri Masjid–Ramjanmabhumi issue is drawn in to illustrate, rather than to illuminate, the more general argument of this essay.

Both as an ideology and as a movement, communalism derives ideological sustenance from the view, which was popularized by Henry Elliot and other colonial writers, that Islam and Hinduism, as indeed their followers, co-existed uneasily in India and that religious conflicts rather than harmonious living was the hallmark of the medieval Indian ethos. In fact, the dominant images of the Muslim presence, nurtured by publicists and major literary writers, were concerned with the degradation of the Hindus through forcible conversions, imposition of the *jaziya* (tax levied on non-Muslims to guarantee their safety and protection), strict application of the *shariat* (Islamic Law) and the desecration of the places of worship.[8]

Such distorted images do not portray the true and real nature of medieval society: they merely serve to reinforce latter-day prejudices. Admittedly, there existed a fragmented and differentiated form of religious consciousness, which may have led the Sultans and their ideologues to offend religious sensibilities. But religious solidarity was not the basis of collective socio-economic experiences. The ideology of the State, trimmed to suit the interests of the ruling elites, accommodated religious concerns. Yet, it did not rest on the notion of a unified 'community', with identifiable interests, which forms the main pillar of modern day 'communalism'. Moreover, while there were stray, localized and sporadic incidents of conflicts over religious symbols, the integrative and syncretic forces were at work amongst the elites as well as the common people. The dominant picture of the seventeenth and eighteenth centuries is not of the Hindus and the Muslims forming exclusive and antagonistic categories but of their cooperating in cultural life and social affairs.[9]

This scenario, however, underwent a change with the coming of the British. For the first time, signs of Hindu–Muslim friction surfaced in some areas and amongst certain groups. Now, the terms of dispute were articulated differently. The language and vocabulary of discourse changed. Muted expressions were replaced with angry exchanges. Mild protests took the form of violent outbursts. The reasons for this were quite numerous, ranging from the introduction of western-style institutions to the emergence of religio-revivalist trends, stimulated by powerful socio-religious reform movements in Bengal, Punjab and Maharashtra.

No summing up of late nineteenth century trends can be complete without reference to the activities of the Arya Samaj, the spurt in cow-protection activity and the vigorous campaign in support of the Nagri script and its use in government and law courts. These were not isolated assertions of militant, religio-revivalist tendencies. They were manifestations of the new and burgeoning Hindu consciousness.[10]

There were similar trends among the Muslims. The Greco–Turkish War of 1897 stimulated pan-Islamic feelings. Islamization in Bengal and parts of northern India, inspired by Shah Waliullah (1702–63) and his successors and bolstered by the Faraizis in Bengal, was an equally potent force. Insistence on a revitalized consciousness and identity, with its corresponding denigration of Islam's local roots, began to erode syncretistic traditions and undermine religious peace and understanding.[11] The massive communal rioting in 1893, preceded by sporadic but violent altercations, was a grim reminder to the nationalists that the fabric of Hindu–Muslim unity was too fragile to withstand the onslaught of various revitalization movements. 'If the smouldering fire of religious enmity is not put out,' warned an observer, 'it will before long be kindled into a mighty flame and destroy the noble edifice which the Congress has built with so much pains.'[12]

The prophecy did not come true. Though relations between *certain* sections of Hindus and Muslims were *sometimes* strained, their deterioration was neither deep nor irreversible. 'Nothing strikes the intelligent traveller in India more forcibly,' observed a senior police official in 1894, 'than the friendly peacable attitude of all castes and classes towards each other'.[13] He was right. Friction between religious groups was not ordinarily a major source of disturbance in the last quarter of the nineteenth century.[14] During 1889–94, there was no violence in Bengal, except once in Calcutta and its suburbs.[15]

Such sporadic outbursts did not signify, as some writers are wont to suggest, the fragmentation of society along communal lines. Intercommunity tensions and disputes were counterbalanced by the quiet, commonplace routines in which Hindus and Muslims intermingled without notice or incident and they could still be found involved in a range of 'religiously promiscuous' practices. In 1909, the *Imperial Gazetteer of India* stated that it was the regular practice of 'low-class Muhammadans' to join in the Durga Puja and other Hindu festivals; it mentioned Muslim consultation of Hindu almanacs, worship of Sithala and Manasa, use of vermilion and joint offerings to village deities before the sowing or transplanting of rice seedlings.[16] Another inspiring legitimation of the more mundane expressions of peaceful co-existence came daily in the sounds of Muslim *shehnai* players joining in the *arti* at Hindu temples, including the *arti* of the Vishwanath temple in Benares.[17] Two America-based scholars—Sandria Frietag and Nita Kumar—have recently shown how in this holy city of the Hindus, Muslim weavers actively participated in public ceremonials expressing a shared Benarasi culture, including 'the marriage of the Laut' (Bhairava), Bharat Milap and the day-to-day observances related to particular figures and shrines.[18]

Contemporary writings took note of cordial Hindu–Muslim relations and projected the ongoing process of social and cultural fusion. The poet Mohammad Iqbal (1876–1938) shared the vision of a united India—one that was free of both alien domination and inner dissensions. He called his land of birth a garden where the people inhabiting it were members of a *qaum* (nation), with the two circles of Islam and *watan* intersecting and at several places coalescing into a coherent whole. *Himala*, the first poem in *Baang-i-Dara*, was inspired by the beauty of his land of birth. *Hindustani Bachhon ka Qaumi Geet* (National Anthem of Indian Children) and the *Tarana-i-Hindi* (The Song of India) were refined, buoyant and non-communal expressions of patriotic sentiments. In *Naya Shiwala* (New Temple), Iqbal chided both Hindus and Muslims for their narrow mentality and appealed to the keepers of the temple and the mosque to foster mutual goodwill and understanding.[19]

Akbar Allahabadi (1846–1921), a merciless satirist equipped with an irrepressible sense of humour, had similar concerns. He subjected to ridicule, to scathing criticism or damning exposure the social and political strategy of imperialism and Syed Ahmad Khan's (1817–98) policy of loyal cooperation with the Government. And, like Iqbal, he championed Hindu–Muslim unity. Both Hindus and Muslims, he wrote, have to bear the blows of those who wield the rod of worldly power, but they should respond by being like water on which the blows of a rod have only a momentary effect.[20]

Iqbal and Akbar were stating the obvious. They recognized, as indeed did the others, that the direction in which patronage, economic welfare and authority flowed in everyday life indicated the continuing importance of cross-communal networks.[21] Syed Ahmad Khan's Aligarh project was backed by the Hindus and Muslims alike. He encouraged, despite his misgivings over the Nagri resolution of 1900 (which sparked off a Hindi–Urdu controversy), a Hindu–Muslim *entente* in cultural and religious matters. His contemporary, Ajudhia Nath Kunzru, owed his fortunes as much to the wealthy Muslim landholders as to his extensive banking and commission agencies.[22] In east UP and Avadh generally, the dominant factor in the politics of the towns tended to be an Urdu-speaking elite connection based on landed interests. Communal considerations did not always foul the path of politics.[23]

The competing units in early municipal politics, as in the case of Faizabad, were multi-factions, not antagonistic groups. In the composition of early municipal factions, caste and communal considerations played a secondary role to personal rivalries, family linkages and economic ties. The lawyer, Maulvi Sirajul Islam, was elected from Chittagong to the Bengal legislative council, largely on the strength of the 'Hindu vote'. Surendranath Banerjea (1848–1925), on the other hand, was backed by Muslims for a seat in the prestigious Calcutta Corporation. Around the same time, a similar move was afoot in UP, where the Congress backed Hamid Ali Khan for a seat in the council.

Nor did communal divisions last long after they had been politicized. Soon after the violent eruptions in 1893, tempers began to cool everywhere and there was much display of 'mutual love and affection' in the riot-torn cities of UP.[24] Public statements and newspaper editorials on national unity and the commonality of Hindu–Muslim interests were matched by strenuous efforts of local reconciliation committees to resolve and defuse tensions.[25] When asked how the 'upper classes' of the two communities behaved when the riots occurred, the Assistant Magistrate of Gorakhpur replied:

> By taking leading Hindus and Muslims into confidence, matters are satisfactorily arranged. . . . In Aligarh, we left the whole matter to leading Hindus and Mussalmans and everything went off without hitch.[26]

Such was the pattern everywhere, reinforcing the argument that, by the end of the nineteenth century, there was no sign of the Hindus and the Muslims going their separate ways. If anything, the lines of cleavages in north India were more sharply drawn between the Shias and the Sunnis rather than the Hindus and the Muslims.[27] Though expressed in exaggerated terms, there is merit in the observations of W.S.Blunt and Henry Cotton that the Hindu–Muslim animus was accentuated only after the Government translated the principle of divide and rule into formal constitutional arrangements.[28]

With the onset of the twentieth century, there was a tendency towards the use of religious solidarity as a basis of political action. It started with the Nagri resolution of April 1900 which created fissures among the professional classes in UP. The prospect of reforms and of a greater share in the expanding administrative and bureaucratic machinery triggered off the Shimla deputation and the establishment of the All India Muslim League in December 1906, while widespread religio-revivalist movements aided the mushrooming growth of Defence Leagues, Anjumans and Sabhas. The Turko–Italian War of 1911 fanned pan-Islamic passions leading to intense religious activity among Muslims.

Many of the controversies, both political and religious, subsided during the Khilafat and Non-cooperation movements when Mahatma Gandhi was able to cement an extraordinary alliance between different segments of Indian society.[29] But not long afterwards, the edifice of inter-communal unity, so passionately built by the Mahatma, began to crumble. The Khilafat movement itself got bogged down in religious issues instead of concentrating on the consolidation and integration of anti-colonial forces. Consequently, a popular political movement, a gift of history, was a great opportunity absurdly wasted.

Still, it would be wrong to either conclude that the gulf separating the Hindus and Muslims was unbridgeable or that they were hopelessly polarized after Gandhi had called off the Non-cooperation campaign in February 1922. Most people, especially in the countryside, were unruffled by communal controversies and continued to live, as they had done in the past, in peace and harmony. This was so because bonds of socio-economic interests, centuries of common experiences and shared memories were strong enough to withstand the onslaught of religious fundamentalists and political propagandists. The Governor of Bengal commented on how the 'rank and file' of the two major communities in his province cooperated with each other in all 'daily business of life'; it was 'only at rare intervals, when religious feelings become inflamed, that they treat each other as enemies and clashes occur'. O.M. Martin, who served in the same province from 1915 to 1926, made similar observations. Hindu–Muslim unity, he added, was not a temporary occurrence but an old and cherished tradition.[30]

The pan-Islamic euphoria, which had caused so much excitement in the subcontinent, did not take much time to disappear as the Turkish nationalists began to rewrite their political agenda without a Khalifa/Sultan. Faced with this reality, unpleasant though it was to committed pan-Islamists, there was an unmistakable reordering of priorities.[31] From then onwards, Islam was once more firmly rooted in the Indian subcontinent and the interests of its followers were much more closely linked with their country and their countrymen. That is why the *ulama*, based at the Deoband seminary in the Muzzaffarnagar district of UP and connected with the Jamiyat-al-ulama, emerged as powerful advocates of composite nationalism and rejected the two-nation theory. Their arguments in defence of their position was backed by the theological weight of Islam.

It is assumed that the perspective of the Deobandi *ulama*, with its emphasis on composite nationhood, was rejected by large sections of the Muslim community and that the creation of Pakistan was a testimony to the validity of M.A. Jinnah's two-nation theory.

These are questionable assumptions. The Muslim League's success neither vindicates nor legitimizes the ideological underpinnings of the two-nation theory, for the birth of Pakistan in that summer of discontent in August 1947 was neither imminent nor historically inevitable. It symbolized, more than anything else, Jinnah's personal triumph, his answer to the obdurate Gandhi–Nehru–Patel leadership which had persistently refused to treat him on equal terms or discuss the blueprint of a free and united India. In the end, the creation of a new nation seemed more of an aberration, a historical accident, caused by a complex configuration of forces at a particular juncture. Sadly, Indian nationalists of all shades, including the socialists and communists, failed to grasp this reality. As a result, they bowed to the mounting pressure of the League and acquiesced in India's partition, though for different reasons.

This is not all. In the behind-the-scenes negotiations that took place on the eve of the Independence and the Partition, nobody tried to ascertain the views or the wishes of the people—both Hindus and Muslims. The predictable collapse of the interim ministry and the fire of violence in Bihar and Bengal, which so few tried to extinguish, offered the Congress and League leaders the opportunity and an excuse to hammer out the modalities of transferring power to two separate nations. Lord Mountbatten, the impetuous representative of the Crown, was anxious to hasten the process and preside over the liquidation of an Empire which had lost its *raison d'etre*. Asking the people to sit in judgement on an issue that was virtually settled during the prolonged confabulations at the Viceregal Lodge was an act of deception, a monumental fraud. Those privileged to vote in the 1946 elections did so in an atmosphere vitiated by communal rancour and strife. The die was cast and they could not, even if they wanted to, reverse a process that was well underway. Never before in South-Asian history did so few decide the fate of so many. And never before did so few ignore the wishes and sentiments of so many in the subcontinent.

One final point. In the debates that preceded and followed the birth of Pakistan, communal rivalries alone were projected as *the* stark Indian reality. It is necessary to provide a corrective to this approach, for there still existed, despite the trauma and agony that accompanied the vivisection of the country, large areas of Hindu–Muslim cooperation and tangible expressions of cultural fusion and religious syncretism.

Most people, Hindus and Muslims alike, clung to their inherited ideas, traditions and customs. This was so in the case of, for example, the Meos, the Malkana Rajputs, the Khojas, Bohras and Memons in western India and the Mappilas in Malabar.[32] Given their long, uninterrupted history of social mingling and cultural fusion, it is hard to conceive of a different scenario. Similar trends, syncretic and composite, were at work elsewhere. Islam in Punjab provided a repertoire of concepts and styles in authority which had served to encompass potentially competing values, including the values of tribal kinship, within a common Islamic idiom. [33] Islam in Bengal took many forms and assimilated values and symbols not always in conformity with Koranic ideals and precepts. Cultural idioms of Islam underwent a rapid transformation, giving birth to a set of popular beliefs and practices which, in essence, represented the popular culture of rural Bengal rooted in the pre-Islamic past. [34] Finally, Islam in South India evolved a tradition of worship which was marked by a striking capacity to accommodate itself to indigenous patterns of faith and worship. It gained a foothold in the region because of its capacity to forge links with the religions and peoples of the wider society, to offer a form of access to the divine which could be grasped and built upon through means which were already present within these societies. [35]

True, the rise of communal and 'separatist' politics diminished the importance of certain religio-cultural symbols which had, in the past, transcended caste and community distinctions. Yet, one could still find Hindus observing Muharram—which marks the martyrdom of Prophet Mohammad's grandson and his seventy-two companions. [36] Thousands continued to gather around shrines of the Sufis and other venerated men and sought their intercession to avert calamities, cure diseases, procure children for the childless, or even improve the circumstances of the dead. [37] Frederick Graham Cracknell, Magistrate and Collector of Etawah and Kanpur, reported that the *mela* commemorating Shah Madaar, who settled at Makanpur in Bilaur tahsil in the fifteenth century, was attended by 50,000 people, mostly Hindus. Unmoved by a Hindu–Muslim fracas in the area in 1931, Hindus and Muslims flocked to his shrine in equal numbers. The pattern was largely the same elsewhere. [38] Even when Hindu–Muslim relations had reached their lowest watermark in 1946–47, Mohammad Mujeeb, Vice Chancellor of Jamia Millia Islamia, noticed in the course of his travels:

> I remember that shortly after the orgy of violence in Bihar
> I visited the grave of a Sufi on the banks of the Ganges.
> The Muslims living in the *dargah* had fled and the place
> looked desolate. But soon a group of Hindu women appeared.
> They performed circumambulations and prostrations, as if nothing had happened that affected their

sentiments of veneration for the tomb of a Muslim saint.[39]

The extent to which narrow religious barriers were transcended and strict codes of behaviour transgressed is evident from Bahraich in eastern UP, where an outbreak of cholera in 1930 prompted Muslims to join the Hindus in great force to worship the goddess Bhawani to induce her to remove the pestilence.[40] In the Bengal countryside, pre-Islamic ceremonies relating to birth, marriage and death continued to be observed. As a concession to the 'reformist' movements, the 'outer labels' were discarded to make the rituals and practices look 'Islamic'.[41] The *Census of India* report of 1921 summed up the situation as:

> There are. . . communities among the Muslim population, chiefly among converts from Hinduism, whose religious ritual and exercises have a very strong tinge of Hinduism and who retain caste and observe Hindu festivals and ceremonies along with those of their religion. . . . The rigidity of intolerance of view, which is a marked feature of the religion of Islam in its purer form, does not extend to the masses, who are quite willing to recognize and assist the efforts of their neighbours to keep on peaceful terms with the unknown powers.[42]

It is not intended to portray an idyllic picture as such but to highlight an aspect of contemporary Indian history which is largely unexplored on account of stark and irrefutable evidence marshalled to detail the history of Hindu–Muslim animosity. Harping on antagonisms alone and turning a blind eye to areas of inter-community cooperation and fraternization, has distorted perspectives, deepened prejudices and, as in the case of the Babri Masjid–Ramjanmabhumi issue, strained India's fragile social fabric. To discover the roots of religious conflicts and comment on its intensity, even if one is thrown back into India's colonial past, is a legitimate historical exercise in so far as it does not offer a one-sided view.

Faizabad district in UP, once the capital of the Avadh Nawabs and an important Muslim centre, mirrored national and provincial trends in large measure. The Muslim population was relatively small—11.11 per cent in 1901. Most of them belonged to the weaving community, followed by the Sheikhs who held considerable land in Mangalsi, Haveli, Avadh and Khandansa, and the Syeds whose vast estates lay in Pirpur, Samanpur and Bhadarsa. In fact, Faizabad was among those districts of UP where a large proportion of land was held by Muslims. There were 2,051 separate estates at the beginning of 1905. Of these, 1,115 were owned by Rajputs, 366 by Brahmins and 286 by Muslims.

In general, Faizabad and its adjoining areas, including Ayodhya, was not different from other places in UP: it was equally affected by religious and revivalist currents. The militancy of the cow-protection agitation, which led to widespread rioting in 1893 in Azamgarh and the neighbouring districts of Bihar, caused much excitement in Faizabad. Yet there was no outbreak of violence. When the 'cow-question' surfaced in 1906 it was amicably settled by local leaders. During 1910–12, however, the consensus broke down largely in reaction to extensive cow-riots in certain areas of eastern and western UP.[43] A 'snowball plan', based on the 'heavenly voice' heard at Hanumangarhi in Ayodhya, was in circulation in Faizabad district.[44] But its impact was blunted by alert district officials. Backed by the UP Government, local and provincial leaders, including the Raja of Mahmudabad (1889–1931), were able to soothe frayed tempers. By September–October 1915, the Provincial Government, headed by James Meston (1865–1943), evolved a compromise formula acceptable to various contending groups.[45]

Hindu–Muslim relations in Faizabad were only marginally soured by the cow-protection movement and the great 'communal' debates, which started with Syed Ahmad Khan's crusade against the Congress and culminated in the Lahore Resolution of 1940. A major source of irritation was the mosque at Ayodhya which was allegedly built on the site of an ancient temple raised on the actual spot of Rama's birth. Evidence on the destruction of the temple is disputed.[46] Most historians at the Centre for Historical Studies, Jawaharlal Nehru University, point out that neither Abul Fazl, the sixteenth century author of *Ain-i-Akbari*, nor Tulsidas, a celebrated devotee of Rama, mention the demolition of a temple at the site of Rama's birthplace. They conclude, 'It is in the nineteenth century that the story circulates and enters official records. These records were then cited by others as valid historical evidence on the issue.'[47] H.R.Neville, who compiled the *District Gazetteer of Fyzabad*, recorded a view that was widely shared by British civil servants. He observed:

> The materials of the old structure were largely employed, and many of the columns are in good preservation; they are of close-grained black stone, called. . .*basauti*, and carved with various devices. Their length is from seven to eight feet, and the shape square at the base, centre and capital, the rest being round or octagonal. The mosque has

two inscriptions, one on the outside and the other on the
pulpit; both are in Persian and bear the date 935 Hijri. Of
the authenticity of the inscription there can be no doubt,
but no record of (Babur's) visit to Ajodhya is to be found
in the Musalman historians.[48]

What is perhaps not in dispute is that Ayodhya was, well before the
sixteenth century, a centre of pilgrimage for the Buddhists, the Jains and
Hindus. It is known that Hindu worship remained possible in the compound of the Babri mosque and the activities of the Brahmin *pandas* of
Ayodhya are recorded by the first European visitor to the place, William
Finch, between 1608 and 1611.[49] When Ayodhya first became an important pilgrimage centre in the eighteenth century it was as much due to the
activities of the Ramanandi sadhus as to the patronage of the Nawabi
court. The Diwan of Nawab Safdarjang, Raja Naval Rai, built and repaired
several temples in Ayodhya, while Safdarjang himself gave land for
building a temple on what is known as Hanuman's hill. Asaf-ud-daula's
Diwan, Tikayat Ray, supported the building of the important temple-
fortress Hanumangarhi on this land. Peter Van Der Veer refers to documents which indicate that Muslim officials of the Nawabi court gave away
gifts for rituals performed by the *pandas*,[50] i.e., Hindu priests on the site
of pilgrimage centres.[51]

Peter Van Der Veer also makes the important observation that when the
power of the Nawabs gradually eroded due to the influence of the British
in Avadh politics the peaceful co-existence of Hindus and Muslims in
Ayodhya came to be threatened.[52] He, along with Michael H. Fisher and
J.R.I. Cole, have shown how the changes in the configuration of forces
under Wajid Ali Shah deepened religious conflicts and, in 1833 and 1855,
nearly exploded into civil war.[53] Though the last Nawab of Avadh dealt
with the recalcitrant forces, headed by Amir Ali, he did not emerge
unscathed from the incident. His power and authority, already clipped by
the British, waned as the firebrand agitators chose the reckless course of
waging a holy war against each other. The British intervention in the Mandir–Masjid fracas was decisive. Its immediate effect was that an ambivalent
Nawab was goaded into taking action. At the same time, it sealed his fate and
gave the British an excuse to annex the kingdom of Avadh.

The confrontation in 1855 was serious, bitter and violent. But it did not
take long for the wounds to be healed. Apart from litigation between 1883
and 1886,[54] the Masjid–Mandir dispute remained dormant until 1934
when a communal riot near Ayodhya, triggered off by cow-slaughter,

inflamed passions in the area. Again, between 1950 and 1984 there was no movement to demand occupation of Rama's birthplace, except for legal actions destined to remain endlessly unfruitful.

There can be no doubt that the Ayodhya mosque was a powerful symbol of communal mobilization in UP. Yet, it was not strong enough to polarize sentiments to a degree where Hindus and Muslims in the province or in the locality would be arrayed against each other. Even when religious sentiments ran amok in the towns of UP from 1 February 1986 onwards, Ayodhya remained unaffected by communal frenzy. 'It is remarkable,' reported a newspaper correspondent, 'that while the controversy surrounding the Babri Masjid–Ramjanmabhumi has aroused religious passions elsewhere, Ayodhya and its surrounding areas have been able to maintain communal peace.'[55]

This was not an uncommon feature in Ayodhya. For nearly a century, most Hindus and Muslims in the area did not allow their daily lives to be influenced by the Masjid–Mandir controversy. They conducted their affairs and performed their usual chores without being swayed by religious passions. Their political life was not moulded by religious considerations alone. In the 1989 elections, for example, most people in a predominantly 'Hindu' constituency voted for the candidates of the Communist Party of India (CPI) who had stood for Hindu–Muslim amity and opposed the communalization of Faizabad polity and society by 'outside' forces. In this way communal groups and parties were humbled soon after the Shilanyas ceremony. This was an extraordinary develop-ment, especially in the light of the fact that the then ruling party capitulated on the occasion and legitimized the activities of the Vishwa Hindu Parishad (VHP), the RSS and the Shiva Sena.

It was, however, not a surprising occurrence. Generally speaking, political affairs in Faizabad were conducted on a supra-communal network. Before independence, this process was aided by professional ties, cultural links and common landed interests which bound the Urdu-speaking elites and helped to create a strong and powerful composite cultural tradition. More often, caste loyalties rather than religious affiliation moulded public life. This is illustrated by the strong links between the Kayasthas, who occupied one-quarter, and the Muslims, who held two-fifths, of the municipal board seats in the last quarter of the nineteenth century.[56] Between 1905 and 1911, Muslims, in general, were attracted to Balak Ram and his Kayastha party whose *taluqdari* links gave it a class dimension, a more cosmopolitan, cross-communal image.[57] Until after the first general elections in 1952, municipal bodies in Faizabad-*cum-*

Ayodhya remained in control of the Kayastha party and its Muslim allies.[58]

In the late 1930s and 1940s, however, there were visible strains in such cross-communal alliances. This was largely due to the failure of the Congress to thwart the communal forces. It allowed the Muslim League to wrest the initiative, as in the 1937 elections to the Faizabad–Sitapur–Bahraich urban constituency, when the Congress did not press its claim and literally surrendered the seat to the Muslim League. What happened in the 1946 elections is a different story altogether. Like the rest of the country, Faizabad district was communally polarized. Here, as elsewhere, the success of the League candidates was a foregone conclusion.

In the aftermath of Independence and Partition, the Congress made no effort to strengthen secular forces in Faizabad. On the contrary, it seized on purely religious issues and exploited religious sensibilities to secure electoral gains. Harold Gould has shown how the Faizabad district became the focal point of a political showdown between Acharya Narendra Deva, the fiery socialist leader, and his Congress rival Baba Raghava Das. In the course of the by-election campaign in 1948, Pandit Govind Ballabh Pant visited Ayodhya and declared that the Acharya did not believe in the divinity of Rama as proven by the fact that he did not wear the *chhot*, or tuft of hair at the back of the head, displayed by all devout, genuine Hindus. Baba Raghava Das, for his part, moved among his followers distributing *tulsi* leaves to emphasize the spiritual difference between him and his socialist adversary. Ayodhya voted overwhelmingly for the Baba. This is how, concludes Gould, the 'Ayodhya strategy' had worked to perfection.[59]

It is easy to establish the connection between this election campaign and the event on the night of 22 and 23 December 1949 when an idol of Rama suddenly appeared in the Babri mosque, which had been guarded by a posse of policemen. Baba Raghava Das and his Congress patrons in Lucknow not only revived but exploited the Masjid–Mandir issue which had remained dormant for decades. They pressed into service the Bairagis and the Mahants who, in subsequent years, were at the head of a vigorous movement to 'liberate' the mosque at Ayodhya. In this way, the Congress introduced a discordant note in an otherwise harmonious society of Faizabad.

The 'Ayodhya strategy' was also used in a different context but with similar results. In May 1986, the Rajiv Gandhi Government capitulated to the strident clamourings of some Muslim groups by introducing the retrograde Muslim Women (Protection of Rights on Divorce) Bill.[60] The motive was simple: the rising tide of anger over the Shah Bano verdict had to be stemmed if the Congress was to retain its Muslim votes which, in the wake of the momentous Supreme Court judgement, had tipped the balance in favour of the opposition parties.[61] At the same time, the growing Hindu sentiment over the Ayodhya mosque, voiced by the VHP, the Bajrang Dal, the Shiva Sena and the RSS, had to be assuaged. Rajiv Gandhi's former associate and ministerial colleague, whose own conduct in the murky happenings on 1 February 1986 is not beyond reproach, is reported to have stated the following:

> In early 1986 the Muslim Women's Bill was passed to play the Muslim card; and then came the decision on Ayodhya to play the Hindu card. It was supposed to be a package deal. I knew it was a dangerous thing to do and I did not agree. . . . When I asked Mr Rajiv Gandhi who is showing the worship in the disputed shrine at Ayodhya on Doordarshan two days after it was unlocked, he did not reply; he merely smiled and observed it was tit for tat for the Muslim Women's Bill.[62]

The 'Ayodhya strategy' worked in 1948 but not in 1989. The Congress gained a prestigious seat in a constituency then but was thrown out of office in 1989. The goodwill of the Muslims, achieved in 1986 through cynical means, was frittered away by a reckless act. 'The alienation of the Muslims,' commented a newspaper editorial, 'will undoubtedly rank as the most grievous lapse of the Rajiv Gandhi government.' The paper added:

> In retrospect the laying of the foundation stone of the Rama temple in Ayodhya on November 9 can be seen to be a dangerous turning point in the history of independent India. The seeds for a disintegration of the secular vision of the country were sown on that day. History cannot easily pardon the Congress for its direct and indirect contribution to the spectacular growth of Hindu chauvinist forces today and for the tightening hold of the fundamentalists on the Muslim community.[63]

The use of the 'Hindu card' by a party that laid claims to the secular legacy of Gandhi and Nehru proved counterproductive. The BJP rather than the Congress was the beneficiary of an ill-conceived and ill-advised electoral plan.[64] Communal mobilization not only divides people but often devours its own protagonists.

Competing symbols are supposed to cause friction and create cleavages. Not so in Faizabad, where the people, with some exceptions, have withstood the communal onslaught for well over a century. There is much room for optimism that they will be able to weather the present crisis, which has been deliberately created to serve short-term political interests. The people of Faizabad have done so in the not so distant past. There is no reason why they cannot do so now.

The *real* issue is not the future of the Babri mosque or of Rama's birthplace; in fact the seemingly endless debate among scholars over the existence of a temple on the present site of the mosque or the actual birthplace of Rama is of academic interest. The main concern of the people of Faizabad and their brethren in other parts of the country must be to create an ethos and a social order in which competing symbols can be blended into a harmonious whole. Individuals and groups have quite successfully done so in the past and there is no reason why it cannot be done in our times.

In the ultimate analysis, India's hope lies in areas like Faizabad where shared memories and common historical experiences should slowly but steadily strengthen bonds of unity and promote consensus and accommodation between different segments of society.[65] Even though strewn with obstacles and difficulties, it is worth fighting for the realization of such an ideal.

Notes

1. Mohammad Mujeeb, *The Indian Muslims*, George Allen and Unwin Ltd.: London, 1967, p. 485.

2. The official count of the deaths due to communal riots in 1990 put the number at 831. A report compiled by the Delhi unit of People's Unit for Democratic Rights (PUDR) lists 116 places where riots took place in the wake of the *rath-yatra*. An agonized journalist commented, 'The 831 or 1,662 or more deaths due to the mandir–masjid row were not due to material causes, and the dead did not belong to an alien land. Think in the way poets think, and you are hit by the indicting realization that Indians as a nation are not growing, but diminishing... The only way we can grow, individually and nationally, is by struggling to stop this *tandava nritya* (devil's dance) of communal violence.'

Sudheendra Kulkarni, 'India Brutalised', *Sunday Observer*, New Delhi, 30 December 1990. Also, see editorial comments, 'Bestiality in Bhagalpur' *Sunday Observer*, 5 November 1989; 'Stop the Carnage'; *Times of India*, New Delhi, 17 October 1989; 'Anguished India'; *Times of India*,; 31 October 1990.

3.   Rajiv Gandhi conceded that 'shilanyas played a crucial role in the (Congress) debacle' *Times of India*, 30 November 1989 and 15 December 1989 for analysis of the UP elections where seven of the nine Muslim candidates elected to the Lok Sabha belonged to the Janata Dal. Also, Zafar Agha, 'UP Muslims Desert Congress-I', ibid., 26 November 1989.

4.   This view has found much support and is echoed in the writings of leading journalists like Chandan Mitra, editor of the *Sunday Observer*, and Swapan Dasgupta, assistant editor of the *Times of India*. Dasgupta has argued that the fragmentation of India can only be arrested by creating alternative focal points of national consolidation. For this reason, he backs the 'movement in Ayodhya', pointing out that the defeat of the BJP (Bharatiya Janata Party) on this issue 'will, in one important sense only aggravate the crisis of Indian nationalism'. 'Nationalist Disarray: Renewed Importance of Ayodhya', *Times of India*, 10 September 1990. Also, 'Journey to Ayodhya: Hindu Nationalism Comes of Age', ibid., 23 October 1989. However, the views of Swapan Dasgupta have been effectively challenged in the columns of the *Times of India* itself. For example, Arvind N. Das, 'Pathology of Uncivil Society: Ritualism United Mandal–Mandir Moves', 5 October 1990; Praful Bidwai, 'BJP in a Clef Stick: Yatra's Success is a Liability', 12 October 1990; Harish Khare, 'Sparring with Communalism: Why Sadhus are Setting National Agenda', 20 October 1990; H.M. Seervai, 'NF–BJP Divorce: Hinduism Not Above the Constitution', 2 November 1990.

5.   The Jagatguru Shankaracharya of Dwarka Peeth announced that 'as long as the three sacred places, which the Muslims had destroyed to build mosques, are not restored to the Hindus, no peace or communal harmony is possible'. *Times of India*, New Delhi, 9 September 1990.

L.K.Advani, President of the BJP, and his colleagues have also made similar statements. While announcing his plan of undertaking the *rath-yatra* from the Somnath temple to Ayodhya, the BJP President declared, 'So far as the question of the birthplace of Lord Ram in Ayodhya and Lord Krishna in Mathura and the Kashi Vishwanath temple is concerned, the Hindu community cannot compromise.' ibid., 13 September 1990.

6.   See the collection of essays in *Hindu Temples: What Happened to Them*, Delhi, 1990.

7.   Balraj Madhok, 'Persecuted or Pampered', *Illustrated Weekly of India*, 9 January 1983. The thrust of this article is that Indian Muslims 'have no legal or moral claim or right on *(sic)* this country'.

8.   Mushirul Hasan, *Nationalism and Communal Politics in India, 1885–1930*, Manohar: Delhi, 1991, ch. 8.

9.   Satish Chandra, *Parties and Politics at the Mughal Court 1707–1740*, People's Publishing House: Delhi, 1972, pp. 261–66.

10. John R. McLane, *Indian Nationalism and the Early Congress*, Princeton University Press: New Jersey, 1977, pp. 271–331 (for an insightful account of the cow-protection movement). See Francis Robinson, *Separatism Among Indian Muslims: The Politics of the United Provinces' Muslims, 1860–1923*, Cambridge University Press: Cambridge, 1974, pp.

66–78, for a sensitive analysis of revivalist tendencies, including the development of the Hindi–Urdu conflict and the campaign for Hindi.

11. Asim Roy, *The Islamic Syncretistic Tradition in Bengal*, Princeton University Press: New Jersey, 1983, p. 251; and Rafiuddin Ahmad, *Bengal Muslims, 1871–1906: A Quest for Identity* , Oxford University Press: New Delhi, 1981, p. 184.

12. *Al Waqt*, Gorakhpur, 21/26 February 1894, Selections from Native Newspapers, UP.

13. T.C. Arthur, *Reminiscences of an Indian Police Official*, London, 1894, p. 145. Both British and Indian witnesses before the Public Service Commission testified to the harmonious relations between the Hindus and Muslims and took note of the cross-communal links. See *Public Service Commission*, NWP & O Sub-Commission, Calcutta, 1888, pp. 15, 23, 26.

14. McLane, op. cit., p. 318.

15. Rajat Kanta Ray, *Social Conflict and Political Unrest in Bengal 1875–1927*, Oxford University Press: New Delhi, 1984, p. 121. The Commissioner of Dacca noted the 'extraordinary fact' that in five years 'not a single riot of any description should have occurred'.

16. *Imperial Gazetteer of India*, pp. 48–9.

17. Judy F. Pugh, 'Divination and Ideology in the Banaras Muslim Community', K.P. Ewing (ed.), *Shariat and Ambiquity in South Asian Islam*, Oxford University Press: New Delhi, 1988, p. 289.

18. Sandria B. Frietag (ed.), *Culture and Power in Banaras: Community, Performance, and Environment, 1800–1980*, Oxford University Press: New Delhi, 1989, pp. 13–14, 168–69.

19. See the collection of essays in Hafeez Malik (ed.), *Iqbal: Poet-Philosopher of Pakistan*, Columbia University Press, 1971.

20. Ralph Russell and Khurshidul Islam, 'The Satirical Verse of Akbar Allahabadi (1846–1921)', *Modern Asian Studies*, Cambridge, 1974, vol. 8, 1, pp. 44–6.

21. Notice the comment on Benares: 'It should be explained that in Benares the Mahomedan population is nearly entirely dependent upon the Hindus. With the exception of a few members of the old Mahomedan aristocracy, who are now in straitened circumstances, the entire community lives a hand to mouth existence. . . The weavers are without exception dependent on the goodwill of their Hindu employers. The two communities are therefore closely bound to each other by economic ties.' Quoted in Sandria B. Frietag, *Culture and Power in Banaras*, p. 13. Nita Kumar has argued that what seems more influential in promoting harmony is the fact that Hindus and Muslims of 'lower classes' share a similar lifestyle and ideology of work, leisure and public activity. 'Work and Leisure in the Formation of Identity: Muslim Weavers in a Hindu City', in Frietag, op.cit., p. 169.

22. Henry Sender, *The Kashmiri Pandits: A Study of Cultural Choice in North India*, Oxford University Press: New Delhi, 1988, p. 244.

23. Robinson, *Separatism*, p. 79.

24. Hasan, *Nationalism and Communal Politics*, p. 50.

25. ibid., pp. 50–1.

26. *Public Service Commission*, NWP & O, Evidence, p. 158.

27. Mushirul Hasan, 'Sectarianism in Indian Islam: The Shia–Sunni Divide in the United Provinces', *The Indian Economic and Social History Review*, vol. 27, no. 2, April–June 1990.

28. Henry Cotton, *India and Home Memoirs*, London, 1911; W.S. Blunt, *India Under Ripon: A Private Diary*, London, 1909, p. 94.

29. See the collection of essays in Mushirul Hasan (ed.), *Communal and Pan-Islamic Trends in Colonial India*, Manohar: New Delhi, 1985.

30. Earl of Lytton, *Pundits and Elephants: Being the Experiences of Five Years as Governor of an Indian Province*, London, 1942, p. 172; 'Memoirs of O.M. Martin' (Typescript), Centre for South Asian Studies, Cambridge.

31. Mushirul Hasan, *A Nationalist Conscience: M.A. Ansari, the Congress and the Raj*, Manohar: New Delhi, 1987, ch. 6.

32. Mujeeb, *Indian Muslims*, pp. 10–20; and the collection of essays in Imtiaz Ahmad (ed.), *Caste and Social Stratification Among the Muslims*, Manohar: New Delhi, 1984.

33. David Gilmartin, 'Customary Law and Shariat in Punjab', in Ewing (ed.), op cit., p. 44.

34. Rafiuddin Ahmad, 'Conflicts and Contradictions in Bengali Islam: Problems of Change and Adjustment', ibid., p. 115.

35. Susan Bayly, *Saints, Goddesses and Kings: Muslims and Christians in South Indian Society 1700–1900*, Cambridge University Press: Cambridge, 1990, pp 13–14.

36. *Census of India*, 1931, UP of Agra and Awadh, vol. 1, Appendix E, p. 515.

37. See, for example, P.M. Currie, *The Shrine and Cult of Muin-al-din Chishti of Ajmer*, Oxford University Press: New Delhi, 1989.

38. Cracknell Papers, Centre for South-Asian Studies, Cambridge.

39. 'The Partition of India in Retrospect', C.H. Philips and D.A. Wainright (eds.), *The Partition of India: Policies and Perspectives*, George Allen and Unwin Ltd.: London, 1970, p. 407.

40. *Census of India*, 1931, p. 515.

41. Rafiuddin Ahmad, op.cit., p. 134.

42. *Census of India*, 1921, vol. 1, p. 115.

43. Home (Political), B, File No. 109–14, April 1913, National Archives of India (NAI), Delhi.

44. Home (Political), A, File No. 1–4, December 1913, NAI.

45. Home (Political), A, File No. 258–259, October 1915, NAI.

46. R.S. Sharma, *Communal History and Rama's Ayodhya*, People's Publishing House: Delhi, 1990. And the collection of articles in Asghar Ali Engineer (ed.), *Babri-Masjid—Ramjanmabhoomi Controversy*, Delhi, 1990.

47. The document was generally appreciated. 'All those,' wrote a leading journalist, 'who have given up neither their belief in secularism nor the hope that Indians will one day stop killing one another should be grateful to Professors S. Gopal, Romila Thapar, Bipan Chandra and other historians of Jawaharlal Nehru University'. Praful Bidwai, 'Appeasing Hindu Bigotry',

Times of India, 20 November 1989. But there was adverse criticism as well, much of which, quite predictably, came from the ideologues of the BJP and the RSS. The debate was conducted in the letters to the editor column of the *Times of India* (15,21,23 December 1989) as well as in the *Indian Express*. Within the Centre for Historial Studies, Majid H. Siddiqi alone struck a discordant note with the view that 'it is not for historians to "prove" or "disprove" as right or wrong every instance of an assertion made by a political or cultural group as social winds blow this way or that'. Siddiqi, who was not a signatory to the document, concluded with the exhortation: 'Historians must discard their personae as historians if they are to intervene in the dispute without at the same time endangering the very basis of their intellectual stand. They must exhibit intellectual self-confidence in their discipline and determine their own agenda in terms of their own questions and not allow the existence of communalism in this society. . . to force its agenda upon them.' 'Ramjanmabhoomi–Babri Masjid Dispute: The Question of History', *Economic and Political Weekly,* Bombay, 13 January 1990.

48. *District Gazetteer of the United Provinces of Agra and Oudh*, Fyzabad, vol. XLIII, Allahabad, 1905, pp. 173–74.

49. Peter Van Deer Veer, 'God must be Liberated! A Hindu Liberation Movement in Ayodhya', *Modern Asian Studies*, vol. 21, no. 2, Cambridge, 1987, p. 287.

50. For their importance in Ayodhya, see Peter Van Deer Veer, 'The Concept of the Ideal Brahmin as an Ideological Construct', Gunter D. Southeimer and Herman Kulke (eds.), *Hinduism Reconsidered*, Manohar: Delhi, 1989, pp. 71–7.

51. Peter Van Deer Veer, 'God must be Liberated', p. 288.

52. ibid.

53. Michael H. Fisher, *A Clash of Two Cultures: Awadh, the British and the Mughals*, Manohar: Delhi, 1987, pp. 228–36; J.R.I. Cole, *Roots of North Indian Shiism: Religion and State in Awadh, 1772–1859* , Oxford University Press: New Delhi, 1989, pp. 244–49.

54. S.K. Tripati, 'One Hundred Years of Litigation', in Engineer (ed.), op.cit., pp. 15–27.

56. Kuldip Kumar, 'Ayodhya Ready for Compromise', ibid., p. 106. Likewise, several neighbouring areas, such as Akbarpur in Sultanpur district, remained undisturbed. Suneet Chopra, 'Akbarpur: An Island of Communal Unity', *Times of India*, New Delhi, 3 November 1989.

56. Robinson, *Separatism*, p. 64.

57. Harold A. Gould, *Politics and Caste*, vol. 3, Chanakya: Delhi, 1990, p. 49.

58. ibid., pp. 48–49.

59. ibid., pp. 76–77.

60. See Zoya Hasan, 'Minority Identity, Muslim Women Bill Campaign and the Political Process', *Economic and Political Weekly*, Bombay, 7 January 1989.

61. See Mushirul Hasan, 'Indian Muslims Since Independence: In Search of Integration and Identity', *Third World Quarterly*, London, vol. 10, no. 2,

April 1988.

62. Arun Nehru quoted in A.B. Noorani, 'The Babri Masjid–Ramjanamab-hoomi Question', in Engineer (ed.), p. 57.

63. *Times of India*, New Delhi, 28 November 1989.

64. Harish Khare, 'Rise of the BJP: Reemergence of the Right', *Times of India*, New Delhi, 6 December 1989. Notice that in Maharashtra the BJP–Shiva Sena won fourteen seats and emerged as the only credible opposition to the Congress. *Sunday Observer*, New Delhi, 3 December 1989.

65. I agree with R.S. Sharma that 'patient and sustained efforts of right thinking writers, researchers and educators can foil the communalist attempt to use the past as a wedge to divide the people into warring camps'. 'Communal History and Rama's Ayodhya', op.cit., p. 32.

Myth, History and the Politics of Ramjanmabhumi[1]

Neeladri Bhattacharya

Crucial to the controversy over Ramjanmabhumi are differing notions of myth and history and their relation to social practices. Historians have shown that the claims of the Vishwa Hindu Parishad (VHP) are based on questionable historical evidence.[2] The historicity of present-day Ayodhya is debatable, no historical record notes the exact spot of Rama's birth, nor is there any evidence that the Babri Masjid was built on the ruins of a Rama temple.

Yet this critique of the VHP claims may not convince many. And the sceptics are not all Hindu zealots, ardent supporters of the VHP. Popular conceptions of the past are often informed and structured by myths. In these conceptions, myths are true histories; desacralized, demythicized histories based on historical records are false.

We cannot dismiss such myths. We cannot counterpoise history to myth as truth to falsehood. These are different modes of knowledge, varying ways of understanding the world, ordering one's life and defining one's actions. If myths convince people, we must understand why they do so. If fabulous stories circulate and light up the popular imagination, we cannot merely demonstrate the fabulous character of such stories; we must know why they circulate, why they play on popular imagination.

The facts, the events, and the social actors referred to in myths often have no 'real' historical existence. Yet myths do refer to reality. They talk about the world symbolically, metaphorically. The effort to read traditional myths to discover the historicity of events may not be too meaningful. But they reveal a lot about the mind of those who produced those myths, the values of the society which believed in the myths. Since myths are constituted and reconstituted within society through social processes, different versions of the same myth exist. The meaning of each version is different: the symbolic representations of good and evil differ, the same characters embody different qualities. By comparing the different versions, by analysing the alterations and reinterpretations within them, we can understand the societies which sustained those versions, and the function that a myth played in a particular society.

Reinterpretations are often contestations. Within a traditional society, which is ordered through myths, social reordering occurs through a questioning of the dominant myths. Existing myths are not always dismissed—their internal structure is changed. The different layers of meaning in each myth allow a range of possible appropriations. Old myths are sedimented with new meanings, counter-myths are produced, and the hierarchy of values reflected in the myths are altered. All this occurs within the structure of mythic discourse, not outside it. Reinterpretations are not always recognized as such. Myths and counter-myths can reach out only when they share with the audience a repertoire of what is familiar. Structured within the archetypal mythical narratives and hidden behind familiar stories and characters, innovations have a surreptitious existence. Through this familiarization the mythical narrative wins the confidence of the audience and weaves in new stories into the text. Once the audience identifies with some of the stories, they are persuaded by the narrative; all the stories appear plausible, believable. A myth is thus transformed through the introduction of new ideas, new values, new stories; it no longer expresses and reconfirms the values of the people, it modifies them.

The process of mythification has to be understood. We need to study the relation between the production of the modern political myths and the social and political practices within which this takes place—which in turn the myths seek to sanction. By demonstrating the constituted character of myths, we can question the effort to present them as 'eternal' and unchanging, and we can contest the sanction which politics seeks from them.

The Rhetoric of History

The VHP claims about the Ramjanmasthan, however, are not sustained by references to myths and beliefs alone. Integral to their whole argument is the rhetoric of history. Myths and stories about the Janmasthan are persistently presented as 'history' whose facts could be established through historical records and evidence.

In the debate over the issue, conviction in history and the sanctity of historical evidence has been repeatedly emphasized by the BJP and the VHP:

The facts of history appear fiction only to a person suffering from Historologia and not to a balanced mind who is
not afraid of any unpalatable fact whether it is for or
against.

Facts of history cannot be wished away; they must be
realised and imbibed, instead of closing eyes to them.[3]

The popular accounts about the Janmasthan, which would appear
incredible to most historians, claim to be 'true histories'. 'In this book
historical facts have been presented exactly as they were' says the preface
to a booklet which recounts an imaginary story of Ayodhya through the
voice of river Saryu.[4] Other accounts like *Sri Ramjanmabhumi ka Raktaranjit Itihas* by Ramgopal Pandey and *Ayodhya ka Prachin Itihas* by
Acharya Gudunji Sharma may violate all canons of the historian's craft,
but are stated to be 'authoritative history'.

Sri Ramajanmabhumi Mukti Yagya Samiti has collated its own version
of historical and archaeological evidence,[5] and Justice Deoki Nandan
has produced an influential historical pamphlet for this Samiti.[6] The
Organiser, which has been relentlessly campaigning for the construction
of a Rama temple in Ayodhya, has published, on several occasions, what
it claims to be 'authentic' historical facts about the Ramjanmabhumi and
the Babri Masjid.[7]

Thus in both the propaganda pamphlets and popular 'histories', there
is a recurrent reference to 'true history' and 'authentic account'. History
is called upon as a witness to the events recounted. '*Itihas sakshi hai*', is
a phrase often used. 'History speaks',[8] we are told, in support of the
account produced by the VHP; as if we need only listen to this voice of
history to know the truth.

These accounts seemingly conform to the practice of historians; they
quote historical records. Here the procedure of citation is considered more
important than the nature of records cited; when necessary records are
imagined into existence, they are concocted. It is easy to demonstrate that
many of the records referred to do not exist. Yet the fact that citations are
seen as essential to justify claims to truth is significant.

, These narratives appeal to two distinct audiences. On the one hand they
appeal to those who will be persuaded by the validity of mythical truth
and will allow myths and beliefs to be the basis of action; on the other
they appeal to those who would doubt the basis of myths, seek a different
form of historical knowledge and argue for a different order of democratic
practice. So these narratives seek the sanction of myths and beliefs on the

one hand and 'history' on the other. It is a strategy necessary in the modern age when all types of minds have to be united.

What characterizes this mode of argument, therefore, is an ambivalent and sceptical attitude towards myths, beliefs and history. The persistent reference to 'true' history shows a lack of conviction in the power of myths and beliefs in legitimating action, and in their claims to truth. But when the authenticity of historical facts cited in these texts are criticized, then legitimacy for action is sought in myths and beliefs.[9] When there was a proposal to set up a historians' committee to investigate the history of Babri Masjid to help the Court in its decision, the *Organiser* reacted typically, 'With the Hindus it is a matter of faith that Bhagwan Rama was born where the Babri Mosque is. No government or court can sit on judgment over it.'[10] When the historians of the Jawaharlal Nehru University produced a critique of the VHP claims, K.R. Malkani, a VHP historian, again fell back on the same argument. If indeed 'history' and myth were no different, then why does the VHP use the language of the historian's discourse?

If reference to historical documents are so important in the campaign for the Ramjanmabhumi, then a debate over the authenticity of the records and the evidence contained within them is essential.[11] This has been attempted elsewhere.[12] But we also need to go beyond this debate over 'historical' evidence to understand the meaning and structure of the myths and stories which circulate at a popular level, as well as the political context within which they are structured.

The Politics of Ramjanmabhumi

The battle for the Ramjanmabhumi is part of a wider political struggle for a constitution of 'Hindu' consciousness and identity, for the construction of a unified Hindu tradition, and for the assertion of 'Hindu' power over all the other communities in India. The VHP activities acquire their meaning within this broader context.

One major objective of the VHP is to forge a national and international unity amongst all those it defines as Hindu.[13] Hindus, they feel, have been fragmented and divided into groups and castes—in conflict with each other. This weakness has allowed foreigners to invade and rule over India, and the minority communities to become defiant. To reassert their power, the Hindus have to become conscious of their underlying common identity, rediscover and forge the unity which lies submerged. It is essential for all Hindus to realize that 'they respond to the same historical memories. Their hearts beat to the same spiritual tune. They are bound by the same ties of blood'.[14]

This project of forming a Hindu Community, united at the national and international levels, marks a major effort at restructuring religious traditions within India. The diversity and differences within religious traditions, considered by religious reformers a sign of the strength and vitality of tradition, now acquires a new meaning: it becomes a sign of weakness of the community. To overcome the weakness the Hindus must unite, they must act together, they must speak with one voice.[15]

But to what purpose?

All forms of unity are not the same. Their objectives may differ, the basis on which they are forged may vary. So it is important to understand the politics of unification.

Unification is essential, according to the Bharatiya Janata Party (BJP) and the VHP, not merely to bring the Hindus together, but to arouse them—to awaken the Hindu spirit. The struggle for the Ramjanmabhumi has an important part to play in this process. 'The present agitation to liberate the Sri Rama Janmabhumi,' we are told, 'is no less than a battle for national self assertion.' It is, in fact, 'nothing short of a phase of struggle for the liberation of the National Soul'.[16] Rajmata Scindia has repeatedly defined the politics behind the struggle for the Ramjanmabhumi, 'Our target is *jagriti,* awakening and unity among Hindus.'[17] Hindus have to come out of their stupor, overcome their inertia, and regain their *swabhiman* (self-respect). They need to rise and act.

This is not a movement for an awakening of the 'old' Hindu spirit. It seeks to redefine the spirit of Hinduism and the identity of a 'good' Hindu. Underlying the plea for self-assertion is a specific notion of self and an effort to develop an authoritarian Hindu personality.

The need for aggression is a theme which recurs insistently in the speeches and writings of the VHP and the BJP.[18] It is powerfully expressed in a polemic against secularism which first appeared in the pages of the *Organiser* and was then reprinted in a pamphlet for popular circulation.[19] The author, speaking through the voice of an 'Angry Hindu', attempts to explain the reasons and justifications for the Hindu anger:

> Yes, certainly I am angry. And I have every reason to be angry. And it is also right for me to be so. Otherwise I would be no man.

Yes for too long I have suffered affronts in silence. For ever so long I have been at the receiving end... My people have been kidnapped by the hostiles. My numbers have dwindled. . . my adored motherland has been torn asunder. . .

And still you tell me I should not get angry? That I should not stand up and shout 'enough'?

My temples have been desecrated, destroyed. Their sacred stones are being trampled under the aggressor's feet. My gods are crying. They are demanding. . .reinstatement in all their original glory. When I speak out my agony, you of the secular tribe condemn me as a threat to our 'secular peace'. You add insult to my injury. You rub salt into my wounded heart. . . .

For you, our national life minus every bit of Hindu is secularism. In short, you want me to cease to be myself.

Should I, tell me frankly, continue to sit silent in face of all such indignities and exploitations? And do you dare to tell me that I have no right to be angry? Even a worm turns, they say. Do you think I am worse than a worm?

You have derided me as an 'Angry Hindu'. On the contrary, I take it as a compliment. For so long—for too long—I was lost in a deep coma. I saw nothing, I heard nothing, felt nothing—even when my motherland was cut off. But all such incessant blows have at last awakened me. Now I have begun to see, I have begun to hear, I have begun to understand, and I have begun to feel—what tragedies have overtaken me. . . . Hereafter I will sleep no more. I will not remain dumb; I will speak out. I will not remain inert; I will begin to act. I will not run away from challenges; I will face them. . .

I now realise I had been too good for this world of 'hard reality'. I believed that others would respect my gods and temples as I respected other's. . . I believed generosity begets generosity. . . . But alas, again and again I was deceived. I was betrayed, I was stabbed in the back. . . . My goodness has been turned upon me. I know now a bit of the ways of the world. And I have decided to speak to others in the language they understand. . .

And finally, I have come to know the value of my anger itself.

Patience, tolerance, generosity are first claimed as innate qualities of the Hindus—virtues which differentiate them from others. Then the same qualities are identified as signs of weakness, the basis of inertia, apathy and passivity, the cause of all their present problems. To face contemporary challenges, new values had to be developed. The value of aggression and anger had to be realized.

This framework of discourse idealizes masculinity—a specific form of masculinity. Anger and aggression are identified as the qualities of manhood, tolerance and patience are feminine. Manliness symbolizes strength and feminity is a sign of weakness. To overcome their weakness Hindus had to give up their feminity and assert their masculinity.

Beyond anger and aggression, is the politics of vengeance and retribution. Other communities, it is argued, have subjected the Hindus to innumerable indignities and oppressions in the past. The Hindus have foolishly and silently tolerated all this for too long. Now is the time to avenge past injustice: 'For centuries the injustice to the Hindu community by Babur's hordes cannot be allowed to perpetuate.'[20]

The struggle for Ramjanmabhumi is fed by this ideology of retribution. The logic is simple: if Muslim rulers inflicted their tyranny on Hindus, all Muslims today have to bear the burden of this guilt. It is as if the guilt of an individual can be transferred to the entire community to which the individual belongs, and as if guilt is passed down the generations over centuries. If Hindu temples have been destroyed in the past, mosques will be destroyed today.

This is a demand for a re-enactment of medieval politics. Since sacred and temporal authority was closely connected in the past, religious institutions were also symbols of political power. Conquerors often asserted their power by destroying sacred places. This medieval logic is at work behind the struggle for the Ramjanmabhumi. Mosques, like the Babri Masjid, are seen as symbols of Hindu subjection; and their destruction, a necessary part of the liberation movement of the Hindus.[21]

Destruction is not always the inevitable logic of this politics. Institutions and buildings can be appropriated without being destroyed. The strategy here is to deny creativity to the Muslims. Muslims only pillage, not create, 'Islam only destroyed. It never built anything on its own. It captured temples and palaces and advertised them as mosques and tombs.'[22] P.N. Oak has not tired of arguing that Fatehpur Sikri, Buland Darwaza, Taj Mahal were all built by Rajputs.[23] The claim that the Babri Masjid is a Hindu temple is nothing unique.

The new Hindu spirit requires its own popular imagery and symbolic representation. Traditionally, Rama was represented as powerful but restrained; he is Maryada Purushottam (Supreme Man) but tenderhearted. This image of Rama is being transformed into that of an aggressive, masculine, warrior God. Yet, in the present context, Rama cannot provide the symbol of desired aggressive values. Popular communal literature often represents Shiva as the personification of the new ideals. The imagery of death, destruction and fiery anger, and its association with Shankar and Chandi, is emphatically expressed in the followed passage from a poem which attempts to define the identity of a Hindu:

> *Hindu tan-man, hindu jeevan, rag-rag hindu mera parichay*
> *Main shankar ka wah krodhanal, kar sakta jagti kshar-kshar*
> *Main damru ki pralaydhwani hun jismain nachta bheeshan sanhar*
> *Ranachandi ki atripta pyas, main durga ka unmatta has,*
> *Main yam ki pralayankar pukar, jalte marghat ka dhuandhar*
> *Phir antartam ki jwala se jagti me ag laga dun main,*
> *Yadi dhadhak uthe jal-thal-ambar-jar-chetan phir kaisa vismay?*
> *Hindu tan-man Hindu jeevan, rag-rag Hindu mera parichay.*[24]

Here we have a specific interpretation of Shiva. Within Indian tradition Shiva has more than one image. According to one tradition, Shiva, like many other deities, embodies the tension between the opposing principles of chaos and order, of *asat* and *sat*, of violence and creation. The Shaivas in South India erased the violent and destructive side and presented god as *nirmala*—one without taint. Now there is an opposing effort: to idealize the violent and destructive principle. The attributes which are celebrated in the present political context are discovered in and sanctified through the divine figure of Shiva.

If Shiva expresses the new militant, aggressive spirit of Hindutva, Rama is projected as the symbol of the Hindu unity. Here again the symbolism of Rama is being subjected to a new political interpretation. Traditionally, the *Ramayana* has been an open text which has been adapted to local contexts and read in different ways.[25] In some versions, Rama is the personification of the ideal Kshatriya, the perfect man; in others he is also the embodiment of evil—a man who treacherously kills Bali Raja in an unethical combat.[26] In some versions Ravana is a ten-headed monster; in others he is a learned sage, or a hero. Heterodoxical sects like Buddhism and Jainism have their own versions of the *Ramayana*. The Dalits in South India venerate Bali Raja, and contest the representation of Rama as the virtuous king. The efforts by the BJP and the VHP to unify the Hindus around the image of Rama is an attempt to erase the diversity and conflict within a catholic Indian tradition, to repress contestatory voices which question dominant myths, and produce a homogeneous, universalist Hindu tradition conducive to communal politics.

The formation of a new identity and new collectivity also requires the invention of new rituals and practices. In India, rituals and practices are usually specific to sects and castes. Their collective performance binds the members of a sect or a caste together, and separates different sects and castes from each other. To transcend these differences and build a larger 'Hindu' unity, the VHP and the BJP have invented new rituals. These are not traditional religious rituals. They are desacralized, in the sense that their objective is solely political. Through these rituals the VHP and the BJP seek to mobilize the people, instil an aggressive sense of Hindutva, and generate a communal consciousness.

The early 1980s saw the beginnings of a new phase of intensive communal mobilization.[27] The first Hindu Samajotsav (Hindu Unity Conference) was held at Shimoga in Karnataka in January 1981. Since then the VHP has organized similar Hindu Samajotsavs all over the country. In October 1981 a Virat Hindu Sammelan was held in Delhi; in March 1983 a three-day Vishal Hindu Sammelan was organized in Jammu; in January 1982 there was a Hindu Jagriti Ekta Sammelan in Kanyakumari. Subsequent *sammelans* have been held in Ranchi (1987), Tirupati (1988), and Alandi in Maharashtra (1987). Processions and *rath-yatras* have been a regular part of the rituals of communal propaganda: Jana Jagarani Abhiyans, Vishal Hindi Aikya Yatras, Ekatmata Yatras, Rama Ratha Yatras. New bonds of unity are being cemented through earth (consecrated bricks), water (ganga-jal), fire (torch-lights), blood, and ashes of the dead.

These rituals of communal mobilization are rituals of confrontation.

Mobilizations are essentially against other communities. The crude demonstration of 'Hindu' power through the practice of these rituals is meant to intimidate others, and to defy and provoke them. These *yatras* have been invariably accompanied by violent rioting, bloodshed and death. The experience and memories of such hostilities have deepened the divide between Hindus and Muslims and created in turn a further context for confrontations.

'Other' faiths do not provide the only targets of political aggression. The new face of Hindu communalism is characterized by its violent opposition to secularists—to all those who are opposed to the politics of religious intolerance. Such an opposition has always been a part of communal politics, but now it is one of its defining features. The communal argument is simple: experiments in modernity have failed; rationalism and secularism has led to a civilizational crisis in India; assertive Hindutva alone can provide the possibility of the nation's survival. Secularism, we are are told, 'is draining away the nation's "elan vital" of Hindu spirit'.[28] Secularists are identified as 'Hindu baiters', traitors, Muslim communalists. They are 'trojan horses' who 'weaken Hindu strength from within'.[29] These 'traitors' have to be attacked to defend the Hindu nation.

The politics of Ramjanmabhumi is thus part of a wider communal politics which seeks to forge a combative unity amongst Hindus. It seeks to reconstitute Hindu identity as an aggressive, masculine identity. It speaks the language of vengeance and retributive justice.

This effort at a redefinition of the Hindu identity leads to a series of conflicting arguments. The discourse of communalism criticizes other religions for being monolithic, but aspires to build a monolithic unity. It glorifies diversity within Hinduism as a mark of its superiority over Semitic religions, but seeks to repress this diversity. It identifies aggressiveness as an evil intrinsic to other religions, but attempts to instil the same quality in all Hindus. It talks of patience and tolerance as innate virtues of Hindus, yet sees these traits as the basis of Hindu weakness. It condemns other religions for their politics of religious repression and temple destruction, but organizes itself around the same politics.

The politics of Ramjanmabhumi, therefore, does not seek to defend Hindu tradition, religion, myths, practices, values and norms. It legitimates its communal politics through the discourse of tradition, it appropriates tradition in communal ways. In the process it transforms, politicizes, and communalizes tradition and religion. It demeans both religion and 'tradition'.[30]

Mythic History and Communal Politics

Myth, history and the politics of Ramjanmabhumi interrelate in complex ways. Specific appropriations of myths and history give meaning to present communal politics, govern the nature of social action; the specific form of politics in turn is articulated in myths and history, it defines the way myths and histories are constructed.

There are many versions of the history of Ramjanmabhumi which are being popularly circulated.[31] Their details differ in important ways, but in broad outline they are similar. The story inevitably begins in the Treta Yuga when Rama was said to be born in Ayodhya. Here he spent his childhood, and part of his life. After Rama moved his capital to Saketa, Ayodhya went into decline. Despite the desolation of the city, Ramjanmabhumi survived. But it survived in anonymity: its location was lost. Vikramaditya miraculously rediscovered Ayodhya, and built a temple at the Janmasthan. After Vikramaditya, Ayodhya again went into decline but the temple and the place at the Janmasthan survived. When Babur came to India he pillaged and plundered like all Muslims. He destroyed the temple at the Janmasthan and built a masjid. Subsequently Hindus made repeated efforts to recover control over the Janmasthan. But the Janmasthan could not be liberated even after British rule. In 1949 a Ramamurti was miraculously discovered in the masjid: Rama, it was said, had himself appeared to remind the Hindus of the sacred history of the place and their duty to liberate it.

The story thus revolves around several myths: the myth of ancient Ayodhya, the myths of its loss and rediscovery, the myth of the destruction of the temple and the construction of the mosque, the myth of the popular movement for the recovery of the Janmasthan, the myth of the miraculous appearance of Rama's idol. The politics of Ramjanmabhumi flows from this mythic history.

Mythic narratives provide the structure within which these popular histories are framed. Within myths personages appear as archetypes as villains or heroes. The struggle between heroes and villains represent the deeper conflict between the forces of truth and falsehood, justice and injustice, *dharma* and *adharma*, order and disorder, creativity and destructiveness, good and evil. The struggle between gods and demons, between devas and asuras, express the conflict between these opposing principles.

The popular communal histories are cast within this frame. But in the process the mythic structure is filled with a communal meaning. Muslim rulers are transformed into archetypal villains, and Hindus who fought the Muslim rulers or suffered under their rule become the heroes. Muslim rulers are shown as representing the forces of evil: tyranny, injustice, oppression, destruction, repression, disorder. By opposing these forces, Hindus fought for the principle of order, justice, and *dharma*. The struggle around Ramjanmabhumi is depicted as a long struggle between these forces.

Once historical personages are transformed into personifications of archetypal models, all sorts of acts are attributed to them. Events and actions described in the narrative may not have ever actually occurred. They are 'invented' to build up the picture of the archetypal villain or hero. The popular communal histories of Ayodhya produce long lists of misdeeds of all Muslim rulers to demonstrate how cruel and oppressive they were. Having painted this picture, readers are persuaded to believe that such rulers were capable of all heinous crimes, like the destruction of the Ramjanmabhumi temple by Babur and the subsequent ruthless repression of the Hindus who struggled to liberate the Janmabhumi. These stories have no support in any historical evidence. Yet they appear believable to those who are persuaded by the archetypes, those who accept the representation of Muslims as villains and Hindus as heroes.

The demonology of Muslim rulers in the popular communal histories of Ramjanmabhumi goes along with a particular communal representation of the past. Consider the set of articles on temple destruction published in the *Organiser*.[32] Here the story of the destruction of the Ramjanmabhumi temple dissolves into a more general narrative of temple destruction by Muslim rulers, and the mythic story of the decline of India from the age of civilization to the age of barbarism. Each of these articles on different provinces of India is framed within a similar narrative structure. They all begin with the pre-Muslim period. It was an age when India was studded with temples. It was a time of growth and development, a time of progress, of high levels of cultural and intellectual achievements. Then came the Muslims. Death, destruction and decline followed. It was now a time of invasions, cruelty, forcible conversions, religious repression, cultural disintegration, and economic collapse. Destruction of temples epitomized this general phenomenon of decline. Regeneration could only be through a return to the origins, a recovery of the original glory. In a way, the obsessive concern with the place of Rama's birth reveals this vision of a mythic return to the Yuga of Rama, from which India had apparently descended to barbarism.

The popular communal histories of Ayodhya persistently play on the theme that Ayodhya and the Janmasthan are profoundly sacred to the Hindus and that their sanctity has been defiled by Muslims.

One of these histories, *Ayodhyaji ka Prachin Itihas* is presented as the *Ayodhya Guide*. It tells the reader about the sacred history as well as the sacred geography of the place. Ayodhya, we are told, existed before the profane world came into being. To create the cosmos, Manu needed a place to work. He brought Ayodhya from heaven and placed it on earth. After creating the world from his base in Ayodhya, Manu gave Ayodhya away to Ikshvaku. Ayodhya derives its sanctity from being present at the sacred time of creation, from being the centre from which the cosmos was created.

To further emphasize its sacred character, several other mythic marks of sacredness are attributed to Ayodhya. Ayodhya, we are informed, was more sacred than all the other sacred places in India. This is expressed by symbolically associating different sacred centres with different parts of the divine figure of Vishnu. Ujjain was the feet of Vishnu, Dwaraka was the navel, Haridwar was the heart, Mathura was the neck, Kashi was the nose, Ayodhya was the head. Ayodhya is the source of origin of all the worlds: Brahmalok, Indralok, Vishnulok, Golok. It was the original nature from which the human world was created. After enumerating these myths of Ayodhya's ancient origin, the *Ayodhya Guide* proceeds to substantiate the myths through historical evidence.

In a world that believes in myths, the sanctity of a place is often attested by its association with the miraculous, that which does not occur within the sphere of profane experience. The sacred, as it were, reveals itself through the extraordinary, the mysterious, the miraculous. This link with the miraculous is established in the myths of the loss and the rediscovery of Ayodhya.[33] After the Treta Yuga, Ayodhya was lost. Vikramaditya set out to rediscover it. One day a tired Vikramaditya was sitting on the banks of a river. He saw a dark man taking a bath. When the man re-emerged from the river he was no longer dark. Vikramaditya asked the person who he was and how he was miraculously transformed. The man said that he was *tirtharaj* Prayag. When he could no longer bear the burden of other people's sin he came for a bath in the Saryu which flowed next to the sacred city of Ayodhya. The myth again attempts to reaffirm the sanctity of Ayodhya. Saryu was purer than Prayag; Prayag who had the power to cleanse the sin of humanity, came to purify himself in the water of Saryu. And Saryu derived its purity from its association with Ayodhya.

The miraculous reappears in the second myth about the discovery of Ayodhya. Prayag tells Vikramaditya to allow a cow and a calf to roam.

When the calf reached Ayodhya, milk would secrete from its udder. Vikramaditya follows Prayag's instructions and thus rediscovers the exact location of ancient Ayodhya. Location of a sacred place, evocation of its sacred signs, through the help of an animal is common in the world of myths.[34] The secretion of milk is a reference to unilateral creation, to androgynous birth, again common in the sacred myths of India, but not in everyday life.[35] The above myth re-emphasizes the divine character of the place where the unilateral creation occurred.

The miraculous surfaces yet again in other myths. *Sri Ramajanmabhumi ka Raktaranjit Itihas* tells us that Babur confronted an extraordinary problem when he destroyed the Ramjanmabhumi temple and proceeded to build the Babri Masjid. He found it impossible to construct the Masjid. The walls which were built in the day inevitably collapsed at night (p. 16). Babur was told by Hindu mahatmas that Hanuman would never allow a masjid to be built in Ramjanmabhumi, unless the structure of the masjid was changed, Hindu features were incorporated, the place was called Sitapak, and Hindus were allowed to worship in it (p. 17). Babur had to listen to the advice of the mahatmas. The myth asserts the sanctity of the Hindu claim over Babri Masjid and the sacred power of the Rama temple. The divine could not be easily destroyed. It had the power to resist human and natural forces of destruction. Even earlier, we are told, the Ramjanmabhumi had miraculously survived amidst general desolation, first after the Treta Yuga and then after the age of Vikramaditya. The story of the miraculous appearance of the Rama idol within the Babri Masjid in 1949 sought to reconfirm both the sacredness of the place and the Hindu claims over it.

The politics of Ramjanmabhumi derives its sanction from a mythic history of a long heroic struggle for the recovery of the Janmasthan. 'For centuries we have been fighting for Ramjanmabhumi. It's not a new thing of today. Not thousands, but lakhs have perished for the sake of Ramjanmabhumi,' says Rajmata Scindia.[36] All the popular communal histories attempt to describe this long struggle that Hindus have waged over centuries.[37] This unfinished struggle, they urge, has to be carried on.

This is an effort to legitimize the present action by tracing its ancient lineage, to deny the communal character of the present movement by the construction of a mythic sacred history. The recovery of Janmasthan was, in this logic, both a sacred duty and an inherited obligation of all Hindus. The blood the ancestors shed had sanctified their cause and imposed an obligation. Their blood has to be honoured, their goals have to be realized, their martyrdom has to be avenged. And for this the Hindus have to be ready to sacrifice their blood as well as their lives.

This myth of past struggles for the recovery of Janmasthan seeks to authorize the politics of Ramjanmabhumi in yet another way. Therefore a mythological explanation of the present action is not seen as novel: it is a repetition of what has gone on before. The nature of action is governed by archetypal models, and these models are provided by past heroes. The present generation of Hindus have not *begun* the struggle for Ramjanmabhumi, they need only carry on and complete a struggle begun in the past. The ancestors, through their sacrifices, their struggle against the evil, injustice and oppression associated with Muslim rule, set the example which the descendants must follow.

The use of mythic forms and mythic themes makes these communal histories familiar to their audience. The myths appeal because they appear to be part of the known, accepted tradition. Yet the stories which are cast within the traditional mythic forms are invented. This invention often takes place in the course of struggles between communities, and it is the politics of these struggles that are expressed through the myths. The myths about the Janmasthan were invented sometime in the third quarter of the nineteenth century. In the mid-1850s a conflict occurred over the Hanumangarhi temple.[38] Reacting to the tolerant policies of the Nawab, a group of Sunni Muslims claimed that the Hanumangarhi temple was built at a place where a mosque stood earlier. Dispute around the claim led to violent confrontations and bloody fights between the Sunnis and the Bairagi sadhus. Retaliating against the Sunni claim over Hanumangarhi, a section of Hindus produced a counter myth. They retained the structure of the argument put forward by the Sunnis, but reversed the claim. They now asserted that the Babri Masjid was, in fact, built after destroying a Hindu temple. This claim was raised not during the Hanumangarhi episode, but after it. The focus of dispute thus shifted from Hanumangarhi to Babri Masjid. Myths about the Babri Masjid which were now invented in the course of the conflict became part of the local tradition and were reported in British official accounts written after this period.[39]

The mythic histories we have been discussing seek to authenticate themselves through a set of narrative strategies. There is a process of concretization. A mass of concocted figures, dates, names are quoted to create an illusion of concreteness.[40] We are told that there were seventy-six attempts to liberate the Janmasthan: twenty during the reign of Akbar, and thirty-six at the time of Aurangzeb. During the reign of Humayun the Hindus did not remain silent. Three thousand women fought along with Jayrajkumari and 24,000 soldiers were mobilized by Maheshwaranand.

There is actually no historical evidence for any of these struggles. But invented sources are continuously cited to establish the factual authenticity of the text.

Concretization goes along with a method of familiarization. The mythic histories recount some familiar details about the reigns of Humayun, Akbar and Aurangzeb, and cite a few well-known sources. Once the reader is made to identify with such familiar facts, he is persuaded to believe in the authenticity of the narrative. Through this process of familiarization invented details are sought to be authenticated. An occasional criticism of the sources, a discussion of their limitations, makes the texts appear all the more self-critical and convincing.

Myth, history and the politics of Ramjanmabhumi are thus closely linked. Mythic history draws upon a stock of familiar stories and myths. Myths provide open forms which are filled with communal meaning. Through them the struggle for Ramjanmaabhumi is charged with a symbolic, historic and a deeply communal significance. These popular mythic histories structure people's consciousness and beliefs. They provide the frame through which people begin to perceive other communities and conceive of the world. They provide a rationale for communal action. Mythic history appeals to people's emotions and plays upon their religious feelings. It seeks to mobilize people's anger, hatred and aggression and provides them with a target. The struggle for Ramjanmabhumi becomes a metaphor for a war against Muslims.

The politics of Ramjanmabhumi and its effort to legitimize itself through mythic history raises a deeper question about the principles which can govern our actions. We need to demarcate our principles from those that lay behind the actions of individuals in the past. If intolerance, religious repression, and violence have characterized the politics of earlier times, in India and in other countries, we need to distance ourselves from that politics. If other nations and other societies continue to practice such politics, we need not emulate them. The politics of Ramjanmabhumi seeks to reassert the principles of medieval politics. It aspires to re-enact in the present the politics of violence, repression and revenge. This is a politics which negates not only the secular character of the Indian Constitution but the democratic principle of equal citizenship and the rule of law which the Constitution upholds. It is a politics whose profoundly dangerous implications only the future will unfold.

Notes

1. I would like to thank Romila Thapar, K.N. Panikkar and Chitra Joshi for comments on an earlier draft of this essay.

2. K.N. Panikkar, 'Ramjanmabhumi and Babri Masjid:A Historical Overview', *The Political Abuse of History: Babri Masjid–Rama Janma Bhumi Dispute*, Centre for Historical Studies, Jawaharlal Nehru University, New Delhi, 1989.

3. *Organiser*, 20 July 1986.

4. Pratap Narain Misra, *Kya Kahati Hai Saryu Dhara?: Sri Ramjanmabhumi ki Kahani*, Lucknow, 1986, p. 5.

5. Sri Ramjanmabhumi Mukti Yagya Samiti, '*Sri Ramjanmabhumi ke Bare me Tathya*', *Ham Mandir Wahin Banayenge*, Suruchi Prakashan: New Delhi, 1989, p. 17.

6. Justice Deoki Nandan, *Sri Ramjanmabhumi: Itihasik and Vidik Samiksha*, Suruchi Printers: Allahabad, n.d. Deoki Nandan, in fact, wishes away all disputes regarding the historical facts over the Ramjanmabhumi/Babri Masjid issue. 'It is an undisputed historical fact that at Ramjanmabhumi there was an ancient mandir since the time of Maharaja Vikramaditya,' he writes. *Ham Mandir Wahin Banayenge*, Suruchi Prakashan: New Delhi, 1989, p. 17.

7. We are told in one article on the subject, 'There is no room for any doubt that the Babri Masjid was constructed after demolishing Shri Ramjanmabhumi temple and on the very spot. This *fact* has been clearly *recorded* in many *authentic* history books.' (*emphasis mine.*) P. Parameswaran, Director, Bharatiya Vichar Kendra, Trivandrum, *Organiser,* 15 February 1987. See also S.P. Gupta, 'Ram Janmabhoomi Controversy: What History and Archaeology Say', *Organiser,* 29 March 1987.

8. Bharatiya Vichar Kendra, 'Sri Ramjanmabhumi or Babri Masjid?', *Organiser*, 29 March 1987.

9. 'The belief of billions in such matters is enough to bestow upon them the sanctity more than History can. . . . The very fact that Ram is worshipped from far east to Arabian sea, from Himalayas to Kanyakumari, and tradition passing from father to son believes him to be a living person of a prehistoric era is proof enough that a person of that name existed and was born in a city called Ayodhya.' *Organiser*, 5 April 1987. See also M.V. Kamath, 'Myth and Reality', *Organiser*, 13 December 1987.

10. *Organiser*, 5 April 1987.

11. Those who feel that a historian's critique of the VHP claims is illegitimate and misplaced, fail to understand the nature of the present political debate on the issue. The VHP rhetoric uses both the language of History and the language of myth; it seeks to authenticate its account by presenting it as 'history'.

·12. Centre for Historical Studies, Jawaharlal Nehru University, *The Political Abuse of History: Babri Masjid–Rama Janma Bhumi Dispute,* New Delhi, 1989; K.N. Panikkar, 'Ramjanmabhumi and Babri Masjid: A Historical Overview', in this volume.

13. Raghunandan Prashad Sharma, *Vishwa Hindu Parishad ke Uddeshya, Karya tatha Upalabhdhiyan*, New Delhi, n.d.; Ashok Singhal, *Vishwa Hindu Parishad Ke Pachis Varsha*, New Delhi, n.d.; A. Shankar, *Hindu Jago Desh Bachao*, VHP pamphlet, New Delhi, n.d. See also the VHP pamphlet series, Ekatmata Pustak Mala.

14. H.V. Seshadri, *Organiser,* April 1982, reproduced in Seshadri, *Hindu Renaissance Underway,* Bangalore, 1984.

15. A. Shankar, *Chetawani: Desh ko Khatra*, VHP pamphlet, New Delhi n.d.; Sitaram Goyal, *Hindu Samaj Sankat ke Ghere Me*, Lokhit Prakashan: Lucknow; Seshadri, 'Now is the Time for Hindus to Act', *Organiser*, 19 July 1987.

16. H.V. Seshadri, 'Wiping out the Blot of Foreign Slavery', *Organiser,* 5 January 1986. See also Bhanu Pratap Shukla, *Shilanyas se Shikhar ki Or,* Suruchi Prakashan: New Delhi.

17. *Organiser*, 6 July 1986.

18. M. Verma, 'The Beleaguered Hindu', *Organiser,* 24 April 1988; 'Angry Hindu! Yes, Why Not?', *Organiser*, 14 February 1988.

19. *'Angry Hindu!' Yes, Why Not?* , Suruchi Prakashan: New Delhi, 1988.

20. Interview with Rajmata Scindia, *Organiser*, 6 July 1986.

21. H.V. Seshadri, 'Wiping out the Blot of Foreign Slavery', *Organiser*, 5 January 1986. 'How can Babri Masjid be a National Monument? It is a symbol of foreign Turkish attack, of cruelty and bestiality, of Muslim barbarism. It can only be a symbol of Indian subjection.' Pratap Narain Misra, *Kya Kahati Hai Suryu Dhara*, p. 139.

22. *Organiser,* 14 July 1985.

23. P.N. Oak, 'Akbar was only the captor, not the builder of Fatehpur Sikri', *Organiser*, 14 July 1985.

24. 'My mind and heart is that of a Hindu, my life itself is Hindu; I am Hindu to my very core. I am Shankar's fiery anger, I can burn the world to ashes. I am the drum which ushers destruction. I am the unsatiated thirst of Ranachandi (the Goddess of war), I am the wild laughter of Durga. I am the death-call of Yama (the Lord of death), I am the smoke that emits from the cremation ground. The anger which burns deep within me will set the world ablaze. I am in essence a Hindu.' *'Angry Hindu!' Yes, Why Not?*, p.17. On the iconography of Rama see Anuradha Kapur, 'Militant images of a Tranquil God', *Times of India*, 10 January 1989.

25. On the many versions of *Ramayana* see Romila Thapar, 'Epic and History: Tradition, Dissent and Politics in India', *Past and Present*, November 1989; and 'The Many Faces of the Ramakatha: A Historical Perspective on the Story of Rama' in this volume; J.L. Brockington, *Righteous Rama: The Evolution of an Epic*, New Delhi, 1984.

26. David Shulman, 'Divine Order and Divine Evil in the Tamil Tale of Rama', *Journal of Asian Studies*, August 1979.

27. On the activities of the VHP, the BJP and the RSS, see Seshadri, 'The Country-wide Hindu Resurgence: A Bird's-eye View', 'A Yatra for National Union of Hearts', 'Ekatmata Yatra: Setting National Vision Right', *Hindu Renaissance Underway*; Indraprastha Vishwa Hindu Parishad, *Sri Ramjan-*

mabhumi Mandir Mahabhiyan mein Kiye Gaye Mahatwa Purna Karyakram, New Delhi, n.d.

28. *Organiser,* January 1988.

29. P.C. Asdhir, 'Do not push the Hindu Psyche too Hard', *Organiser,* 6 September 1987.

30. See also Sudipto Kaviraj, 'On the Discourse of Communalism' (mimeo). Ashis Nandy has written entensively on this theme of transformation of Hinduism.

31. Pratap Narain Misra, *Kya Kahati Hai Saryu Dhara?*; Ram Gopal Pandey, *Ramjanmabhumi ka Raktaranjit Itihas;* Acharya Gudunji Sharma, *Ayodhyaji ka Prachin Itihas: Ayodhya Guide;* Gumanmal Lodha, *Ayodhya Mein Sri Ram ka Apaman Kab Tak Hoga?,* VHP, n.d.; Raghunandan Prasad Sharma, *Sri Ramjanmabhumi ki Balidangatha,* New Delhi, 1989. I would like to thank Urvashi Butalia for giving me access to two of the above booklets.

32. *Organiser,* 21 Oct 1984; 12 May 1985; 23 June 1985; 18 Aug 1985; 22 Dec 1985; 27 April 1986; 4 May 1986; 7 Dec 1986; 24 Aug 1986.

33. Myths of discovery are important for the consecration of sacred spaces. For, a sacred space is not supposed to be chosen by man, it is discovered by him. Sacredness manifests itself through appropriate signs. See Mircea Eliade, *The Sacred and the Profane,* New York, 1959.

34. ibid.

35. Wendy Doniger O'Flaherty, *Sexual Metaphors and Animal Symbolism in Indian Mythology,* Delhi, 1981.

36. *Organiser,* 6 July 1986.

37. This claim has no real historical basis. My concern here is not to disprove the claim, which can too easily be done, but to understand it.

38. British official reports on the incident are extremely detailed and interesting. See in particular *Foreign Political Consultations,* 28 December 1855. For a discussion of the incident see Panikkar, 'Ramjanmabhumi and Babri Masjid: A Historical Overview' in this volume; G.D. Bhatnagar, *Awadh Under Wajid Ali Shah,* Varanasi, 1968.

39. P. Carnegy, *Historical Sketches of Tahsil Faizabad, Zillah Faizabad,* Lucknow, 1870; H.R. Neville, *Faizabad District Gazetteer,* Allahabad, 1905.

40. See in particular, Misra, *Kya Kahati Hai Saryu Dhara?*; Pandey, *Ramjanmabhumi ka Raktaranjit Itihas;* Sharma, *Ayodhyaji ka Prachin Itihas;* Sharma, *Sri Ramjanmabhumi ki Balidangatha.*

A Historical Perspective on the Story of Rama[1]

Romila Thapar

It is popularly believed today, especially in northern India, that there have been only two important versions of the *Rama-katha* or the story of Rama in Indian civilization: the earliest being the Sanskrit version of Valmiki, the *Ramayana,* and the Hindi version of Tulsidas, the *Ramacharitamanas*. However, historically, what is of the greatest interest about the *Rama-katha* is its multiple versions. Each major version reflects a substantial change both in how the role of the story was perceived, and in the acceptance of each of these different versions by their audience as the authentic one. This places the Valmiki and the Tulsi texts in a broader civilizational context rather than solely in a religious one—a context which I hope to explore in this essay.

As each of these many different versions makes a particular statement as part of an ongoing dialogue over time, some versions contradict the others in both narrative and intent. As the same story or a relatively similar story is treated variously in terms of ethics, values, social and political norms and religious identities, the purpose and function of each version are significant and they cannot all be labelled as manifestations of a single religious expression. Even an overview of these variants provides rich material for the historical and cultural understanding of the role of the story. The variations introduced into the story by specific authors are for specific reasons and constitute a debate whose parameters change with historical change. It becomes necessary then to make a distinction between versions which are cultural idioms and those which are essentially propagating a religious sectarian point of view. Historically, the significance of the cultural idiom is in many ways richer, with many more levels of symbolic meaning, than the more narrowly religious, sectarian form. However even among the latter, the contradictions and deviations are in themselves very valuable pointers to the cultural idiom.

The Valmiki *Ramayana,* in its original form, was not a 'sacred book' as we understand sacred books today. It was a narrative, a story, cast in an epic mould. It was not even described as a text on *dharma*. Nor is it generally classified as an *itihasa*—that which was believed to have happened in the past. It is more frequently referred to as a *kavya* or an *adikavya*, a poetic composition. Unlike sacred books which are rarely questioned or altered (and if they are, the change is marginal) the *Ramayana* was refashioned time and again, sometimes to convert it into a religious text and sometimes for other purposes.

That the Valmiki *Ramayana* was not originally treated as a sacred book becomes apparent from the difference between its recording, orally at first and later in writing, and the recording of the Vedic corpus. The hymns of the Vedas were meticulously memorized using a range of mnemonic devices taught to and restricted to Brahmins performing priestly functions—as they still are. This ensured a remarkable reproduction of the original composition;[2] and the hymns being regarded as sacred, such correct recitation was a precondition to their effectiveness. By contrast, texts such as the *Ramayana* had a much more open method of preservation. Its oral memorization did not preclude changes and later interpolations such as perorations on good government and the observance of the rules of *dharma*. In fact that very act of converting the text from an epic poem to the story of Rama as an *avatara* of Vishnu, required that there be substantial additions.

Literature which is recorded orally in a fashion as free as that of the epics of early India cannot be dated to any one time period as it has constantly undergone change. It can only be precisely dated from the time when the earliest manuscripts of the text survive. In the case of the Valmiki *Ramayana* this would be quite late. However, other texts of earlier periods refer to the *Ramayana* and we know that at least the oral form was current in earlier centuries. As to when even this originally oral form was composed, remains uncertain and has its own history.

Epics do not date to a particular period for they are in essence the literature of a later age looking back on an earlier one. Events and characters are fictionalized to such a degree that even if there is a kernel of history embedded in them, it is often not in conformity with the narrative. The importance of the epic for the historian lies not in the narrating of events which may be believed to have happened, but in the perception of the past which is encapsulated in the text, a vision which portrays a society of earlier times and thereby also provides a commentary on the social assumptions of the age when the epic was composed.

Some decades ago historians using the data from the two epics, the

Mahabharata and the *Ramayana*, argued for what was termed 'the epic age' in Indian history.[3] This age has now been eroded from historical periodization for the original epics are embedded in the versions which have survived. Attempts to find a solution to the date of the Valmiki *Ramayana*, by excavating sites mentioned in the text, have been disappointing for those who believe in the great antiquity of these places. Thus excavations in and around Ayodhya do not take the settlement back to earlier than the seventh century BC. The artefacts of this period suggest a very simple way of life, which in no way can be regarded as urban living; nor can it be regarded as the archaeological counterpart to the descriptions in the text.[4]

There have been many interpolations over the millennium from 500 BC to AD 500, and therefore only episodes can perhaps be dated on comparative evidence.[5] This would imply that the epics do not belong to a specific period because they are part of an ongoing tradition and that the epic itself is made to change its function over time when it is converted from bardic to religious literature.

Poems as literary forms, even if they should be dealing with historical themes, cannot in themselves be regarded as historical texts. They can at best provide clues to the ways in which people perceived the past or their own times. Such clues are important to the historical reconstruction of ideologies and attitudes, but are not evidence of historical events unless proven to be so from other contemporary historical sources.

Epics are not religious documents in origin. But some versions of an epic story can be transformed into religious statements, as was done in the rewriting of the Valmiki *Ramayana*. The emphasis on the sacred has tended to make this text the preserve of specialists in religion. Some analyses of its religious concepts and philosophical ideas are valuable to the study of Hinduism, as is also the unravelling of its mythology. What has however been neglected is the comparative study of the large range of substantially variant versions. Frequently intended for a popular audience, they incorporate changes which have a significance other than just a sectarian religious statement or a deviation in mythology. The change of function is in itself of historical importance and the range of variations suggests that the historian should view the variants as recounting historical change. I hope to show that this is pertinent even to the contemporary use of the epic, both in defining social attitudes and in manipulating political conflicts.

Epics are frequently an amalgam emerging out of a number of ballads, folk tales and myths. Stories are threaded together by a bardic poet and these linkages give a different form to a literary genre. The *Rama-katha*, put together from a number of floating, bardic compositions, is believed to be the first form of the epic and it no longer exists in its original form. Even the earliest surviving versions, dating in their present forms to the turn of the Christian era, have each been worked over from particular perspectives. Among the early versions was the literary epic composed by the poet Valmiki, the *Ramayana,* which has come to be popularly accepted as the standard version. The story incorporates the usual raw material and stereotypes of epic tales: the changing fortunes of the hero, the kidnapping of the princess, the quest for rescuing her, the heroic battle interspersed with flying monkeys, demons and an aerial chariot.

The hero, Rama, is the eldest son of king Dasharatha, who rules from the city of Ayodhya over the kingdom of Koshala situated in the middle Ganges plain, and claims descent from the Suryavamsha or solar line. The neighbouring forests are the haunt of demons, the *rakshasas,* who continually interfere with the sacrificial rituals in the forest hermitages of the ascetics. Rama and his younger brother, Lakshmana, are called upon to rid the forest of the demons. This they do and then proceed to the court of king Janaka in the foothills of the Himalayas. The daughter of Janaka, Sita, is to be wed. The choice of her husband is dependent on which of the heroes gathered at the court can lift and bend a massive bow. The young Rama alone succeeds, and Sita becomes his bride. On their return to Ayodhya, Dasharatha announces the installation of Rama as the future king. But Rama's stepmother, prodded by her hunchbacked maid, reminds her husband of a promise which he had made to her earlier. She demands that her son succeed Dasharatha and that Rama be exiled to the forest for fourteen years. Dasharatha, true to his word, sadly gives in. Rama, Sita and Lakshmana, the latter two voluntarily, go into exile, wandering in the forests of the Vindhya hills to the south of the Ganges plain. Here the inevitable happens. Sita is kidnapped by the powerful demon Ravana, who takes her away in his aerial chariot to his home in Lanka. Rama and Lakshmana discover the whereabouts of Sita with the help of the chief of the monkeys, Hanuman. Rama in order to recover Sita, goes into battle against Ravana. Ravana is eventually defeated. Sita is rescued but has to undergo a fire ordeal to prove her chastity. The three then return to Ayodhya where, the period of exile being completed, they are warmly welcomed. Dasharatha having died meanwhile, Rama is crowned and his reign is symbolic in social memory with a mythologized utopian period of prosperity and well-being, reflected in the phrase *Rama-rajya.*

The original epic, composed by bards as part of the oral tradition, was recited at sacrificial rituals, at feasts and at the courts of the *rajas*—the chiefs and kings. Its origin could be seen as a eulogy to a patron or else the eulogistic functions could be seen as a simile. The story involved the families of the Kshatriyas, chiefs and warriors, with other social groups playing lesser roles. The hero had often to be distinguished by a special birth. Thus, Rama and his brothers were born only after the performance of a sacrificial ritual by a particular sage.[6] Exile was a useful device. It gave the bard occasions for fresh incidents if the narrative was wearing thin. Time was not rigid. It could move back and forth with a continuum between mythic, heroic and historical time. Narrating the previous incarnations of various persons was a way of playing with time. The conflict between Rama and Ravana has been described as a prototype myth echoing the earlier conflict described in Vedic sources between Indra and Vritra, and exalting the heroic ideal. Rama is the personification of the ideal Kshatriya. He is referred to as a human hero and in these references there is no question of his being identified with Vishnu.[7] He is however the perfect man.[8]

That the story gained popularity is evident from its inclusion among the narratives, the *akhyanas*, of the sixteen great heroes as given in the *Mahabharata*. The 'Ramopakhyana' as it is called is not just a summary of the Valmiki text as is often assumed, but a rendering of the story with distinct changes. Whether it preceded the Valmiki version or was composed later remains controversial. The popularity of the story has been attributed to various factors such as that it was a compendium of nature myths with Sita as a fertility goddess and Rama as the solar deity, given his descent from the solar line. Perhaps it was because of this increasing popularity that the Valmiki *Ramayana* was now converted into a religious text[9] through a new edition which was a refashioning by Brahmin authors. Appropriate changes were made in the text and two further books were added at the beginning and the end, the 'Balakanda' and the 'Uttarakanda'.[10] The pre-eminence given to the Bhargava Brahmins is noticeable in both these additions.[11]

The hero Rama was now said to be an *avatara* or incarnation of Vishnu, one of the two major deities of the emerging Puranic Hinduism. The *Ramayana* therefore becomes a text for the propagation of the worship of Vishnu with the suggestion that the reading of the story might free one from sin. The additional book at the beginning and end of the text gathered to it a variety of myths, legends, genealogies and changes in the narrative which drew on features of the religious sects of the Bhagavatas. Furthermore, an elaboration on the character of the protagonists led to an exaggeration of their earlier depiction. Thus Ravana emerges as a ten-headed monster, and so much the personification of evil as to be almost a caricature. Yet at the same time, in a lengthy interpolation at the end we are told that Ravana was descended from a line of Brahmin seers and was himself an ascetic whose power had to be broken because of his turning to evil actions.[12] Many see it as a battle between good and evil where the narrative encapsulates a theory of ethics. One of the explanations for its popularity originated from a nineteenth century Indologist, Christian Lassen, who argued that the story describes the Aryan invasion of the non-Aryan south, and the conflict is between Aryan and Dravidian culture.[13]

Substantial changes introduced into the story have their own interest, such as those referring to the birth of Sita. Further, when Rama and Sita return to Ayodhya after the exile, Sita's chastity is again questioned and on this occasion she is banished and goes to live in the hermitage of the sage Valmiki. Here twin sons are born to her and named Kusha and Lava, a curious choice because *kushilavah* came to be used as the technical term for a bard.[14] It is said that Valmiki composed the *Ramayana* and taught it to the sons of Sita, directing them to recite it on appropriate occasions. This is a curious turn to the story. The main thrust of the Brahminized version which continued to be referred to as the Valmiki *Ramayana* was of course the glorification of Vishnu incarnated as Rama.

The arena was that of clans in conflict, in a situation of new settlements encroaching on forests and the migrations of peoples.[15] The Valmiki *Ramayana* has obscured the identity of the *rakshasas* by describing them as demons, where the fantasy of the poet has had full play. Nevertheless it is evident that these were not demons but a people with ways of life different from those of Ayodhya and into whose territory the hermits and the exiled heroes were intruding. The original *Rama-katha* probably attempted to describe a conflict between chiefdoms prior to the rise of monarchies. Subsequent rewriting changes the focus to a strong endorsement of the monarchical state. Monarchy is now regarded as the ideal political form and there is an implied disapproval of pre-monarchical or of variant systems such as among the *rakshasas*.[16]

The *Ramayana* repeatedly states that a people without a king is conducive to general anarchy.[17] Ayodhya is the capital of a monarchical state, Rama endorses the duties of a king, primogeniture becomes a crucial issue when the eldest son is exiled and debarred from kingship, contrary to the norm. Society in Ayodhya is ordered according to the rules of caste.[18] Its citizens count their wealth in grain and in valuables which they exchange even over long distances.[19] The *rakshasa* territory by contrast has no boundaries, lacks the authority of a state and its society is not ordered according to caste. Decisions are taken by Ravana the *rakshasa* chief and his kinsmen for there is neither consultation with ministers nor a hierarchy of status. Lanka, his island stronghold, is described as a city of gold, gems and untold riches but there is no obvious source of wealth.[20] The luxury may well be an example of extravagant poetic imagination. The *rakshasas* are unfamiliar with agriculture and know no trade. The hermits are the vanguard, as it were, of encroachment into the hunting grounds and forests of the *rakshasas,* for they are, in effect, also the precursors of an agricultural society which would clear and settle the forested areas. This may well have occasioned the need for the *rakshasas* to disturb the rituals of the hermits. The *rakshasas* were looked down upon. Yet they are also said to have access to magical powers and objects among which the most impressive was the aerial chariot of Ravana. The demonizing, as it were, of the *rakshasas,* could be the projection of a feared enemy. There is both a putting down as well as a looking up to Ravana in the Brahmanical version.

The lesser persons who became the allies of Rama in exile, such as the Nishada chief and the kinsmen of Hanuman, have been viewed as possible hunting and gathering tribes of the forests, who in early myths were expelled to less accessible areas.[21] These were people bound by elaborate rules of gift-giving and reciprocal obligations, more so than in the monarchy. The text therefore might seem to incorporate a continuum of social and economic forms, moving from hunting and gathering peoples to chiefdoms, and reserving the accolades for the monarchical State. With each major version of the text, there is an increasing emphasis on the monarchy as the model, but some of the non-monarchical forms are retained for contrast or else manage to slip through.

The *Rama-katha* was part of a floating tradition of bardic stories which were picked up and reworked into variant versions. This is confirmed also by versions which occur in the literature of what are generally regarded as the heterodox religions, Buddhism and Jainism, the heterodoxy being opposition to Brahmanism. From the Buddhist sources comes the story as narrated in the *Dasaratha Jataka*[22] dating to anywhere between the fourth and the second centuries BC and which is in effect the briefest of summaries of part of the *Rama-katha.* Some scholars have argued that this version of the *Rama-katha* predates Valmiki whereas others maintain that it is later.[23] There is a significant change in the story, for here Sita is not the wife but the sister of Rama. At the end of the exile when Rama returns to Ayodhya, Sita is made the queen-consort of Rama and they rule jointly for sixteen thousand years. This version may reflect the tradition of brother-sister marriages in Buddhist origin myths, including that of the Buddha himself. It can be interpreted in many ways: as a symbol of the purity of blood or, possibly, a demarcation of a distinctive status. A comparison with Buddhist origin myths suggests that Rama and Sita may have been seen as the originators of a royal clan and therefore placed in this particular relationship for the ancestry of Rama is traced back to the eponymous ancestor Ikshvaku, from whom incidentally the clan of the Buddha also claimed descent.[24] Sibling incest is not to be taken literally but seen as a cultural signal. Written in Pali for the edification of Buddhist audiences, the function of the story was different from other versions of the *Rama-katha*. The Buddhist ethic is underlined in the consolation which Rama offers to his brother Lakshmana on the death of their father.

The Jaina version of the *Rama-katha*, the *Paumacharyam*, is aggressively different from the others and sets itself up as the counter epic.[25] Composed by Vimalasuri in about the third century AD or a little later, it was written in the popularly used language, Prakrit. It contradicted the *Ramayana* as reworked by Brahmin authors and which it describes as part of the false tradition propagated by Brahmin heretics, the Brahmins being heretical from the Jaina point of view.[26] The Jaina version, framed in the perspective of the Jaina ethic and doctrine, was in a way the mirror image of the Valmiki version as revised by the Brahmins. Vimalasuri naturally claims veracity for his narrative but also introduces a new dimension of historicity in arguing that his version conformed to what actually happened. Historicity is not one of the claims of the Valmiki *Ramayana*.

The Jaina version starts by giving the genealogy and background not of Rama, as in the Valmiki version, but of Ravana and then of Hanuman.[27] We are told that the *rakshasas* were not demons but normal humans. Ravana was not a ten-headed monster but was described as such because he wore a necklace of nine large gem-stones which reflected his face. Similarly Hanuman was not a monkey but the leader of a clan with a monkey emblem on its standard. His role as mediator rather than one who loyally serves Rama, is more pronounced in this version. Ravana, we are told, belongs to the Meghavahana lineage, the word literally meaning that he was 'cloud-borne', which also links him to his other epithet, *akasha-margi,* he who travels through the sky—both epithets are suggestive of aerial chariots.

At the time when the Jaina version was written the Vindhyan region had witnessed earlier settlements growing into trading centres, cities and the nuclei of small kingdoms. Patronage to Jainism came to be associated with some of these. Not unexpectedly, Ravana in the Jaina version far from being a villain, is a devoted Jaina who practised all the required religious precepts and austerities and acquired considerable ascetic power. At the end of the story, Dasharatha, Rama and Lakshmana, all become Jaina ascetics and Sita takes herself off to a nunnery. The question of self-perception therefore takes on a different definition. The ethic of the warrior so evident in the Valmiki version now changes to that of the Jaina ascetic. At the same time the Jaina epic is a powerful contradiction of the Brahmanic version.

There now begins a tradition of a series of Jaina versions of the *Rama-katha*.[28] These coincide with the period when Rama as an *avatara* of Vishnu begins to gain popularity, although an increase in the number of Jaina versions dates to the later time when Rama emerges as the focus of *bhakti* worship. The Jaina texts are composed in various languages: Prakrit, Apabhramsha and Sanskrit. The characters are all human heroes but placed in a setting of Jaina ethics. Even within the Jaina tradition there are variations in the story for in some texts Sita is the daughter of Ravana but is brought up by Janaka, a theme which was to be popular in other late versions. This makes the abduction doubly heinous but adds a further layer to the symbolic meaning. The accusation that the Brahmanical version of the story was incorrect continues to be made. What the Jaina and Buddhist versions point to is that the *Rama-katha* was a popular story which was picked up by a range of sectarian interests for a variety of purposes and at the same time, there was a continuing controversy as to the authenticity of event and character. The historically interesting question is whether Vimalasuri's version draws from an earlier tradition which might explain the contradiction in the treatment of the story, or does it reflect an increasing confrontation between Jainas and Brahmins.

The *Rama-katha* provided familiar stories to many different audiences. These themes found their way into yet another and entirely separate genre, namely, plays and poems written for the royal courts and the literati. They were reworked into the classics of creative literature in Sanskrit and many underwent major changes conforming to the requirements of courtly literature. Among the better known and more frequently quoted are the narrative poem of Kalidasa, *Raghuvamsham,* the play of Bhasa, *Pratima-nataka* and Bhavabhuti's *Uttararamacharita*. Some compositions even took the form of a literary *tour de force* as in the ninth century biography of a contemporary east Indian king, Ramapala, where the *Ramacharitam* of Sandhyakaranandin can be read equally easily as the story of Rama or as the biography of the king. Such compositions were not treating the *Rama-katha* as sacred literature but as a source for literary themes and demonstrations of poetic virtuosity.

The emergent regional languages also produced at different times their own versions of the *Rama-katha,* such as the Tamil epic of Kamban, *Iramavataram* or the Telugu, *Ranganatharamayana,* or the Kannada *Pampa Ramayana,* or the later Bengali, Krittibasa *Ramayan,* or that of Ekanatha in Marathi, the *Bhavartha Ramayana.*[29] The writing of the *Rama-katha* in regional languages nas been a continuing process and many of these versions introduced innovations in response to changes in Indian society and regional perspectives. The innovations were both of event and of character. Thus the treatment of Ravana in many of these versions is that of a hero in decline rather than a villain and is distinctly different from that of Valmiki. The Tamil poem draws a little more heavily on the Bhakti tradition of devotion to a deity.

By the early second millennium AD there had been an enormous geographical spread of the Rama story. This had less to do with *Ramabhakti* as such and more with the fact that in its variant forms, local traditions were expressing themselves in a common cultural idiom which was widely dispersed and understood. A distinction therefore has to be made between the story as a cultural metaphor and as sacred literature. In the reworked Valmiki text it remained the sacred literature of the Vaishnavas, but many other variants were treating it as a cultural metaphor. The latter were popular in central Asia, China and Tibet,[30] sometimes drawing on the Buddhist originals, although these versions had their own variants reflecting the social and cultural norms of the society from which they arose. In south-east Asia there was an avid appropriation of the story frequently drawing on Indian folk and regional versions, with clear variants deriving inspiration from local geography, tradition and events. In one version the area of north Vietnam (Annam) is identified as the Ayodhya of the text and that to the south of it (Champa) as Lanka, a considerable shift in geographical identification. In some versions Sita appears, unknown to him, as the daughter of Ravana. The more up-to-date versions in south-east Asia incorporate Islamic legends, some even featuring the prophet, Adam.[31] In the Malayan version of the legend, Ravana is exiled to Serendib, where Adam sees him and pleads for him before Allah, who grants him a kingdom.[32] It has been argued that the sculptured reliefs at major sites in Indonesia are more likely based on folk versions of the story than on any text.[33]

Narrative art in painting and sculpture had also begun to draw on the local version of the story from the middle of the first millennium AD. Gupta period sculpture at the temples of Nachna Kuthara and Deogadh have been interpreted as depicting scenes from the *Rama-katha*. The depiction of the *Rama-katha* was part of the general theme included among the *avataras* of Vishnu. The treatment of Rama as an individual deity in his own right, with temples dedicated specifically to him is, however, a much later development.

When we ask why there was this mushrooming of the story in India, the notion of cultural idiom appears to take precedence over the religious text. One obvious reason was that it was a tale well told, personifying the conflict between good and evil with the virtuous eventually triumphant. Equally obvious was the use of the text for the propagation of the cult of Vishnu. Specialists in the history of Indian literature have argued that the spread of Sanskrit to new areas which were until then using their own local language, was facilitated by the use of the simple Sanskrit of the Valmiki epic. This became the model for epic genres in the new regional languages although the narrative was changed in accordance with the demands of popular culture and local tradition. Such explanations are entirely feasible, but perhaps not sufficient. An investigation of the historical background may further fill out the picture.

If the *Rama-katha* was also seen as a charter of validation for monarchy then it was an appropriate text for historical changes taking place from about the eighth century AD. There was a noticeable growth of a large number of small kingdoms. Barring a few major dynasties, these were generally short-lived kingdoms of no great pretension to extensive territory but each claiming and indulging in the full panoply of monarchical status. Minor rulers rushed to take grandiloquent titles and did not hesitate to call themselves Maharajadhiraja, great king of kings. Local courts boasted large retinues of retainers whose code of behaviour laid emphasis on heroic chivalry combined with blinkered devotion and loyalty to the king. The subsistence of these kingdoms came in large part from the steady encroachment of the agrarian economy into erstwhile forested regions. Waste land was brought under cultivation, not necessarily by the State directly but also through a system of granting land to learned Brahmins and those holding high administrative office. The ancestors of many of the lesser kings were such grantees in origin and the more ambitious among them aspired to the monarchical model. Some came from families of tribal chiefs who through administrative office had moved into the hierarchy of the State. In this situation access to economic resources implied increasing the land under cultivation. Forest tribes were under all circumstances to be subjugated, a strategy which has continued through the centuries. The triumph of Rama over Ravana therefore provided a powerful metaphor for a process which was actually taking place.

Where royal courts came into existence, there the Brahmins legitimized the king by providing him with a genealogy and by performing rituals through which his divine status was proclaimed.[34] There is a frequency in this period to claims to ancestry in the two royal lineages—the Suryavamsha and the Chandravamsha. By means of the genealogy the status of Kshatriya, now seen as that of the landed aristocracy was bestowed on the family irrespective of its actual origins. Those who claimed descent from the Suryavamsha had Rama as a distant ancestor. The *Ramayana* would then become the story of the royal ancestor. That the ancestor was an incarnation of the god Vishnu, helped underline the divinity of kingship which by this period was more generally asserted than in earlier times.

The settling of Brahmins in areas previously unfamiliar with Brahmanical culture brought about an acculturation through which a familiarity with the Sanskritic tradition was introduced to these areas. But such acculturation increasingly required that the Sanskritic tradition incorporate manifestations of the local culture. Thus new versions of the *Rama-katha* were composed in which the ingredients of local culture predominated.

One form taken by these manifestations was the use of historical geography. The geography of the earlier Valmiki *Ramayana* remained confused. Thus, the location of Lanka, never made precise, may have moved from the Vindhyan region south-eastward following a known route of migration and trade.[35] According to popular belief today it could even be the island of Ceylon or Sri Lanka. This geographical flexibility could be put to good use. The theme of exile came in very handy. Originally a bardic device used in virtually all epics to stretch the story or incorporate other fragments, it became, in this case, part of the process of acculturation. Local opinion could claim that exile had actually brought Rama to that area. Topographical features and local cults were gradually linked to the story. This enhanced the cultural prestige of the site, assisted in the proselytizing of people to the religious cults of Vishnu and his incarnations and incidentally also helped to strengthen the theory of the genealogical links of the local ruling family where it claimed descent from Rama. In a sixteenth century version of the *Rama-katha* from Orissa, the exiles are depicted as travelling through the then contemporary kingdoms.[36]

Parallel with these developments but of a qualitatively different kind was the emergence of a specific sect focussing on the worship of Rama and dating to the early second millennium AD. This was the influential sect of Ramanandins. For them the worship of Rama or *Rama-bhakti* was the most effectual form of devotional worship and ensured the salvation of the individual. *Rama-bhakti* was of course part of the Vaishnava Bhagavata tradition even earlier, but the focus which the Ramanandin sect provided was new. They drew on those versions of the story which emphasized *Rama-bhakti* and the texts associated with them were distinct. The focus shifts somewhat from Vishnu to more specifically Rama, but the concern of these texts was not so much the activities of Rama as the prescription for the attaining of *moksha* (release from the cycle of birth and death).

Among these texts the *Adhyatma-Ramayana*, dating to about the fifteenth century AD[37] carries the notion of *maya* or illusion to its logical conclusion, when it argues that the very story of Rama is an illusion and that the importance of the text is less the story and more what the text has to say about devotional worship. The *Rama-katha* is set in the frame of Shiva telling the story to Parvati for the salvation of all. This is yet another idea which changes the function of the story. There is also a listing of benefits derived from the recitation of the *Adhyatma-Ramayana*. This points to a move in the direction of making the text into a sacred book for the *Rama-bhaktas,* even though at many crucial points there are differences with the Valmiki *Ramayana*. Echoes of the Krishna legend are introduced from time to time as in the description of the childhood of Rama.[38] The legend of how Valmiki took to the ways of a low-caste thief but eventually came to compose the *Ramayana*, is also related.[39] We are told that Rama being in fact Vishnu, knew that Ravana would kidnap Sita, and therefore places her in the safe-keeping of Agni by making her enter the fire and she is replaced by the shadow or *chaya* Sita.[40] The real Sita returns to Rama after the fire ordeal. Ravana in turn knows that Sita is in fact Lakshmi, therefore, although he kidnaps her, he treats her like his mother.[41] Ravana also knows that Rama is an incarnation of Vishnu, so, by kidnapping Sita and being therefore killed by Rama, he ensures that he will go to heaven. When Sita is banished for the second time, the author does leave us with the question of how could Rama, knowing Sita to be his own Shri, have banished her? Yet Rama tells Sita of his plan to banish her, so that she can return to heaven and he will follow later.[42] This altogether changes the ethical implications of the banishment. The obvious logical inconsistencies in this version of the story are subordinated to the text being sacred and devoted to the worship of Rama. The problem for the author was to reconcile the story with the necessary religious explanations. Hence the deviations. The importance given to the Rama-gita recited by Rama towards the end of the story,[43] would seem to point to parallels with *Krishna-bhakti*. Many of these features derived from the differing versions related in the major Puranas, which either refer to the story or carry a summary of it. The influence of the *Bhagavata Purana* is particularly noticeable in the *Bhushundi Ramayana,* where the treatment of Rama's early life is modelled on that of Krishna, and Sita is surrounded by *gopis*.[44]

The notion of a shadow Sita or even a substitute Sita, was to become extremely popular in the later versions. Sita's fire ordeal in these is less a test of Sita's chastity and more a mechanism by which the real Sita is reunited with Rama. This idea, apart from its link with the philosophical notion of *maya* or illusion, was perhaps also a concession to the popular goddess cults of this time which not only insisted on the power and presence of the female principle, but also may not have allowed a goddess of fertility to be subjected to such ordeals.

The influence of the now powerful Shakta tradition on the *Rama-katha* is clear from further changes in the narrative and treatment of the story in other texts. Shiva had already been introduced as the narrator of the story. More interesting is the change in the role of Sita, where she, whether the shadow or the actual Sita, goes into action single-handed against Ravana and finally kills him, episodes narrated in the Sanskrit *Adbhuta* and *Ananada Ramayanas*. Sita, as an incarnation not of Lakshmi but of the Shakta concept of Devi, is common to many Shakta versions of the story and does not hesitate to kill the hundred-headed or the thousand-headed Ravana. From the Shakta tradition such a change in the story is of course predictable, given that the goddess is all-powerful. But it converts the image and role of Sita into something completely different from that of even the revised Valmiki *Ramayana*. The relationship between Rama and Sita changes, as does the delineation of Sita as the ideal woman in the earlier version.[45] Some of these versions also retain the story of Sita being the daughter of Ravana, a fact not known to him.

The increasing influence of the Ramanandin sect led to a physical focus being located for the *bhaktas* of Rama in the city of Ayodhya, which had over time become the centre for many different religions and sects. The focus on Ayodhya was directed through the pilgrimage circuit and this in turn required the demarcation of a sacred topography locating the events of the *Rama-katha*. The *Ayodhya-mahatmya* was compiled in the early part of the second millennium AD, one among a genre of such texts which deal with the local history of a sacred site as part of a remembered tradition and which include myth, narrative about the cult and descriptions of the places regarded as sacred and required to be visited by the pilgrim.[46] Pilgrimage to Ayodhya associated specifically with the *Rama-katha*, seems to have begun only at this time.

In the sixteenth century Tulsidas composed the *Ramacharitamanas* in Hindi, which became the most popular version in northern India. This was not surprising as the Ramanandin sect, with which Tulsi was associated, required a text which would be comprehensible to a larger audience than the limited one of those who knew Sanskrit. For Tulsi, Rama was essentially the divine being present among humans. We are continually told that he is adored by all, even by ascetics who gaze on him like 'a bevy of partridges gazing at the autumn moon'. Tulsi's view of the world made such devotion imperative. He saw his contemporary times as a period of declining morality, the fall from the initial golden age to the present age of iron, the Kaliyuga (the age of Kali), accompanied by inevitable decline in social and ethical norms. He states that caste rules are now ignored, upstarts and low-caste people come into prominence and succeed through fraud and cheating. It is indeed a world turned upside down. The only consolation is the worship of Rama, which alone could bring back the utopian society once ruled by Rama.[47]

A section of popular opinion today maintains that this picture of decline was Tulsi's protest against the Mughal rulers who were Muslims and that his *Ramacharitamanas* consolidated and saved the Hindu ethos. But the text does not bear this out. The evils of the Kali age were conjured up repeatedly by Brahmin authors whenever they felt that Brahmanical authority was in crisis, and this had happened at various times even before the coming of Islam to India.[48] Tulsi as a Brahmin was doubtless disturbed by many of the current religious movements within the fold of what is today called Hinduism, which denied the authority of the Brahmins and the texts which they respected, which propagated alternative religious ideologies and attracted large audiences of non-Brahmins. Sects deriving from Puranic and Shakta worship were often opposed to the more conservative Brahmanical tradition. Thus, far from seeing the decline of Hinduism, India under Muslim rule witnessed the vibrancy of a large number of Hindu sects. Some of these competed for patronage, a competition which was at times to take violent turns as in the battles between the Bairagis and the Sanyasis. Even among the Vaishnava sects there was some competition for patronage. The Krishna cult at Vrindavana was becoming increasingly important. The *Ramacharitamanas* is not only a Vaishnava text but one which focuses more narrowly on *Rama-bhakti*. Yet it is not just a Hindi rewrite of the Valmiki *Ramayana* as revised for Bhagavata worship. It does carry differences of religious meaning. Tulsi's version also gains in importance today because of the status of Hindi in relation to other regional languages.

The popularity of Tulsi's text encouraged a new idiom, that of the *Ramalilas*. These were in the nature of folk plays enacting the *Rama-katha* and performed in the Hindi-speaking areas of north India. The time of year coincided with the autumn harvest and the worship of the ancestors (*shraddhas*), as well as the major seasonal worship of the mother goddesses. Possibly the *Rama-katha* ousted the worship of the goddess in these areas, for elsewhere the festival continues to be associated primarily with the goddess.

Yet another very different use to which the story was put was the mobilization of peasants in Uttar Pradesh by Baba Rama Chander in the early part of this century. Its dual objective was to support the national movement and to oppose the large-scale landlords of the area. Selected verses of the Tulsi version were popularized as part of the resistance to colonial rule. The virtuous characters in the story, Rama, Lakshmana and Sita, were identified with the peasants. The *rakshasas* who were the villains were identified with the landlords, capitalists and the British.[49] Baba Ram Chander does not speak of the return of the *Rama-rajya* or the golden age of the reign of Rama, but since he identified Rama with the peasants, the fulfillment of the dream of peasants in power would virtually amount to a *Rama-rajya*.

Local versions of the story differing in narrative and symbolism from the Valmiki and Tulsi versions have continued to be performed or even read, sometimes as a parallel tradition and sometimes as the central tradition in certain communities. Among these, by way of an example, is the popular Tamil version which was earlier handed down orally, but since the beginning of this century has been made available in printed form. This is the *Chatakantakatai* or the *Story of the Ten-Headed Ravana*.[50] Here once again it is Sita who, with Rama as her charioteer, goes into battle against Ravana and in single combat kills him. Clearly the imprint of the powerful, assertive goddess overrides the more accommodating and gentle image of the Valmiki or Tulsi versions and follows the narrative of the Shakta versions. These are not marginal traditions for they are central to the societies from which they emerge. In many of the folk versions the role of Hanuman changes. He remains a devotee of Rama but is in addition associated with popular humour and jokes, and speaks in a more indigenous style suggesting indirectly that he represents the local people.

The popular depictions in the *Ramalilas* found a place in the movie industry and since the early 1900s, films have been made on the themes of the *Ramayana* and advertised as 'mythological'. The films being largely in Hindi and propagating *Rama-bhakti*, it was almost inevitable that they would rely on the Valmiki and Tulsi versions. The films in turn have influenced the most recent form of the *Rama-katha*—as the most successful soap opera on national television—again drawing on Valmiki and Tulsi, now regarded as received versions.

Thus the *Rama-katha* in India has had a chequered history and has performed many functions, not all of which were solely religious. There are parallel traditions of the story which continue to this day and which relate to diverse social perspectives. There was a floating, oral tradition which probably began with ballads and epic fragments, narrating stories which were finally woven together into epic poems or the *Jataka* stories of the Buddhist tradition. Such forms continue to dominate folk traditions which have on occasion been incorporated into the many manifestations of the *Rama-katha*.

The *Rama-katha* as a story, important to religious sectarian positions, comes into its own in the second millennium AD. This tradition of *Rama-bhakti* becomes more focussed and powerful and the new versions are treated fundamentally as the texts of *Rama-bhakti*. But the variations among religious sects are also reflected in the treatment of the story. Thus the Tulsi version is different from the Shakta version and if the Tulsi version is popular in the Hindi-speaking areas, the Shakta version is popular elsewhere.

There is therefore, no single authentic version of the *Rama-katha,* for each version is authentic to the particular sect to which it is addressed or to the local community from which a version may emanate. By and large, and even when it is included in canonical or semi-canonical literature (as in the case of the Buddhist and the Jaina versions), the story is imbued with a sectarian perspective, but is not necessarily regarded as a sacred text. Only a few versions have latterly been treated as sacred. The multiplicity of folk versions in function go back to the epic tradition. These obviously are not regarded as sacred texts but are a significant part of the cultural idiom.

The *Rama-katha* has thus itself been through many incarnations and has changed its function in society over time. So no particular version can be treated as a specific sacred book, sacred to all Hindus whether of high or low caste or whether conforming to elite or popular religious traditions and irrespective of region and language. Nor is it possible to argue that the topography of pilgrimage at Ayodhya goes back to the centuries BC when, it is supposed, the events of the *Rama-katha* took place. What is of interest in looking at the historical perspective on the *Rama-katha*, is the role which the story has played in articulating a range of dialogue in the context of Indian civilization. This is not to suggest that those who wish to treat any of these many versions of the *Rama-katha* as a sacred book should not do so: but it is to insist that those who wish to see the *Rama-katha* tradition in its totality outside of a religious context, also have the right to see it that way. The differentiation between a cultural idiom and a religious, sectarian, sacred book should not be ignored. That this distinction was not ignored in the past, also becomes fundamental to our understanding of the role of the *Rama-katha* today.

The political exploitation of the worship of Rama has not only been visible but has been forced to the forefront in recent months, culminating in the fall of a government. This has added yet another dimension to the ways in which the *Rama-katha* has been used. Its roots lie in the realization that in the same way as once long ago the story was used to propagate a new religious idea (Bhagavatism and the concept of Rama as the *avatara* of Vishnu), the worship of that *avatara* could now be used to build up a political base and political demands. This first required the annulling of different versions and the projection of a single version as the authentic one. In this the media was of considerable assistance.

Because the medium of television is becoming the most powerful in the country, in places superseding even the entrenched oral tradition, its use of this theme has to be seen in context. The versions selected, with no attempt to suggest that there were other versions contradicting it, is a Hindu Vaishnava text, centring on the worship of Rama, familiar to north Indian Hindi speakers and broadly to the literate few elsewhere. The choice of this version therefore makes a specific social and political statement, becoming all the more significant given that television is part of the Government-controlled media. With such powerful backing the serial comes to be seen as the national culture of the mainstream. This eliminates the range of folk and popular versions or alternative versions even within the same religious tradition. There is a very deliberate choice of one tradition and the elevation of this tradition (remoulded in accordance with contemporary tastes and values) to national status. The differences, the debates, the discussions implicit in the interplay of variants are thus nullified. It is made impossible in the present context even to discuss on television, the specific variants in the Buddhist, the Jaina and the Shakta versions or in folk motifs, leave alone show them as serials. The richness of the themes in contradictory or alternate versions is suppressed and the story is underlined as a sacred story, which therefore cannot be questioned. This is a very different treatment from that given to the *Rama-katha* by Indian civilization. The manifestation of diversity and its accommodation was characteristic of Indian culture in the pre-colonial period and enriched every tradition. To accept and conform to a single version erodes cultural flexibility as well as the encouragement to innovate, so necessary to any cultural idiom.

Inevitably this is also part of the attempt to redefine Hinduism as an ideology for modernization by the middle class. Modernization is seen as linked to the growth of capitalism. In terms of its religious associations, capitalism is often believed to thrive among Semitic religions such as Christianity and Islam. The argument would then run that if capitalism is to succeed in India, then Hinduism would also have to be moulded to a Semitic form: although this desired change is often disguised in the theory that what is actually happening in the new resurgence of Hinduism is a return to Hindu traditions.

Characteristic of the Semitic religions are features such as a historically attested teacher or prophet, a sacred book, a geographically identifiable location for its beginnings, an ecclesiastical infrastructure and the conversion of large numbers of people to the religion—all characteristics which are largely irrelevant to the various manifestations of Hinduism until recent times. Thus instead of emphasizing the fact that the religious experience of Indian civilization and of religious sects which are bunched together under the label of 'Hindu' are distinctively different from that of the Semitic, attempts are being made to find parallels with the Semitic religions as if these parallels are necessary to the future of Hinduism.

The parallel can be seen for example in the recent resurgence of the worship of Rama, where the control of this religious articulation is politically motivated. The characteristics of the Semitic religions are introduced into this tradition. The teacher or prophet is replaced by the *avatara* of Vishnu, Rama; the sacred book is the *Ramayana*; the geographical identity or the beginnings of the cult and the historicity of Rama are being sought in the insistence that the precise birthplace of Rama in Ayodhya was marked by a temple, which was destroyed by Babur and replaced by the Babri Masjid; an ecclesiastical infrastructure is implied by inducting into the movement the support of Mahants and the Shankaracharyas or what the Vishwa Hindu Parishad calls a Dharma Sansad; the support of large numbers of people, far surpassing the figures of earlier followers of *Rama-bhakti*, was organized through the worship of bricks destined for the building of a temple on the location of the mosque. There has been an only too apparent exploitation of belief. The current Babri Masjid dispute is therefore symbolic of an articulation of a new form of Hinduism, militant, aggressive and crusading, which I have elsewhere referred to as Syndicated Hinduism.[51]

In earlier times a dispute over a location would not have arisen, since the historicity of the deity being worshipped was not a matter of significance. These are new strategies for mobilizing political power by exploiting belief. The dialogue between culture and power is directed towards political purposes although the front of a religious movement is sought to be projected. The worship of bricks is new to Hinduism and has been effectively demonstrated as a form of mobilization in the recent Shila puja. Syndicated Hinduism has little in common with either the openness of philosophical Hinduism or the catholicity of the rituals and beliefs of innumerable sects and cults all labelled as Hindu. These latter groups may eventually protest against a uniform religion imposed on them by those who are in power, but if such a religion becomes essential to upward mobility, then the protest will be muted.

Religious movements, by virtue of being social movements and therefore not limited to the salvation of the isolated individual, have at all times had a social base. Some have been movements of intolerance, excluding particular groups in society, whereas others have been movements of accommodation and have assimilated groups thought to be alien. Some have had a larger degree of religious concern, others have merely been a mask for social and political concerns. The movement which has grown around the demand for the replacement of the Babri Masjid by a temple to Rama has been of the latter kind. It has not only politicized the worship of Rama, but has equally unfortunately denied the validity of the variant versions of the story of Rama.

Notes

1. This essay is drawn in part from a paper entitled, 'Epic and History: Tradition, Dissent and Politics in India', published in *Past and Present*, November 1989, 125, Oxford, pp. 1–26.
2. L. Renou, *The Destiny of the Veda in India*, Motilal Banarsidass: Delhi, 1965; J.F. Staal, *Nambudri Vedic Recitation*, Mouton: The Hague, 1961.

3. See the discussion in A.D. Pusalkar, *Studies in the Epics and the Puranas,* Bharatiya Vidya Bhawan: Bombay, 1955.

4. B.B. Lal, 'Historicity of the *Mahabharata* and the *Ramayana*: What Has Archaeology to Say in the Matter?', Paper presented at the International Seminar on 'New Archaeology and India', Indian Council for Historical Research, New Delhi, 1988.

5. Attempts to do this have been made and point to various periods of composition and interpolation, as for example in H.D. Sankalia, *Ramayana: Myth or Reality,* Munshiram Manoharlal: New Delhi, 1982.

6. *Ramayana,* 1. 12 1–34; 13. 1–46, Critical Edition, Baroda.

7. H. Jacobi, *The Ramayana, (trans.),* MS University Press: Baroda, p. 59; for references also see J.L. Brockington, *Righteous Rama,* Oxford University Press: New Delhi, p. 218–9.

8. R.P. Goldman, *The Ramayana of Valmiki,* Volume I: Balakanda, Princeton University Press: New Jersey, 1984, p.43.

9. R.G. Bhandarkar, *Vaishnavism, Shaivism and Minor Sects,* Stassburg, 1913, p. 46 ff.

10. A recent discussion of these interpolated layers is to be found in J.L. Brockington, *Righteous Rama,* Delhi, 1984. An earlier and pioneering analysis of the text, is that of C. Bulcke, *Ramakatha,* Prayaga Vishvavidyalaya: Allahabad, 1950. See also A. Guruge, *The Society of the Ramayana,* Maharagama: Colombo, 1960, and especially p. 32ff.

11. N.J. Shende, 'The Authorship of the Ramayana', *Journal of the University of Bombay,* 1943, 12, pp. 19–24.

12. *Ramayana* 7. 9–34.

13. C. Lassen, *Indisches Alterthumskunde,* Leipzig 1847–62, I, p. 596 ff. The Aryan is represented by the orderly and advanced society of Ayodhya and the Dravidian by the uncouth wildness of the *rakshasas.* This dichotomy was a direct transplant from European ideological obsessions with 'the Aryan' and does not reflect indigenous identifications. This explanation had a politically explosive effect on Tamil nationalism during this century.

14. Kautilya, *Arthashastra,* 1.12. 9; 2.1.34; 2.27.7.

15. For a discussion on the background to this early society, see Romila Thapar, *From Lineage to State,* Oxford University Press: New Delhi, 1984.

16. Romila Thapar, *Exile and Kingdom: Some Thoughts on the Ramayana,* The Mythic Society: Bangalore, 1979; Romila Thapar, '*Ramayana*: theme and variation', in S.N. Mukherjee (ed.), *India: History and Thought,* Subarnarekha: Calcutta, 1982, pp.221–53.

17. *Ramayana,* 2.16.7ff.

18. ibid. 1 1.75; 2.13. 1-2; 5. 33. 11; 6. 115. 13.

19. ibid. 2.29.15; 32.6.

20. Devaraj Chanana, *The Spread of Agriculture in North India,* People's Publishing House: New Delhi, 1963, pp. 27–29.

21. Romila Thapar, 'Origin Myths and Early Indian Historical Tradition', *Ancient Indian Social History: Some Interpretations,* Orient Longman: New Delhi, 1978, pp. 307 ff.

22. V. Fausboll, *The Dasaratha Jataka, Being the Buddhist Story of King*

Rama, Copenhagen, 1981; *Dasaratha Jataka*, No. 461.

23. J. Przyluski, 'Epic Studies', *Indian Historical Quarterly*, Trivandrum, 1939, 15, pp. 289–99. C. Bulcke, *Rama-katha*, pp. 84–105. D.C. Sircar, 'The Ramayana and the Dasaratha Jataka', *Journal of the Oriental Institute*, Baroda, 1976, 26, pp. 50–5.

24. Romila Thapar, 'Origin Myths and the Early Indian Historical Tradition', *Ancient Indian Social History: Some Interpretations*, Orient Longman: New Delhi, 1978, pp. 294ff.

25. The text has been edited by H. Jacobi, *The Paumacariyam of Vimalasuri*, Prakrit Text Society, Varanasi, 1962, reprint. See also K.R. Chandra, *A Critical Study of Paumacariyam*, Research Institute of Prakrit Jainology and Ahimsa Vaishali, Bihar, Varanasi, 1970; V.M. Kulkarini, Prakrit Text Society, *Vimalasuri's Paumacariyam*, Kasi, 1962.

26. *Paumachariya*, 2.116; 4. 64ff.

27. ibid., 5.16ff.

28. V.M. Kulkarni, *The Story of Rama in Jaina Literature*, Saraswati Pustak Bandhar: Ahmedabad, 1989.

29. Virtually every regional language had many versions of the story and it is not possible to discuss them all in a short essay.

30. J.W.de Jong, *The Story of Rama in Tibet*, Franz Steiner: Stuttgart, 1989.

31. As in the Javanese version, *Serat Kanda*.

32. W. Stutterheim, *Rama-Legends and Rama-Reliefs in Indonesia*, Abhinav Publications: New Delhi, 1989, p. 23 ff.

33. ibid.

34. D.C. Sircar, 'The Guhila Claim of Solar Origin', *Journal of Indian History*, 1964, XLII, pp.381–7. Romila Thapar, 'Genealogy as a Source of Social History,' in Thapar, *Ancient Indian Social History*, pp. 326–60

35. Romila Thapar, 'Ramayana: Theme and Variation', op. cit.

36. N.N. Misra, 'Folk Elements in the Jagmohan Ramayana,' in A.K. Banerjee (ed.), *The Ramayana in Eastern India*, Calcutta, 1983, pp. 74ff.

37. N. Siddhantaratna, *Adhyatmaramayana*, Calcutta Sanskrit Series: Calcutta, 1935; F. Whaling, *The Rise of the Religious Significance of Rama*, Oxford University Press: Delhi, 1980. B.H. Kapadia, 'The Adhyatmaramayana', *Journal of the Oriental Institute (Baroda)*, 1964–5,14, pp. 164–70.

38. *Adhyatma-Ramayana*, 1.2.54–55

39. ibid. 2. 6. 65ff. This idea catches on in folk versions, as for example in Maharashtra, where in one version he is a thief of the Koli caste to begin with. G.D. Sontheimer, 'The Ramayana in Contemporary Folk Traditions of Maharashtra', in M. Thiel-Holstmann (ed.), *Contemporary Ramayana Traditions* (in press)

40. ibid. 3.7.1.ff.

41. ibid. 3.7.65.

42. ibid. 7.4.32ff.

43. ibid. 7.5.2ff.

44. Brockington, *Righteous Rama*, Oxford University Press: New Delhi, 1984, op. cit., p. 257ff.

45. W.L. Smith, *Ramayana Tradition in Eastern India,* University of Stockholm: Stockholm, 1988, p. 136ff.

46. A. Bakker, *Ayodhya,* Egbert Forsten: Groningen, 1984.

47. *Ramacharitamanas,* 7. 97–103.

48. *Mahabharata,* 3. 186-188; *Matsya Purana,* 273; *Vishnu Purana* 6.1; *Vayu Purana,* 58; *Brahmanda Purana,* 2.3.74.; B.N.S. Yadav, 'The Accounts of the Kali Age and the Social Transition from the Antiquity to the Middle Ages', *Indian Historical Review,* 1978–79, 5, 1 and 2, 31–63.

49. Kapil Kumar, 'The Ramacharitamanas as a radical text; Baba Ram Chandra in Oudh 1920–1950', in Sudhir Chandra (ed.), *Social Transformation and Creative Imagination,* Oxford University Press: New Delhi, 1984. See also M.H. Siddiqi, *Agrarian Unrest in Northern India,* Vikas: New Delhi, 1978.

50. D. Shulman, 'Battle as Metaphor in Tamil Folk and Classical Tradition,' in S.H. Blackburn and A.K. Ramanujam (eds.), *Another Harmony,* Oxford University Press: New Delhi, 1988, pp. 105–30.

51. Romila Thapar, 'Syndicated Moksha', *Seminar,* New Delhi, September 1985, 313, pp. 14–22. See also, 'Imagined Religious Communities? Ancient History and the Modern Search for a Hindu Identity', *Modern Asian Studies,* Cambridge, 1989, 2, 23, pp. 209–39.

Colonialism and Communalism[1]

Aditya Mukherjee

Communalism is above all an ideology. It is a particular way of looking at and mobilizing society which began to be promoted in India in the second half of the nineteenth century. The communal view assumed that Indian society was divided into homogeneous religious communities which shared common secular interests, i.e. economic, political, social and cultural interests, which were different from and antagonistic to the interests of those belonging to other religions. In other words, it was assumed that among the Indian people it was the religious identity which dominated (their entire social existence being organized around this identity), subsuming other identities such as class, linguistic, regional, cultural and national identities. Perpetuating yet another orientalist stereotype, it was made out that Indians were 'unique' in this regard, as other societies, particularly advanced Western societies, were not seen to be organized in this manner.

This was a view of Indian society which the British colonial rulers did much to create and propagate. Their success is evident from the fact that decades after independence many Indians, from academicians to ordinary citizens, still tend to analyse their own society, from the ancient past to the present, in religious, communal or casteist categories while using secular categories of class, nation, etc., to analyse Western societies. For years no one flinched at ancient, medieval and modern Indian history being periodized, *à la* James Mill[2] (a major influence on British thinking on India since the early nineteenth century), as the Hindu period, Muslim period and British period (note the switching of categories, it is not called the Christian period). This despite the existence of a substantial secular current which has been critical of this irrational switching of categories while dealing with similar phenomena in different societies. W.C. Smith (1946) was among the first to brilliantly highlight this aspect by repeatedly demonstrating how communal categories, which were readily used for describing aspects in Indian society, appeared absurd when used to describe the same aspect in the West.

As an aside it may be noted that 'communalism' is supposed to be so 'peculiar' to the Indian context that even the meaning of the word is not understood in the West except among those closely familiar with India. However, the easiest comparison with a phenomenon the West is familiar with is racism. All one needs to do is substitute colour of skin for religion. The ideological underpinnings of both the phenomena are very similar. Anti-Semitism is another comparable phenomenon.

Without entering into debate on the historical roots of racism and anti-Semitism in the West, it can be said with a considerable degree of confidence that Indian society was *not* split since 'time immemorial' into religious *communal* categories. Nor is it so divided today in areas where communal ideology has not yet penetrated. In traditional Indian society there were different religious groups, with different ritual practices, social customs and ritual taboos in relation to each other.[3] There was also evidence of religious fanaticism and oppression. However, communalism as it is understood today (where religion is used to mobilize all sections and classes of a religious community basically for achieving political and economic goals), is a *modern phenomenon,* which took root half way through the British colonial presence in India—in the second half of the nineteenth century. Communal ideology and politics emerged simultaneously with, and in distorted response to, the emergence of *modern politics* based on generating public opinion, popular participation and mass mobilization.

The parallel with the rise of modern nationalism is instructive. Though different religions and religious differences have existed for centuries, communalism was a modern phenomenon, a product of modern historical developments, in the same way as (despite the existence of empires and large regional political entities since ancient times) nationalism as a modern ideology emerged all over the world only in the modern period with the development of a specific historical conjuncture. It would be as absurd and anachronistic to call a medieval religious bigot like Aurangzeb 'communal' as it would be to call an ancient empire-builder like Chandra Gupta a 'nationalist'.

In this essay, I will address myself to the question of how communal ideology, which made its appearance in the late nineteenth century, became a mass force over the following decades, and will discuss the role of colonialism and the policies of the colonial government that helped in propagating communalism in India and encouraging it to take deep roots in Indian society.

By the second half of the nineteenth century, certain objective conditions emerged which created fertile ground for communal and communal-type ideologies or movements to take root. Many of these conditions related particularly to the potential of a Hindu–Muslim divide and partially explain why it was this division, among so many others that were tried (based on caste, region, language, class, etc.), which caught on and grew so rapidly. Very briefly these conditions are discussed here.

First, due to a large number of factors, which were not designed to produce this result, there was an uneven development among the Hindu and Muslim middle and upper classes. The fact that colonial rule came first to coastal areas like Bengal where the Muslims belonged largely to the poorer classes, meant that they, unlike the well-to-do Hindus, were unable to take advantage of 'modern' colonial education and thereby enter government service (the main employment opportunity outside agriculture in that period) or other middle-class occupations which required such education. British rule came only later to areas like the North-Western Provinces (present UP) where a substantial section of the upper classes were Muslims. By the time 'modern' education spread among the Muslims, in the late nineteenth century, the limited opportunities in administration, business and the professions had shrunk even further, creating the potential for dissatisfaction among the 'late-comers'.

There were some other factors which contributed to the share of the Muslims in Indian middle class development being relatively weak. The social and religious reform movements, the so-called 'Renaissance' that India witnessed in the nineteenth century, which exposed the Indian people to rationalism, western ideas and thought, etc., remained largely confined to the Hindus. The Muslim masses continued for long (even after the advent of Syed Ahmad Khan in the 1860s) to be led by conservative and reactionary upper classes which were hostile to modern education and other aspects of social change. The main impact of the forward-looking, reformist, modern intelligentsia was among the Hindus.

To add to all this, the mistaken British understanding of the imperialist government that it was the Muslims who were particularly seditious, and that they were chiefly responsible for the Revolt of 1857, made them adopt a policy of suppressing the Muslims. For nearly two decades after the Revolt, the Muslims were subjected to political and administrative discrimination. Consequently, the percentage of Muslims employed in the administration fell steeply in many areas. The increasing shift from Persian to English in conducting official business gave the English-educated Hindus a clear advantage over the Muslims, further accentuating the imbalance.

Second, while the above factors created a situation tailor-made for promoting a communal divide, particularly among the middle-class Muslims and Hindus, there were certain other developments which engendered divisions of this kind in general. For example, by the second half of the nineteenth century, the colonial structuring of the Indian economy, the thwarting of the potential of rapid economic development and the structuring of backwardness, produced conditions of economic stagnation if not decline. Scarcity, unemployment and even famines became rampant. This created a situation conducive to aggressive competitiveness among groups formed around narrow identities, where one group's gain was seen as the other's loss. As W.C. Smith put it, 'A circumscribed capitalism produces the conditions under which communalism, or some parallel form of group discord, flourishes.'[4]

In effect, colonial intervention dislodged the traditional order in Indian society without bringing in its place an adequate modern structure. The traditional identities, the moral order as well as the economic support system provided by the village communities and other traditional institutions began to give way under the colonial impact. Hurled into a new situation of social and economic insecurity and finding the traditional identities and moral order inadequate to deal with it, the Indian people were faced with a situation where they had to look for and evolve new identities (and ideologies based on those identities) which could encompass, explain and enable them to handle the new, modern, colonial reality. Communal ideologies now competed with the emergent modern secular ideologies to provide precisely such a framework.

However, while the various objective conditions discussed above certainly provided the *basis* for the growth of communal-type ideologies it cannot be argued deterministically that these conditions would inevitably have led to their acceptance and spread on Indian soil. This was particularly so because around the time that the divisive communal ideology began to make its first forays into Indian society, there had already emerged a powerful alternate current under the aegis of the Indian national movement which attempted to weld India into a nation, and to give a fillip to the process of the Indian 'nation in the making'. This was a current which attempted to explain the same 'objective conditions' not on the basis of the competing indigenous groups, sections, religious communities, etc., but on the basis of an anti-colonial ideological discourse. It tried to meet the identity crisis of a society in transition from the pre-capitalist, medieval system to the 'modern' colonial one, not by rallying people around narrow caste or religious identities but by attempting to forge broad secular identities like that of the nation—followed later by other secular identities such as class, region, language, culture, etc., all promoted as complementary and not antithetical to the national identity.

The fact that despite the best efforts of the varied secular currents in the Indian national movement, the emergence and spread of the communal virus could not be contained, has a lot to do with the critical role played by the colonial government.

The role of government can be critical in spreading communalism or communal-type movements in several ways; it can use state power to rapidly communalize the state apparatuses—from the bureaucracy, the police and the judiciary to the education system and the media. With government backing and the state apparatuses communalized, the promoters of communal politics find it infinitely easier to spread communal consciousness in civil society.

There is another little-noticed aspect. The study of mass movements in history in various parts of the world shows that it is extremely difficult to make the masses accept a programme or demand and be willing to launch a movement on that basis unless in their consciousness it was a morally legitimate demand. This legitimacy could be derived from a traditional notion of justice passed down the generations. In a situation where no such clear sanction from the past was available, 'legality' or acceptance by the state apparatuses of the fairness or correctness of such a demand, went a long way towards lending it legitimacy.[5]

How was communalism, a new ideology, to find acceptance among the masses and get them to move on that basis to the extent that they would be willing to riot and loot, and in total contravention of the traditional moral code, commit crimes like rape, murder and mutilation of their fellow citizens, neighbours, business associates, co-workers, etc.? It was difficult to find legitimacy for such a course from the past, from within the historical memory or the existing sense of history of the people. Hence the need felt by communalists to distort history and, through continuous and repeated propaganda, attempt to introduce a false notion among the people of their own history. This was however a slow and prolonged process that would yield results only *after* the communal view had already spread sufficiently. In this situation, the legality, the legitimacy and, to use Francis Robinson's term, the 'prestige', lent to communal ideology and politics by the government and various other state apparatuses, played a critical role in their acceptance and spread among the mass of people. Interestingly, even in the communal falsification of history (which, in turn, created a communal historical memory) the role played by the British government and the government-controlled education system, media, etc., was very important, even as early as the beginning of the nineteenth century.

The potential of the colonial regime to push the forces of communalism was great, a potential fully utilized by it. It did so for several reasons.

Most obviously the colonial government promoted communalism to weaken the rising anti-imperialist movement in India *inter alia,* by pitting loyalist communal forces as political adversaries of the nationalist mainstream. It is not an accident that communal and communal-type political forces in India have historically by and large ended up playing a socially reactionary and politically loyalist role. This was because on the one hand they hampered any mobilization based on secular categories like class, or nation, which cut across religious categories, and on the other hand they focussed their attack on the 'other' i.e., the other communities and not imperialism.

It bears emphasis (as the contrary view is often projected) that it was not only the minority communalists represented by the Muslim League, a section of the Akalis, etc., but also the majority communalists, the Hindu Mahasabha and the Rashtriya Swayamsevak Sangh (RSS), who performed this essentially loyalist role. Both the rival communalist forces concentrated their attack on the Congress, the leading anti-imperialist organization, as the secular assumptions of this organization threatened to erode the very basis of the communal formations. The members of the opposite community came a close second on the hate list. At the peak of the nationalist agitation in 1942 it was not only the Muslim League which stayed well away from the movement but the Hindu Mahasabha and the RSS also advised their cadres to keep aloof and 'conserve' their energies for the struggle against the real enemies and not fritter it away in anti-imperialist agitations.

Second, the spread of communalism enabled colonialism to expand its social base to classes and sections of Indian society which had nothing to gain and everything to lose from colonialism. To begin with, the social base of colonialism and communalism had been the same, consisting of the landed gentry, the princes, the higher bureaucracy, etc., sections which also benefited economically and otherwise from colonialism. However, with the spread of communalism among large sections of the lower middle class and even sections of the working class and the peasantry, these chief victims of colonial exploitation were rendered objectively at 'the command of colonialism'.[6] This was a major gain for colonialism. It would not have been possible to secure the support of these classes through concessions which would effectively end their exploitative relationship with colonialism, as that would threaten the very *raison d'être* of colonialism.

Third, for a regime that was based not on coercion alone but also had certain ideological or hegemonic foundations, a degree of moral legitimacy both among the rulers and the ruled was necessary. It was the spread of communalism that increasingly provided the most important legitimation for the continuance of colonial rule.

The traditional arguments in favour of colonialism, 'the civilizing mission' or the 'white man's burden', were wearing thin. The modern Indian intelligentsia, which in the early nineteenth century saw in British rule a 'gift of divine providence' which would pull India out of the backwardness of centuries and expose it to modern civilization, were by the second half of the nineteenth century totally disillusioned. Now they saw colonialism as the chief obstacle to modernization. In Britain itself radical trends began to emerge which began to question the legitimacy of imperialism.

In this context the argument of the necessity of maintaining the colonial presence in 'defence of the minorities' proved very useful. The arguments that Britain was staying on to prevent a communal civil war in which the weak minorities would be suppressed and that they were unable to leave because the warring groups could not come to a mutual agreement, were used to legitimize British presence in India till the very end. Britain used similar arguments (in Africa it was to prevent tribe from killing tribe) to deny autonomy to the peoples of various other countries both before and after Indian independence.

It must be clarified that the colonial government, though it claimed the contrary, was never actually interested in a principled defence of the minorities. It promoted only *communal* minority groupings and that too when they served the purpose of weakening the forces of anti-imperialism and did not in any way adversely affect other imperial interests.

For example, the so-called consistent pro-Muslim stance of the British was a myth. As stated above, after the Revolt of 1857 till well into the 1870s, the Government was positively hostile to the Muslims. It was in an effort to win Muslim support for the regime and following the emergence of a loyalist communal stand among the Muslims that the Government reversed its policy. It now began to profess special support to the Muslims while basically patronizing the Muslim communal strand. However, the smallest sign of political opposition evoked threats of withdrawal of patronage—as happened in UP at the turn of the century when sections from within the Government-patronized Aligarh college began to adopt anti-government postures on the language (Hindi vs. Urdu) issue. There were other instances as well when anti-government agitation, even when led by essentially loyalist communal forces (Muslim or Sikh or Hindu), were firmly put down.

Further, the Government, after promoting, and using to the hilt, Muslim communalism for well over half a century, ditched them in the end. Until 1945, i.e., till 'the British had worked on the assumption that the empire must survive', Muslim communalism and its ultimate demand for a separate state were 'a useful counterpoise to the Congress demand for independence'. However, once, in 1946, the decision to leave was clear, the British 'preferred to transfer power to a united India', since that was perceived to better serve British economic and military strategic interests in the post-war world.[7] Unable to actually prevent Partition, since Muslim communalism had by now acquired the character of the proverbial Frankenstein's monster that no longer responded to the dictates of its creator, the British nevertheless showed their unconcern for Muslim communalists by leaving behind 'a moth-eaten Pakistan'.[8]

The cynical use of the minorities and the absence of any genuine interest in them was starkly evident in the manner in which a large number of British civil and military officials, on the eve of their departure, adopted, at best, a laid-back attitude while one of the worst civil wars in modern times was let loose in front of them in the form of the Partition riots. Again, the British made no attempt to insist on safeguards for the minorities in the newly-independent states which were to come up when the empire wound up its interests in this region. It became clear that communalism was promoted because it facilitated the maintenance of the colonial regime, and not because of any inherent affinity to any community.

Communalism was promoted by the colonial government in multifarious ways. To begin with, the very viewing of Indian society communally, the calculation by the Government of a proportion of jobs in the civil and military services, seats in educational institutions, membership in the legislature, even membership of political parties, etc., in terms purely of religious (or caste) origins, itself promoted communalism (or casteism). Colonial writing, both by administrators and historians, enquiries conducted by the Government, statistical surveys, etc., consistently used religious and caste categories to measure the distribution of people in jobs and in general political and economic activity, even when religion or caste clearly had nothing to do with it, and refused to take into account or adopt more meaningful criteria in this context, such as income, ownership of land or other means of production, possession of education or 'intellectual capital', class position, regional cultural traditions, social status, influence of competing ideologies, political beliefs, etc.

The government's attitude and practice encouraged the people to view themselves in these categories, to compete with each other, and try to secure official support for the reservation of a larger share of the national cake for members of their respective religious or caste groups as against members belonging to other groups, rather than turn their attention to the question of the role of the existing system and the colonial government in keeping the size of the total cake stagnant, if not shrinking. This was a situation of obvious advantage to the Government. While sections or groups would come to the Government with demands for reservations, and the like, the Government, by offering or withdrawing concessions on this basis, could arouse communal feelings and split Indian society down the middle. In much the same way today attempts at casteist reservations are arousing casteist passions, and caste wars are breaking out even in areas where caste consciousness had greatly eroded.

The colonial regime also promoted and encouraged the notion that the introduction of the democratic principle and elections on that basis, a long-standing demand of Indian nationalists, would be injurious to minority interests as it would lead to domination by the majority, the Hindus. Instead, the pernicious principle of separate electorates was pushed. Embedded in the idea of separate electorates was the notion that members of one religious community could not represent even the political, economic, and other secular interests of other religious communities, and hence the notion of separate nations. As W.C. Smith pointed out, the institution of separate electorates was the *principal technique* in the hands of the government of spreading communalism by splitting the people into separate constituencies so that they voted communally, thought communally, listened only to communal election speeches, judged the delegates communally, looked for constitutional and other reforms only in terms of more relative communal power and expressed their grievances communally. It is not fortuitous that independent India, while reserving seats in legislatures for certain categories like the Harijans or untouchables, refused to have separate electorates, i.e., voters were not limited to any one category. This meant the candidate had to appeal to members of other castes and religions in order to be elected.

The cynically discriminating manner in which the Government used the State apparatus to promote communalism while coming down heavily on nationalism had a lot to do with the rapid growth of the former. Flagrantly using double standards, the Government ruthlessly suppressed nationalist propaganda while refusing to take action, in the name of civil liberties, against the most virulent communal propaganda. The police and the legal and administrative machinery were quick to nip nationalist agitation in the bud while communal agitation, including communal riots were allowed to fester by a suddenly lax and inactive administration. Concern for civil liberties was again pleaded by the officials to deny the demand of Hindu and Muslim legislators for legislation to curb activity that could lead to communal riots. There is evidence that sometimes the administration even connived at instigating communal riots. Teachers, students, writers, and even government servants were allowed to propagate communal ideas and participate in communal politics often receiving honours and titles for such labours; but if they showed any affinity to nationalism or nationalist activity, firm action was taken. 'The nationalist (historian) K.P. Jayswal. . . was made to resign his post in the Calcutta University. . . Prem Chand was first compelled to destroy a collection of his short stories and later dismissed from the Education Department'.[9] Bankim Chandra Chatterjee, who was also a Deputy Collector, was persuaded under threat to alter, in later editions of his novels, the nationalist anti-British edge into a communal anti-Muslim one.[10]

Yet another major way in which the colonial authorities promoted communalism was by giving recognition to and dealing with communal elements (often exclusively so) as *the* representatives of the religious community to which they belonged. They did this even when these elements could possibly not make such a claim. For example, as noted by Francis Robinson, Sir Syed Ahmed Khan, after he entered his actively loyalist phase (in the latter part of the 1880s), was 'raised up as an advocate of his community', despite the fact that he had 'little in common with either the great Muslim peasant populations of Bengal and the Punjab or with the Muslim artisan masses of the UP towns'. Nor did it matter that 'the majority of his co-religionists branded him infidel'. 'His views were accepted by Government as Muslim views, and *because they were accepted, they found currency among other Muslims* who might otherwise have thought differently. By building up the (Aligarh) College and Syed Ahmed, Government assisted at the birth of a Muslim political party and a Muslim political doctrine.'[11] (*italics mine.*) Interestingly, roughly around the same time, in the 1880s, the claim of the Indian National Congress of representing the Indian people was summarily dismissed with the remark that it represented only a 'microscopic minority' of upper-caste Hindus.

The same pattern was repeated in the twentieth century. Now the Muslim League was promoted by the Government as the voice of the Muslims. This when, as late as 1937, the Muslim League got only 4.4 per cent of the Muslim votes in the provincial elections, in spite of communal electorates and the franchise being restricted to eleven per cent of the population consisting largely of the upper and middle classes, among whom the League had a greater following. The League, thus, did not have the allegiance of more than a small proportion of the Muslim population till the 1940s when the situation underwent a radical change. The Congress could easily claim far greater support among them. Despite this, the Government branded a secular mass party like the Congress as merely a Hindu organization. The narrow-minded, communal Muslim League was projected as the real and sole representative of the Muslims and was on that basis treated on par with the Congress! In the 1940s the Muslim League was given a virtual veto on all Constitutional proposals, effectively thwarting Congress moves. This attitude of the Government naturally enhanced the prestige of the League among the Muslims, and demoralized the nationalist forces among them.

The manner in which the British Government promoted communalism had clearly undergone a substantial change. From the 1870s till about the end of the nineteenth century, the effort, mainly through support to the Aligarh movement, was to 'woo the Muslims back to the fold of the colonial regime' by offering them special concessions and to 'discourage popular political agitation among Mahomedans',[12] and thus keep them away from the Congress. At the turn of the century, when especially the younger elements among the Muslims were getting restive and the national movement had entered a more militant phase, the policy was changed from that of trying to keep Muslims out of all politics to promoting loyalist, constitutional, communal politics of the Muslim League to neutralize the anti-imperialist agitational politics of the Congress.

Though communal politics was now promoted actively, the Muslim League was not yet given all out support. The overall policy remained one of what Bipan Chandra has described as 'controlled communalism'. An anti-British Hindu backlash could result from too great an identification with the League. Pushing Hindu communalists too far, on the other hand, had the danger of welding the Hindus, splintered into castes and sects, into one community, and also the threat of majority communalism turning anti-government could not be countenanced. Further, too much communal disturbance could cause an administrative law and order problem; though, if the choice was between the politically dangerous unity of the Indian people and the administratively troublesome 'divergence of ideas and collision', then British officialdom was quite clear that 'of the two the latter (was) the least risky'.[13]

It was with the commencement of the Second World War that the British threw caution to the winds and gave all out support to the Muslim League. The fact that the national movement had to be checkmated at any cost in the critical war situation, and that the Hindus had in any case been largely lost to the nationalist camp, may have contributed to this stance. This all out government support to the Muslim League, the fact that the political arena was now open to the League without challenge, with the Congress banned and a large number of Congressmen including most of the leaders in jail, and, very importantly, that the League now acquired limited access to State power with the Government helping to dislodge non-League Ministries and install League-dominated Ministries in all the provinces of prospective Pakistan except Punjab, combined with the deliberate cry of 'Islam in danger' raised by the League, helped the League to grow rapidly and acquire a firm mass base for the first time.

With the rapid growth and 'massization' of Muslim communalism, and it reaching an aggressive, separatist phase, Hindu communalism, which had remained a relatively weak force, also began to acquire strength. The stage was set for the dreadful holocaust of the Partition days—an event which communalized Indian society as never before. The wounds in some regions were so deep that they are yet to heal. This was the legacy for which the Indian people continue to pay a heavy price.

Though the role of colonialism and particularly the colonial government was critical in the growth of communalism, the end of colonial rule did not lead to the fading away of communalism as was hoped by many nationalist leaders. (A hope which might have contributed to no major sustained struggle being mounted against communalism after independence.)

The approach towards communalism of the post-colonial regimes in India (Pakistan followed a different path) was vastly different from that of colonial regimes. Communalism was not the chief prop of these regimes for staying in power. While communal parties, in various incarnations of the Hindu Mahasabha, Muslim League, Akali Dal etc., survived the colonial era, their distance from political power, except for a brief interregnum between 1977–79, and again since end-1989, has been a saving grace.

However, even the secular forces after independence made certain compromises with communalism though for reasons different from the colonial regime. In a society already communalized to a considerable extent, the logic of electoral politics led even secular parties of all hues, including those of the Left, to resort, in varying degrees, to short cuts to popular mobilization, by appealing to or allying with parties that appealed to the existing communal consciousness rather than attempting the relatively difficult and long-term task of altering it.

The ruling regimes, like the Congress, which has ruled for most of the post-independence period, have tended to meet the challenge of communalism inadequately. Often the problem was approached in economistic terms—a tendency, which so committed an anti-communalist as Jawaharlal Nehru, shared, with the rest of the Left. It was hoped that economic development or growth of economistic class struggles would by itself lead to the erosion of communalism (a hope which has been repeatedly belied) and hence a sustained ideological battle against what is above all an ideology was neglected.

Also, the technique of trying to meet the communal challenge by accommodating or absorbing a section of the communalists within the ranks of the secular parties (witness, for example, the repeated merger of Akali factions into the Congress) or by trying to give concessions to and *dealing* with moderate communalists in an effort to first neutralize the extremists and then marginalize the moderates, have failed miserably. The result has been, in the first case, the dilution of the secularism of the secular parties and in the second, the lending of legitimacy to communal politics and the constant upping of the demands of the so-called moderate communalists.

The secular forces outside the Congress, including the Left, which have largely remained out of power have fared no better. In their desperation to dislodge the Congress and come to power they have tended to line up opportunistically with avowedly communal forces. In the process they have let loose dangerous political forces.

The communal forces on whose backs these secular parties tried to achieve petty political gains have now grown menacingly. The 'untouchables' in Indian politics for many years after independence, they now occupy centrestage in the political arena. They have demanded their share of state power—and to the extent they achieved it they have and are using it effectively to communalize the State apparatuses and civil society in a manner reminiscent of the colonial State. After all, for these forces, their very survival, like that of the colonial State, depends on the growth and maintenance of communalism.

Today, more than forty years after independence, after having successfully overcome many of the legacies of colonialism, India's failure to deal with what was one of the chief props of colonialism looms large. Communalism and communal-type movements like casteism have emerged as the main threat to the Indian nation and the unity of the Indian people. Forces which split the country in two in 1947 threaten to fragment it into many more pieces. The irony is that this is happening not under the aegis of an alien colonial regime but under the direct patronage or indirect acquiescence of indigenous political forces whose primary aim is supposed to be nation-building.

Notes

1.   The works listed below are among those which have made a basic contribution to this subject. I have drawn on them heavily particularly the first two. The references in the text to these works are however generally restricted to occasions where direct quotations have been used. W.C. Smith, *Modern Islam in India*, Victor Gollancz, London, 1946; Bipan Chandra, *Communalism in Modern India*, Vikas Publishing House, New Delhi, 1987 (2nd edition); S. Gopal, *British Policy in India*, 1858–1905, Cambridge University Press, Cambridge, 1965; K.B. Krishna, *The Problem of Minorities*, George Allen and Unwin, London, 1939; Francis Robinson, *Separatism Among Indian Muslims: The Politics of the United Provinces' Muslims, 1860–1923*, Vikas Publishing House, Delhi, 1975; Romila Thapar, Harbans Mukhia and Bipan Chandra, *Communalism and the Writing of Indian History*, People's Publishing House: New Delhi, 1977, 2nd edition; Anita Inder Singh, *The Origins of the Partition of India, 1936–1947*, Oxford University Press: New Delhi, 1987.

2.   The reference here is to James Mill, *History of British India*, London, 1826, reprinted by Associated Publishing House, New Delhi, 1982. Also see Romila Thapar, et. al., *Communalism and the Writing of Indian History*, pp. 4ff.

3. However, that did not necessarily lead to a communal divide. Indian history and Indian society today is replete with examples of how despite ritual differences among Hindus, Muslims, Christians, etc., no communal developments occurred for centuries—until they were deliberately promoted.

4. W.C. Smith, *Modern Islam in India*, p.177.

5. See, e.g., Rodney Hilton, "Peasant Society, Peasant Movements and Feudalism in Medieval Europe" in H. Landsberger (ed.), *Rural Protest: Peasant Movement and Social Change*, Macmillan, London, 1973; E.P. Thompson, *The Making of the English Working Class*, Penguin Books, Harmondsworth, 1968; James C. Scott, *The Moral Economy of the Peasant: Rebellion and Subsistence in South East Asia*, Yale University Press, New Haven and London, 1976, and Mridula Mukherjee, "Peasant Resistance and Peasant Consciousness in Colonial India: 'Subalterns' and Beyond", *Economic and Political Weekly*, Bombay, 8 and 15 Oct. 1988.

6. Bipan Chandra, *Communalism in Modern India*, p.289 and Ch.4.

7. Anita Inder Singh, *The Origins of the Partition of India*, pp.244–55.

8. A phrase used by Jinnah to describe a truncated Pakistan which would be on the two extremities of a hostile India. See Bipan Chandra, *Communalism in Modern India*, p.260.

9. ibid., pp.282–83.

10. Ibid.

11. Francis Robinson, *Separatism Among Indian Muslims*, p. 131, and S. Gopal, op. cit., pp. 158ff.

12. This was the objective of the Mahomedan Anglo-Oriental Defence Association of Upper India, an association founded in 1893. The 'chief organiser' behind it was Theodore Beck, the principal of Aligarh College. See Robinson, op. cit., pp. 121–22.

13. S. Gopal, op. cit., p. 201.

Hindu–Muslim Relations Before and After 1947

Asghar Ali Engineer

Modern industrial societies are becoming increasingly multi-religious in structure thanks to the rapid means of transport and internationalization of commerce and industry. There was a time when European society was mono-religious. But from the beginning of the twentieth century it tended to become multi-religious due to the migration of people from colonial to the metropolitan countries in search of better prospects. After the Second World War, this trend grew very fast with rapid industrialization. Today hardly any European society can boast of being uni-religious. With the emergence of multi-religious societies, racial and communal tensions are growing in these countries.

However, in India, society was multi-religious from the earliest period in history with different waves of migration from outside, beginning perhaps with the first wave of Aryan migrants entering into India. Many others came subsequently, the latest being the Muslims who came into the south as traders and into the north as conquerors from the seventh century AD onwards. There were far-reaching consequences, both positive as well as negative, of the coming of Muslims into India. Complex processes started with the coming of Islam into India at different levels. At one level there was rejection of Islam while at another not only accommodation but synthesis resulted. The Brahmins, by and large, refused to be drawn into the process of synthesis, whereas the lower castes, mostly untouchables, either embraced Islam or accommodated to it to lesser or greater degrees.

The sectarian writings on both sides often stress that Hinduism and Islam are incompatible. Those belonging to the privileged upper castes maintained that Islam is a closed religion and could not be integrated with Hinduism, though all other religions which entered into India could become integral parts of Hinduism. Islam, a sectarian, doctrinaire religion, refused to be assimilated. Though this view has some element of truth, it is, nevertheless, an oversimplification. The Muslim theologians, often part of the ruling establishment, also adopted a rigid stance towards Hinduism and dubbed Hindus as *kafirs* (non-believers) with whom there could be no accommodation at the religious level.

More sociological insights are needed to understand the relations between Islam and Hinduism in India during the medieval ages. As pointed out above, it was not always a confrontation between the two. One cannot understand this relationship merely on a theological and doctrinaire level. One has to take caste and class interests into account. The upper-caste Hindus dominated the cultural and religious scene in India; in fact they had a monopoly over it. Cultural hegemony often ensures political hegemony or results from it. In other words they are always interacting. The upper castes were, therefore, rather reluctant to accept the legitimacy of Islam and Islamic culture by accommodating it into the Brahmanic fold. The Muslims, therefore, remained *yavanas* (foreigners, those with whom one should not mix) and had to be kept at a distance. The Muslim ruling classes, on the other hand, had their own reasons: they had to maintain 'religious' distance from the Hindus to keep up their own political and cultural hegemony. The theologians, more often than not of West Asian or Central Asian extract, were part of the ruling establishment, and hence treated Hindus as *kafirs*.

However, it does not mean that there was no accommodation on social and political levels between the upper-caste Hindus and the upper-class Muslims. There was. Political exigencies have their own logic. The Hindus had to collaborate with Muslims and Muslims with Hindus. Many Brahmins and Rajputs held high administrative posts during Muslim rule. The two ruling classes which collaborated with each other also evolved a composite culture of sorts. It can thus be seen that the social and political processes were extremely complex, even contradictory. There were uncompromising stances as well as opportunistic compromises with creative synthesis, too, thrown in. Only a historian with a proper historical perspective and a firm grasp of the socio-political realities can comprehend the complex nature of this mutual protagonist–antagonist relationship between Islam and Hinduism in the medieval ages.

So far we have been discussing the relationship between upper-caste Hindus and upper-class Muslims. But the bulk of Hindus and Muslims were from the lower castes and classes. Their relationship was of an assimilative nature. Most of the conversions to Islam occurred at the lower levels of the social strata. At these levels not only was there no confrontation between Hindus and Muslims but, on the contrary, the lower-caste Hindus found in Islam a liberating force and embraced it. One can debate whether or not their social status improved by embracing Islam but there is no doubt that they could freely enter mosques and pray standing in the same line with the upper-class Muslims. For the untouchables it was no mean achievement. It gave them a sense of pride. Deprived of Sanskritization, they welcomed Islamization. The masses of untouchables who embraced Islam did not take a scriptural view of religion, rather they took a folk view of it.

Thus Islam was Indianized. The Sufis who became models of Islamic virtues, adopted not only the local idiom but also local customs and rituals. The *urs* (death anniversary) rituals had many similarities with the temple rituals, for example, taking out a sandal procession to wash the grave of a Sufi saint or the idol of the temple, with sandal paste.[1] These temple rituals were extremely popular among the Hindus at all levels and adopting these rituals, in the teeth of opposition from the Muslim theologians, created a popular base for Islam in Indian society. There may have been confrontations between Islam and Hinduism as far as the scriptural view of religion was concerned but there was no confrontation (but assimilation) as far as the folk view of Islam and Hinduism was concerned.

Thus we see that there were two models of Islam before the Indian people: the theological model and the Sufi model. The theological model of Islam tended to be, for the reasons enumerated above, confrontationist; whereas the Sufi model of Islam was assimilationist. While upper-class Muslims tended to adopt the theological model both for religious and political reasons, the low-class and low-caste Muslims adopted the Sufi model as it was close to their folk traditions and it provided them escape from the harsh realities of life. One cannot understand Indian Islam without understanding the Sufi model which was assimilationist and avoided confrontation. However, what is most tragic is that upper-caste Hindu historians often take a purely scriptural view of Indian Islam and concentrate their whole attention on the Muslim ruling classes and often draw the wrong conclusions.

The south presents another scene altogether. There Islam did not come through political conquests as in the north but through Arab traders. There were trade relations between Kerala and the Arab world even in pre-Islamic days. When the Arabian peninsula was Islamized, these Arab traders adopted Islam and brought it to Kerala along with them. Thus, in the south, Islam spread in the most peaceful manner. It was assimilationist like the Sufi model of Islam. In fact the south was not devoid of the Sufistic model. So in Kerala, and likewise in Tamil Nadu, Islam was highly assimilationist and hence non-confrontationist.

It was somewhat different in what is known as Andhra Pradesh today. There Islam developed somewhat confrontationist postures as it became the religion of the ruling class led by the Nizam dynasty. The Nizam's rule did not adopt the local language and culture. It was a part of the Muslim rule of the north and it preserved Persian and later Urdu as the language of the administration, whereas the local language was Telugu. The ruling class culture was north Indian composite culture in orientation. Thus we see that the south Indian scene was not uniform.

There is one more fundamental question to be considered before we proceed further on the subject of the Hindu–Muslim relationship. Is the nature of confrontation theological or political? Can there be a purely theological confrontation, or confrontation on grounds of religion, as is often made out? It is very difficult to find evidence for confrontation purely on religious grounds. While the instrumentality of religion in political matters cannot be denied, it is difficult to find historical evidence for wars between Hindu and Muslim rulers solely on religious grounds. The priests or theologians may denounce followers of other religions as *maleccha* (unholy) or *yavana* and *kafirs* respectively, but they confine their war to words, not to swords.

We also have to remember that a society is not constituted purely by religion. There are other equally important constituents of society, economic and political in nature, which motivate human behaviour. For that matter human behaviour, be it towards one's fellow religionists or followers of other religions, has very complex motives; its determinant is usually not one single factor. It has several determinants and more so if one happens to be a politician and a ruler. Neither Hinduism, nor Islam can be the sole determinant of a ruler's behaviour. It would be a gross simplification of history if one sees religion as only the motivating force of a ruler. Also, one should distinguish between consciousness and behaviour. Consciousness may be determined by ideological factors alone but not so human behaviour. Behaviour is much more complex and interest-oriented whereas consciousness is often ideologically-oriented. The communal problem cannot be judged purely from the ideological viewpoint; one has to take into account its interest-orientation too, as well as other aspects.

It is in the light of the above discussion that we must try to understand the communal problem and relations between Hindus and Muslims. It is important to note that communalism is a modern phenomenon and is a product of colonial society. Its seeds were sown after the failure of the Revolt of 1857. At that time Hindus and Muslims made common cause to throw the British out and united under Bahadurshah Zafar, the last Mughal ruler. The revolt was crushed and the feudal structure of society was replaced by the colonial system. It is this shift in social structure that brought about the genesis of communalism. Communalism is not a feudal phenomenon but as far as India is concerned, it is a product of colonial society.

However, it does not mean that complete responsibility of the genesis of communalism goes to the 'divide and rule' policy of the British. All rulers, including democratic ones, follow such a policy, and the contemporary democratic rulers of India have been no exception to this. We must try to understand the genesis of communalism in a deeper sense. It is as much a structural as a political problem. In the political sense it was the divide and rule policy of the British which generated it, and in the structural sense it was generated not only by the limited capacity of the colonial economy to grow but also by keen competition for jobs and political positions and sinecures between the two major communities of India, i.e. Hindus and Muslims.

A feudal structure of society does not generate much competition between different communities either in the sphere of economy or in that of polity. Nor is there any competition for public offices in that society. Public appointments are based on rewards for loyalty to the ruling dynasty, rather than on competition. Also, there is no political competition in a feudal society as the ruler more often comes to power by force than by contested elections. The colonial society established by the British in India ushered in restricted democratic competition as well as competition for jobs. In an ideal situation the competition would be between individuals but in a backward society like India there was little competition on merit between individuals and instead competition took place more on the basis of community thus giving rise to communal tensions.

The first important event which generated communal tensions in Indian society was when the language of administration was changed from Persian to Urdu at lower level courts. Some Hindus of Benares agitated for replacing Urdu with Hindi written in the Devanagari. The implications were obvious. If Urdu was replaced by Hindi written in the Devanagari, many Muslims would lose their court jobs and Hindus would qualify more for them. Sir Syed resented this as he considered Urdu 'a memento of the Muslim rule in this country'.[2] Replying to a British official called Shakespeare, who was his friend, Sir Syed wrote, 'Now I am convinced that both these communities will not join whole-heartedly in anything. . . . On account of the so-called "educated" people, hostility between the two communities will increase immensely in the future. He who lives will see.'

In a way Sir Syed's words proved to be prophetic. He blames educated people for developing communal hostility. The modern theorists of communalism, including this author, consider communalism a product of the educated middle-class, and not of the illiterate masses. Why does hostility develop between educated people of different communities? Here it developed on the question of language, as on language depends job potentiality. Throughout the freedom struggle it can be observed that the middle classes fought both for jobs as well as elective political positions. Even in post-independence India, as we shall see in the next section, political and economic competition generates powerful hostility between the two communities. Sir Syed's prophecy that 'hostility between the two communities will increase immensely in the future' and that 'he who lives will see' found fulfillment not only immediately after his death but even in contemporary Indian society.

There is one more instance from Sir Syed's life which illustrates well the nature of communal conflict in colonial India. When Lord Ripon introduced the Local Self-Government Bill in the Council, Sir Syed made a plea for separate nomination of Muslims to local boards and district councils in January 1883. It is interesting to quote the speech at some length as it throws important light on our thesis on communalism:

> The system of representation by election, in countries where the population is composed of one race and one creed, is no doubt the best system that can be adopted.
>
> But, my lord, in a country like India, where caste distinctions still flourish, where there is no fusion of the various races, where religious distinctions are still violent, where education in its modern sense has still not made an equal or proportionate progress among all sections of the population, I am convinced that the introduction of the principle of election, pure and simple, (to) the local boards and district councils would be attended with evils of great significance. . . .
>
> The larger community would totally over-ride the interests of the smaller community. . . and the measures might make the differences of race and creed more violent than ever.[4]

Sir Syed's words once again proved prophetic. He correctly diagnosed the genesis of hostility between the two Indian communities. He knew that it is not religion or the respective belief systems of Hindus and Muslims which are the cause of this hostility. They lived in peace and harmony otherwise—despite differing belief systems. It is only the competition for elected posts which has generated tensions. He was right that unless all the communities acquire education in the real modern sense in equal measure (i.e., acquire equal merit in the search for jobs as well as elected posts) democratic competitiveness would continue to generate powerful hostility between these castes and communities.

The Muslim separatist movement which ultimately culminated in the creation of Pakistan should not be seen as religious in orientation. Muslim theologians like Maulana Abul Kalam Azad, Shibli N'umani, Maulana Husain Ahmad Madani who were all towering religious personalities of international fame, never approved of the Muslim League and its separatist politics. They either remained independent or became allies of the Congress or joined it. No theologian of any repute or standing supported the League. The Jami'at al'Ulama-i-Hind, an organization of theologians of the Deoband school, steadfastly supported the Indian National Congress.

Maulana Shibli, a noted historian of Islam and a theologian, sharply criticized the Muslim League and called it a strange creation and ridiculed it.[5] Shibli was also highly critical of the deputation of the League which met the Viceroy at Shimla in 1906. In his words, 'It (i.e., the deputation) was a great *tamasha* enacted on the national stage.'[6] Shibli also says that Muslims wanted to share the rights which the Hindus obtained (from the British rulers) after twenty years of struggle, simply by joining the League (without any struggle). The refrain of the League was that 'the Hindus are trying to suppress us and hence we should protect our interests'.[7]

Shibli greatly admires the Congress and its demands. He feels that if these demands are accepted the destiny of the country would change. In comparison to that the Muslim League's demands are, according to him, much inferior. He also severely criticizes the feudal, slavish leadership of the League pursuing its vested interests and the titles of the Raj.[8] He even advises the League to give up communal politics and think in the context of the whole country.[9]

Another outstanding theologián, Maulana Azad, was also irreconcilably opposed to separatist politics. He was a great champion of Hindu–Muslim unity and found legitimacy for this unity in the holy Koran. He came up with the concept of *wahdat-e-din*, i.e. unity of religions. According to this concept, laws and rituals might differ but the essence of religion is one. Azad quotes profusely from the holy Koran to prove his point. Azad believed in composite nationalism and a united struggle against the British. He was highly critical of those who blindly supported British policies. He wrote in one of his articles:

> Indian Muslims followed blindly the policy of the British government. . . (They) broke off all relations with the Hindus who were the real active group in the country. . . .We were warned that the Hindus were a majority and if we went along with them they would crush us. . . . The result was that the government which should otherwise have become the target of the Muslims' spears was saved, and their own neighbours became their mark instead.[10]

The noted Muslim theologians were not supportive of a separate homeland for Indian Muslims. Instead, they upheld the concept of composite nationalism. They took an example in this respect from the holy Prophet of Islam who drew up a convenant with the non-Muslim residents of Medina where he migrated to from Mecca. The Prophet came to terms with the Jews and Pagans of Medina and recognized their religious rights and gave them equal rights of citizenship thus evolving a composite political community. The *ulama*, therefore, drew inspiration from the covenant and argued that Hindus and Muslims could evolve a composite nationalism following in the Prophet's footsteps. They saw no theological grounds for the creation of Pakistan or a separate homeland for the Muslims.

Neither was Jinnah's concept of Pakistan a theological one. He did not envisage an Islamic state. He dreamt of a secular bourgeoisie state for the Muslims. It clearly shows that those behind the Pakistan movement represented either feudal or middle-class interests. Hamza Alavi, a Pakistani sociologist maintains that Pakistan was created by the Muslim *salariat* (salaried) class. No wonder then that the Pakistani movement did not have a democratic and a mass base. The two-nation theory resolution passed on 25 March 1940 in Lahore was opposed not only by the theologians but also by the Muslim masses.

Jinnah, the champion of Pakistan after the late thirties, was neither a theologian nor knew much about Islam. He was, until the late twenties, opposed to mixing religion with politics. He was even cool towards the Khilafat movement which was dominated by the Muslim divines. He was very close to Gokhale and was described as the Muslim Gokhale. In a speech at Ahmedabad in 1916, he said:

> For a real New India to arise, all petty and small things must be given up. To be redeemed, all Indians must offer to sacrifice not only their good things, but all those evil things they cling to blindly—their hates and their divisions, their pride in what they should be thoroughly ashamed of, their quarrels and misunderstandings. These are a sacrifice God would love.[11]

In fact in 1927 the prominent Muslim leaders under the presidentship of Jinnah had formulated certain proposals whereby, if the terms were accepted by the Indian National Congress, the Muslims would give up separate electorates and accept joint electorates. These proposals were: (1) Sind to be separated from the Bombay Presidency and constituted into a separate province; (2) Reforms to be introduced in the North-West Frontier Province and in Baluchistan on the same footing as in any other province in India; (3) In Punjab and Bengal, the proportion of representation to be made in accordance with the population; (4) In the Central Legislature Muslim representation not to be less than one-third. If all these demands were accepted, the Muslims would accept joint electorates in all the provinces.[12]

If the separate electorates had been given up and these demands formulated by the Muslim leaders accepted, it would have eroded the very basis of vivisection of India. The Motilal Nehru report, which took these demands into account but did not accept them all, was a watershed in the history of the creation of Pakistan. Then a series of developments took place, right from the implementation of the Constitution of 1935 to the controversial Cabinet Mission Plan of 1946, which ultimately sealed the fate of the unity of India. It would thus be seen that no religious issue was involved in all these controversies. One can easily conclude that Pakistan was the creation of secular interests rather than of any religious concept of a theocratic state or a concept of *millat* (nation) or Muslim *umma* (followers). Prominent theologians and freedom fighters like Maulana Husain Ahmad Madani and Maulana Azad had understood this well and that is why they never accepted the demand for Pakistan. Islam was used only as an instrument as Hinduism was used by the Hindu communalists. Thus one can say that it is conflict of interests that leads to the conflict of ideas and ideologies. The ideology of Pakistan was also a result of conflict of interests of the Muslim elite with the Hindu elite. There was no religious confrontation involved between the two communities. Merriam Hayes is closer to reality when she observes:

> Muslim businessmen foresaw new markets free from Hindu competition. Landlords hoped for a perpetuation of the zamindari system. Intellectuals envisioned a cultural rebirth free from the British and Hindus. To the orthodox, Pakistan promised a religious state. . . . To officials and bureaucrats a new nation offered a short-cut to seniority. . .[13]

Thus while trying to understand the Pakistan movement, no historian can disregard the socio-economic interests of different classes and groups of Muslims in India. This is the real key to its understanding.

Even after the creation of Pakistan, the Hindu–Muslim confrontation did not finally end, as was expected by many. It has continued in independent India and, recently, with the two major controversies about the Shah Bano judgement and the Babri Masjid–Ramjanmabhumi controversy, it has assumed dangerous proportions resulting in violence and death of several hundred innocent people. However, we would miss the point if we make these controversies central to the dispute. These are, rather, symptoms of a much deeper malaise of political, economic and social developments which have taken place in India since 1947.

We gave ourselves a secular and democractic Constitution in January 1950. This Constitution was quite radical in many respects. It accepted universal franchise which was by any yardstick a radical step. This enfranchisement brought tremendous political consciousness among the masses. Also, over the years, since 1947, the democratic processes continued to deepen and widen, bringing more and more political consciousness among the common people. Meanwhile economic development under the five-year-plans was also underway. Within the capitalist framework, economic development resulted in widening the gap between the rich and the poor. What is worse, this widening of the gap was not on an individual basis but on the basis of castes and communities. The upper castes of the majority community notched up the greatest share of the development while the lower castes and the minority communities had to content themselves with much less. With the deepening of political consciousness over the years, this sense of deprivation became increasingly acute.

There is one more sociological factor in this respect to be borne in mind. Our social structure is such that caste and community consciousness often has precedence over individual consciousness whereas our political structure is such as to make an individual supreme. This has resulted in yet another malaise. One has to come to grips with this malaise to understand the developing confrontation between various castes and communities in our society today. Our political processes, in view of our given social structure, tend to become caste nd community oriented rather than based on individual rights alone, as ideally required. The political processes cannot steer clear of the inherited social structure.

The Hindu–Muslim confrontation should not be oversimplified as a religious confrontation alone, though it often manifests itself through this channel. This channel is used only to legitimize this confrontation. If we have to understand the real nature of the developing confrontation we will have to trace the social, economic and political roots of the Hindu–Muslim relationship. Also, apart from this, there is an increasing tendency of religious assertion among Hindus as well as Muslims popularly called religious fundamentalism. Unfortunately, it is more condemned than understood. What is needed is to understand the reasons of this religious assertion.

Sectarianism, fanaticism, religious assertion or fundamentalism, by whatever name we call it, is not a purely religious phenomenon either. It is as much social, political and economic as religious in nature. If a community is politically and economically on the ascendant, it would tend to be liberal and less assertive of its religious beliefs. However, if a community is faced with hostile circumstances and threats to its existence, it tends to assert its religious zeal to strengthen its defences. The rise of Hindu, Muslim and Sikh fundamentalism in recent years must be seen in this perspective.

Hindu fundamentalism particularly has shown a great deal of aggressiveness in the last few years. It began with the incident of the conversion of a few Dalits (low-caste Hindus) to Islam in the early eighties in Meenakshipuram in Tamil Nadu and culminated in the Babri Masjid–Ramjanmabhumi controversy recently. What was the cause of the aggressive assertion of religion by the Hindus? One can very well argue that Hinduism is not only a liberal, much less rigid and non-doctrinaire religion but that the Hindus are better off both politically as well as economically. Why should there then be a manifestation of such fanaticism on their part?

It is true Hinduism is liberal, less rigid and non-doctrinaire. But this is the scriptural view of Hinduism. Hindu behaviour is not necessarily governed by the scriptural view of religion; instead it is governed by the realities of life and one's own interests. In other words it is interests, and not ideals which govern human behaviour (speaking in the general sense). Secondly, it is true that Hindus, specially the upper and middle classes, are better off both politically and economically; but, of late, they feel threatened by 'aggressive minorities' and have developed, through aggressive propaganda, a sense of encirclement and of being besieged. Here it should also be remembered that it is the perception of reality rather than reality itself which is more important as far as human behaviour is concerned.

A number of developments since the early eighties have reinforced this Hindu upper caste perception of challenge to its social and political hegemony. The first major challenge was, as pointed out earlier, from the conversion of Dalits to Islam. In fact it came as a double threat to Hindu hegemony. First, it was perceived as insolence on the part of untouchables who had, for centuries, abjectly surrendered themselves to the upper-caste Hindus. The untouchables were now raising their heads and challenging upper-caste supremacy. Secondly, it was no ordinary insolence on their part. They had challenged Hindu supremacy by adopting a faith which was never viewed kindly by upper-caste Hindus. That faith itself was perceived as a threat.

The Vishwa Hindu Parishad (VHP), the Rashtriya Swayamsevak Sangh (RSS) and other upper-caste Hindu organizations decided to meet this challenge by asserting Hinduism. It should also be borne in mind that this challenge from Dalits came at a time when the oil revolution in the Arab world had brought about an assertion of Islamic fundamentalism. It was being rumoured that petro-dollars were flowing into India to finance Muslim organizations and with a view to making Muslims a political challenge to the Hindus. In fact it was alleged that petro-dollars were the main inducement for the conversion of the Dalits. The impact of the conversions on the mind of the upper-caste Hindu must be assessed in this context.

Also, for various reasons that need not be discussed here, the Punjab problem assumed menacing proportions around 1983. The Sikhs who were historically not considered different from the Hindus began to assert their separate identity and even to object to being bracketed with the Hindus in the Constitution. Thus the Sikh religious assertion created another major challenge for the Hindus. Sikhism was seen to be so much an integral part of Hinduism that any assertion of separateness on the part of the Sikhs was no less than a traumatic experience for the Hindus. Here also it was perceived as not merely losing a friend but providing an ally to the Muslims. Jarnail Singh Bhindranwale had told a BBC correspondent that the Sikhs should join hands with the Muslims and should together challenge Hindu hegemony.[14]

The Shah Bano movement in 1986–87 also had an adverse effect on the Hindu mind. The Muslims aggressively opposed and rejected the Supreme Court judgement in the case of maintenance claimed by Shah Bano of Indore beyond the period of *iddah* (the three-month period after a divorce during which a divorcee is entitled to claim for maintenance, according to the Muslim law). The Muslims kept on agitating until the Government agreed to nullify the court judgement by enacting a separate law for Muslim women. This was seen as a complete negation of secularism by the Hindus and their perception that only Hindus are secular and the minorities are 'communal' got reinforced.

The then Government, led by Rajiv Gandhi, appeased the Hindus by throwing open the doors of the Babri mosque to the Hindus for worship on 1 February 1986. This 'balancing act' had a very adverse effect on Hindu–Muslim relations in the country. The Hindus led by the Vishwa Hindu Parishad (VHP) and the RSS now began to demand the construction of a Ramjanmabhumi Mandir on the site of the Babri mosque. In order to broaden the movement the VHP, RSS and BJP devised a clever move. They organized the worshipping and consecration of bricks in every village and taking them out in processions. These bricks were to be subsequently sent to Ayodhya for the construction of the temple. Basically it was a clever political move. A large number of Hindus were politically mobilized. But it communalized the whole situation and Hindus and Muslims came dangerously close to confrontation. The processions were organized in October–November 1989 just on the eve of the general elections in the last week of November 1989. It is no wonder that many major riots broke out in Indore (October 1989), Kota (September 1989), Bhagalpur (October 1989), etc. in which hundreds of innocent Muslims were killed.

Thus, it can be seen that the Hindu–Muslim relations are not merely governed by the religious factor alone but, more often, by political and economic developments. The political contour is determined by the social changes brought about by economic development and technological progress which in turn decides the pattern of behaviour and political perceptions. And these perceptions ultimately determine the shape of the relationship between Hindus and Muslims in society. Thus it is the process of economic development, social change and political perceptions which are far more important than the religious factor in determining intercommunal relationships.

Notes

1. Khwaja Hasan Nizami, *Fatimi Da'wat-e-Islam*, Delhi, 1338 A.H.

2. Letter of Sir Syed of 29 April 1870, quoted in Ikram Sheikh Muhammad, *Modern Muslim India and the Birth of Pakistan*, Lahore, n.d.

3. Hali, *Hayat-i-Javed*, quoted in Ikram, op.cit., p. 32.

4. Quoted by Symonds Richards, *The Making of Pakistan*, Faber and Faber: London, 1950, pp. 34–38.

5. Maqalat-i-Shibli, vol.VIII, pp. 161. Quoted by Mehr Afroz Murad in 'Shibli Nu'mani ke Siyasi Afkar', *Islam aur Asr-i-Jadid, vol. XX, issue 4, October 1988, p. 17.*

6. ibid., p. 18.

7. ibid.

8. ibid.

9. ibid., p. 19.

10. Maulana Azad , *Al-Hilal*, Calcutta, 11 September 1912.

11. Quoted by Rajmohan Gandhi, *Eight Lives—A Study of the Hindu–Muslim Encounter,* Roli Publishers: Delhi, 1986, pp. 128–9.

12. Jamaluddin Ahmed, *Historic Documents of the Muslim Freedom Movement*, Lahore, 1970, pp. 86.

13. Merriam Allen Hayes, *Gandhi vs Jinnah*, Minerva: Calcutta, 1980, pp. 91–2.

14. I had heard the interview of Bhindranwale on the BBC Hindi service a few days before he was killed in the Blue Star Operation in 1984.

Predatory Commercialization and Communalism in India

Amiya Kumar Bagchi

The word 'communalism' can be interpreted in numerous ways. In one sense it can mean any feeling of animosity that the members of any community (a *bhaichara biradari,* a linguistic group living side by side with other linguistic groups, a group claiming to belong to a particular 'race' as against other people belonging to other 'races', and so on) entertains against members of any other community defined by criteria which establish the distinctiveness of the latter. But in the Indian context, it has come specifically to mean the feelings of animosity between people who profess different religions. In particular, in post-independence India, it has come to mean feelings of animosity between Hindus and Muslims, and in the 1980s between Sikhs and Hindus in particular pockets of the country. This does not mean that either the Hindus, or the Muslims, or the Sikhs, present a monolithic front to the rest of the world. Apart from the fact that there are many people nominally belonging to each of these communities who do not define their own identities in terms of the religion they actually or nominally profess, there are also divisions within each of these communities. The most pervasive division is between the upper-caste Hindus and the Harijans or Dalits—people who are legally defined as the scheduled castes. The division between the Sunnis, who form a majority of the Muslims in India, and the Shias has sometimes expressed itself in acts of violence; so has the division between the orthodox Sikhs and the Nirankaris. The division between the upper-caste Hindus and the Dalits in many parts of the country has led to a conversion of the latter to Buddhism or Islam, and the older conflicts have then manifested themselves as communal conflicts defined in nominally religious terms.

We have already referred to acts of violence resulting from communalism. How do we, in fact, detect the expression of communalism? I may feel contemptuous or envious of a neighbour who flaunts his wealth or his social standing too blatantly for my taste, but unless he or I have a violent disposition, such a feeling may never come out overtly in public action or behaviour. So it is necessary to gather evidence of public acts as symptoms of feelings of animosity designated as 'communalism'. It might be thought that if we find a group of Hindus indulging in violence against a group of Muslims, it is the clear sign of a communal clash. But this is also not certain: the conflict may arise purely out of a private quarrel, and the Hindus might simply be associates of the Hindu protagonist, and the Muslims those of the Muslim protagonist. It is when these immediate associates are joined by other people with the same religious affiliation, and attack people belonging to another religious community, whether they are associates of the antagonists or not, that the private quarrel turns into a communal conflict.[1] There could also be situations in which members of a particular community would be protesting against the action of a particular individual or a group; when the antagonist has a different religious affiliation, the conflict might appear to be a communal one. This is apparently what happened in the so-called Talla riots of 1897 in Calcutta.[2] That was, properly speaking, a riot of a group of Muslims against the police who had demolished a mosque on disputed ground. In these cases, the specification and the explanation of the so-called communal incident or communal riot are inextricably linked; for, a wrong specification would at once litter the investigator's path with red herrings and the answers would also be misleading.[3]

Two communities may live side by side with feelings of their own identity, and some disdain or contempt for members of other communities, without there being any communal incident or a communal riot. Such, after all, has been the situation of most Hindus, Muslims and Sikhs for most of the period they have lived side by side. There may also be communal 'incidents' without there being communal riots. Very often those who fish in troubled waters try to provoke communal incidents, hoping that there would be a communal riot, or the assertion of the might of one community in relation to the other. What we are concerned to explore here are the conditions which permit mischief-making or politicking by provoking communal incidents. In this exploration we shall confine ourselves mainly to incidents of communalism involving Hindus and Muslims.

Very baldly, the following alternative sets of conditions seem to be necessary for communalist elements to be able to provoke communal incidents and riots. First, the leaders of the community (political or spiritual) perceive themselves and people belonging to their community as losing out in relation to the people of another contiguous community.

Second, the ordinary people of one community suffer a major erosion of their standard of living and identify some or all of the members of the other community (through guilt by association or through personification of a whole community) as being the cause of that erosion. Third, traders or merchants belonging to two separate but contiguous communities engage in competition, and suffer losses through competitive pressures or through the working of exogenous forces and see themselves as competing for the same economic and physical space, and try to use communal solidarity and political instruments to serve their own ends. Finally, there is the ubiquitous fact of politics—whether in a democratic set-up or under a military regime as in Pakistan under Zia-ul-Haq—where some political leaders act as the champions of one community, some others act as the protectors of a threatened community, and some others pose as the champions of communal unity; all the while making sure that the cauldron of communalism continues to simmer.

I take a quick look in this section at some of the ways in which the communal conflict erupted under British colonialism. Under British-style capitalist colonialism, predatory commercialization was let loose in an almost unhindered fashion in most regions of India and it affected most areas of life. The continued operation of a process of commercialization under which the losers are simply proletarianized, or worse, pauperized, is one of the basic continuities between pre-independence and post-independence India. Pauperization is a process under which the property-less losers do not even have access to employment; this can happen both when the losers are willing to behave as 'free' labourers and when they cling to an ascribed status in society and refuse to accept the employment open to them. Ashrafs and Brahmins have often starved rather than accept jobs as unskilled labourers; of course, social mores have also prevented their employment in such capacities, at least within the immediate neighbourhood.

Capitalist colonialism and its inevitable partner, predatory commercialization, did not start out to destroy all communities; they attacked all communal or status attributes that stood in the way of tribute-extraction or private profit-making. But they affected different communities differently, depending on where they happened to be. Take the case of the weavers, for example. Both the Hindu and the Muslim weaver communities were affected by the decline of hand-spinning and hand-weaving after the Indian market was flooded by machine-made yarn and cloth from

Britain. However, in eastern Bengal there was a sizeable amount of forest and swamp land which could be opened up for cultivation. Many peasants moved to clear this land. Some displaced weavers also became cultivators—more often as agricultural labourers than as landowning peasants. Even when the peasants or weavers held land, it was on insecure tenure. This also created problems which took a communal turn when the landlords happened to be predominantly Hindus, and the peasants Muslims. However, the impact was partially absorbed by this kind of population movement. In areas where such prospects of occupational changes were bleak, or where the weavers were highly skilled, urban artisans used to a very different lifestyle from that of the cultivators, they continued to practise a diminishingly remunerative profession. Under Indian conditions, this would mean that they would become even more dependent than before on traders and money-lenders for advances and loans, generally at usurious rates of interest. If again many of the weavers were Muslims and the traders and money-lenders were Hindus, tension between the weavers and money-lenders in the area of commerce and finance would take on a communal turn, especially if the only supervisory authority with which the weavers were in touch happened to be religious leaders. Such conflicts which had a dual edge—an economic and a religious one—have been recorded and analysed by many historians.[4]

But British colonialism damaged the fortunes of many others besides the weavers. The system of revenue extraction and the processes of commercialization instituted under colonialism, affected all Indians. But the effects were felt differentially by different groups. Under the Mughals, revenue was collected only from the land that was cultivated. The effect was that with a relatively sparse population, cattle, sheep and goats had abundant pastures to feed on; the peasants, owning livestock, and the shepherds, especially in northern and north-western India, did well out of this differential treatment, and India perhaps had one of the highest ratios of livestock to people in the world. Under the British, every piece of land was supposed to be owned by a private person or the State. If any piece of land was claimed by a private person, he had to pay rent on it, whether he cultivated it or not. If the land was supposed to be government-owned, the peasants or shepherds had to pay for the use of any of its produce—be it timber or fodder. The relatively favourable treatment of pastures for revenue purposes virtually ceased under this dispensation.

This meant that, over time, it became more and more difficult to keep livestock. As a result, the ratio of livestock to people and of livestock per acre of cultivated land came down.[5] This was because there was pressure to cultivate every piece of land that could yield anything above the cost of cultivation. Earlier on, in many areas, peasants on *khudkasht* (land to which a person has a hereditary right and which he is supposed to cultivate himself; or may designate land tenure incorporating such a right) tenure, *patidars* (persons claiming to belong to the group which has a hereditary right to the ownership of the land in a particular area; a term that was used in Gujarat), or otherwise privileged peasants, could often claim the right to cultivate a piece of land, even if they had not cultivated it for a long time or had not paid revenue on it, provided they could establish an ancestral claim to that piece of land. Under the British, landownership became conditional on prompt payment of the land revenue not just every year, but every *kisht* (instalment of payment of land revenue in British India). Thus even if a particular piece of land gave no certain promise of yielding a surplus above the cost of cultivation, the peasant dare not let it lie fallow. For, he hoped that it would yield some surplus at some future date, and if he failed to meet his revenue demand for a single year, he would lose that land forever, and with that his chance of survival would also decline by a significant margin. The peasants' proverbial attachment to their land was reinforced by the insecurity created by the revenue system.

More livestock for most Indians meant more milk and more butter or *ghee,* and these were major sources of protein and fat. More livestock also meant more manure for the peasants' fields in areas where tillage and pasture were combined. But for shepherd communities—*goalas, yadavs*—livestock was also the source of livelihood. When the government took over common pastures as its own property, or when pastures or forest lands were parcelled out as private domain, the grazers found it increasingly difficult to feed their livestock without encroaching on land claimed by others. Traditional usage, such as keeping the stubble on the fields and keeping the fields open after harvest, provided some relief, but it was not enough. With the low level of monetization in the village economy, the grazers often could not grow fodder crops and make a living after paying for the cost of cultivation and for the state's revenue demand on the land put to fodder. The grazers moved from one area to another in search of empty fields on which they could feed their herds. Often there were no social conventions or regular policing to keep them from letting loose their herds in fields under crop. This led to clashes between peasants and grazers. When the peasants happened to be Muslims and the grazers Hindus, the clashes took on a communal complexion.

However, the 'cow protection movement'[6] in the late nineteenth century which gave rise to a number of communal incidents and helped spread communalism in many parts of northern and eastern India, should not be seen simply as a reflection of the sectional conflict between semi-nomadic grazers and sedentary peasants. The cow, of course, was for ages a symbol of prosperity in Hindu India—both as the source of milk (hence as surrogate mother) and as the mother of oxen, the chief source of power for cultivation. (It is interesting to speculate as to why the buffalo never occupied that space. Was it because Aryan colonizers had already domesticated kine, whereas they had met the buffalo first in their wild state and because the domesticated buffalo was the chief wealth of people who were for long beyond the pale of Brahmanical dominance?) Hence when the peasants and grazers saw one of the main sources of their wealth threatened by alien rule, in a tragic mode of transference of anger to a visible imagined enemy from an invisible system, they took the cow-eaters as their target of attack. Of course, the white rulers also ate cows, but the whites were few and scattered, and in any case, were mostly beyond the threat of violence by the means at the peasants' command. So the Muslim neighbour became the chief target of attack as the cow-protection movement lost its focus.

Neither the anti-Muslim attacks on the cow-protectors nor the anti-Hindu *jehad* (holy war waged in the defense of Islam) of the *julahas* and other poor Muslims, were 'spontaneous'. For anger to express itself in communal violence, some organization and planning are almost always necessary. The Brahmanical hierarchy of the Hindus, strongly supported by the upper-caste landlords (the Maharaja of Darbhanga and his kin were Brahmins, and, along with the Rajputs and the Bhumihars, constituted the dominant landlord element in Bihar and eastern Uttar Pradesh—the chief trouble spot of the anti-cow slaughter riots), provided the ideological underpinnings and the muscle-power of the communal riots triggered by the derailed cow-protection movement. Similarly, the *ulamas* (plural of *alim*: person learned in Muslim scriptures and other traditional Islamic studies) took up the *jehad*—initially against the British who, in their eyes, had converted India from a land favourable to Islam to a country favouring the infidels. But they found it easier to imbue the faithful with a hatred of the infidel next door rather than with a determination to fight the infidel occupying (symbolically speaking first, and literally, from 1911) the *masnad* of Delhi. Moreover, the *ulamas'* movement was soon supplemented by the Anglo–Orientalist movement of Sir Syed Ahmad. The Anglo–Orientalist movement, and the rise of an Anglicized but separatist politics among the upper-class Muslims of Uttar Pradesh illustrate the point that communalism may arise not from processes of absolute deprivation but from perceptions of relative deprivation. According to Paul Brass, the Muslim gentry and the landlords of Uttar Pradesh in the latter half of the nineteenth century were not doing badly at all as compared to their Hindu counterparts.[7] But it is their perception of having felt degraded since at the time a Nawab ruled in Lucknow or a Mughal emperor ruled from Delhi, and this was the major cause of their anti-Hindu sentiments. Of course, not all Muslim gentry or landlords behaved in the same way: there were many who joined the nationalist struggle, just as on the other side many Hindu landlords and professionals remained loyal to the British Government till the very end. Moreover, much of the majority 'nationalism' remained implicated in religious symbolism, vocabulary and sentiment. But among the Muslim masses in most parts of India, it is the communalist ideology of the *ulama* or the Anglo–Orientalist perception of the upper-class Muslims of Uttar Pradesh that came to prevail.

After Independence, there was a large-scale migration of the professionals among the Muslims to Pakistan. Along with that, zamindari rights and the rule of Indian chiefs over their territories ended in the Republic of India. These particular changes hit hard some sections of the Muslims in Uttar Pradesh, the province in which the Muslim landed aristocracy and the professionals had first spearheaded the demand for separate privileges for Muslims and then for Pakistan.[8] Those institutions which had depended on the patronage of the Muslim landlords were impoverished by the changes. Similar changes occurred, though to a lesser extent, in other parts of India also. This meant that, even if there were no concealed processes of discrimination against Muslims working under the surface, with the normal rules of competition in an increasingly commercialized society, the percentage of Muslims making it to the professional classes would decline. Combined with such processes of social discrimination as were operating in predominantly Hindu-administered institutions, the proportion of Muslims in the professional classes could also be expected to be lower than their proportion in the general population. This meant that the average Muslim perceived his advancement being barred in this society, which professed to be secular, but which practised systemic, if not systematic, discrimination against an underprivileged minority.

In this section we turn to an examination of some aspects of the economic and demographic setting in post-independence India, which will help us perceive the operation of predatory commercialization in its true magnitude. If we look at the distribution of the Muslims and Hindus in India as between rural and urban areas (table 1), it becomes obvious that Muslims are a far more urbanized community than the Hindus. In some states (such as Maharashtra), there are more Muslims living in urban areas than in villages (table 1). It is not accidental that most of the communal riots in India have been urban. However, the Bhagalpur riots[9] demonstrate that we should not harbour the illusion that if we understand the predisposing conditions of the urban riots, we will understand the pathology of communal riots in general. Where so many people are dispossessed or threatened with dispossession by processes or predatory commercialization, and where society and the state take little note of the need to succour the victims of such commercialization, the material conditions facilitating communal riots are present all the time.

As we have pointed out earlier, capitalist colonialism under the British already affected the people's livelihood in numerous ways. It led to the erosion of the protection given to members of many communities in precolonial days—however inadequate and unequally distributed such protection might have been in practice—without putting any new protective structures in place. New patronage linkages grew around the zamindari structures and the structures revolving around the more important native princes. But in most cases, the zamindars' economic position deteriorated over time. Moreover, threatened with relative impoverishment, the zamindars increased their demands ferociously—until they were stalled by the resistance of the suffering peasants.

British rule produced landlord domination. This domination was not, however, automatic, and contradictory pulls acted on it: when the zamindars were threatened too extensively with bankruptcy because of their extravagance and because of the newly-instituted right of the moneylender to take over mortgaged properties, the British rulers rushed with Courts of Wards and with special legislation to try and save them as a class. In Punjab the British brought in special measures to protect land from being taken over by non-agriculturists. The imperatives of imperial rule led to authority structures and measures that mainly subserved the colonial regime but could, on occasion, be used to defend some particular rights of members of the patronage network latticing those structures. However, predatory commercialization acted as a corrosive acid on most existing structures, throwing handicraft workers out of work, dispossessing peasants, ruining petty landlords, and enriching traders and money-lenders and leading to new alignments of power under the overarching framework of colonial rule and landlord domination.

After independence, predatory commercialization continued to work through the new structures of a post-colonial, mimetic state apparatus, thrusting forward nodes of industrialization, a countryside dominated by landlords and rich peasants, and urban centres with numerous, jostling, petty merchants and monopoly capitalists. It is a characteristic of predatory commercialization that, acting by itself, it tends to convert people into paupers rather than proletarians. As we have noted already, pauperization is a process under which owners of means of production— whether artisans, peasants or petty landlords—are dispossessed but are not absorbed in alternative gainful occupations, even in the long run. This can happen because the potential employment in alternative occupations does not grow at a sufficiently high rate. This can also happen because the losers refuse to accept the employment open to them, because it does not satisfy the requirements of their ascribed status in the old society. Ashrafs and upper-caste Hindus have often starved (literally to death, in times of famines in colonial India) rather than accept jobs as unskilled labourers, or in menial occupations—at least in the same neighbourhood. One of the motives of migration of such threatened groups has been to achieve a relative freedom from ascriptive status away from prying eyes.

We must not, of course, exaggerate the importance of such barriers. If the searches for jobs have failed, in most cases it is because there are not enough new jobs when old ones are destroyed by shifts in market conditions. Capitalist colonialism and predatory commercialization adversely affected the fortunes of millions of Hindus, Muslims, Sikhs Christians, Buddhists and people outside the reach of the major religions.

Let us try to see whether we can say something more about the predisposing conditions for communal riots by using the data on the urban–rural distribution of populations by community ascription. If we look carefully at tables 1 and 2 we will see that, with the sole exceptions of Assam and West Bengal among the more populous states of India, Muslims are a more urbanized community, in the sense that their proportion in urban population is higher than their proportion in total population. In the more urbanized states such as Gujarat and Maharashtra, the urban Muslims constitute the majority of the Muslim population. The degree of urbanization of the Indians is increasing over time, but in some states the degree of urbanization of Muslims is increasing at a faster rate.

In the jargon of economists, both push and pull factors are acting to affect the process of urbanization. In many states, the proportion of

Table 1   Total population of Hindus and Muslims in different states and their urban areas 1961–81 (in '000)

	Total population						Urban population					
	1961		1971		1981		1961		1971		1981	
	Hindus	Muslims	Hindus	Muslims	Hindus	Muslims	Hindus	Muslims	Hindus	Muslims	Hindus	Muslims
India (a)	366,527	46,941	453,437	61,418	541,779	75,512	60,336	12,698	83,195	17,685	120,653	25,678
Andhra Pradesh (b)	31,814	2,715	38,791	3,520	47,526	4,534	4,759	1,219	6,328	1,667	9,623	2,393
Assam	7,885	2,766	9,490	3,592	—	—	719	114	1,115	145	—	—
Bihar	39,346	5,786	42,589	7,594	58,011	9,875	3,095	691	4,442	986	6,953	1,504
Gujarat (c)	18,356	1,745	17,949	2,249	30,519	2,908	4,108	905	5,887	1,218	8,512	1,647
Haryana	—	—	7,341	405	11,548	524	—	—	1,615	16	2,586	40
Himachal Pradesh	—	—	3,113	50	4,100	70	—	—	211	6	290	9
Jammu & Kashmir	1,013	2,432	1,404	3,040	1,930	3,843	197	370	298	519	420	784
Kerala	10,283	3,028	12,683	4,163	14,801	5,410	1,521	527	2,018	765	2,779	1,048
Karnataka (d)	20,583	2,328	25,332	3,113	31,907	4,105	3,952	1,014	5,227	1,496	7,936	2,198
Madhya Pradesh	30,426	1,318	39,024	1,816	48,505	2,502	3,649	708	5,372	1,009	8,520	1,496
Maharashtra	32,531	3,034	41,307	4,233	51,109	5,806	8,064	1,671	11,195	2,497	15,675	3,552
Manipur	—	—	633	71	853	99	—	—	120	2	296	23
Meghalaya	—	—	187	26	241	41	—	—	71	4	99	7
Nagaland	—	—	59	3	111	12	—	—	28	2	44	5
Orissa	17,123	215	21,121	327	25,162	422	994	81	1,678	100	2,849	159
Punjab	12,930	393	5,087	114	6,200	168	3,117	45	2,135	42	2,982	60
Rajasthan	18,133	1,315	23,094	1,778	30,604	2,492	2,543	518	3,489	757	5,639	1,169
Sikkim	—	—	145	*	213	3	—	—	13	*	33	2
Tamil Nadu (e)	30,297	1,559	36,674	2,104	43,017	2,520	7,485	900	10,323	1,256	13,246	1,579
Tripura	—	—	1,394	104	1,834	139	—	—	157	5	218	6
Uttar Pradesh	62,437	10,788	73,998	13,677	92,366	17,658	6,451	2,765	8,408	3,657	13,856	5,667
West Bengal	27,523	6,985	31,612	9,064	42,007	11,743	7,388	986	9,564	1,243	12,458	1,768

* Less than a thousand

Notes
(a) The population of India includes that of all the component states and union territories, except in 1981, when no census operation could be conducted in Assam.
(b) No census operation could be conducted in Assam in 1981.
(c) Haryana was included in Punjab in 1961.
(d) Karnataka was named 'Mysore' in the census of 1961.
(e) Tamil Nadu was named 'Madras' in the census of 1961.
Sources:
(a) *Census of India 1961*, vol.1, part II, C(i); *Social and Cultural Tables* (Delhi, Manager of Publications, 196), Table CII, Religion, pp. 488–90; *Census of India 1971*, series I, India Part II, C (i); *Social and Cultural Tables* (Delhi, Manager of Publications, 197), Union Table C VII, Religion pp. 92–5; *Census of India 1981*, series I, India, Paper 3 of 1984, Household Publication by Religion by Household (Delhi, Manager of Publication, 1984), Table H H, 15, pp. 6–9.

---

landless labour to the total rural working force has increased. There is also evidence that in Haryana, Punjab, and western Uttar Pradesh the employment of labour per hectare has tended to decline over time. The rate of growth of employment in agriculture has tended to decline drastically in recent years. Along with these developments, unemployment has tended to increase in both urban and rural areas.[10]

On the basis of the data gathered by the forty-third round of the National Sample Survey (NSS), it is found that in 1987–88, the total unemployment was 12.43 million person year, according to the Usual Principal Status (UPS) criterion, 15.3 million according to the Weekly Status (WS), and 18.95 million according to the Daily Status (DS). The proportion of the labour force unemployed was higher in urban than in rural areas, and interestingly enough, higher among females than among males, both in rural and urban areas. A more alarming fact is that the number of unemployed, especially by the UPS criterion, have been rising all through the 1970s and 1980s as table 3 demonstrates. The only break in the series is for unemployed females between 1977–78 and 1983, but it is not clear as to how much this decline in their numbers is a statistical artefact and how much it reflects a real improvement. The rates of unemployment as a proportion of the work force have risen between 1983 and 1987–88, except for unemployment by the DS criterion. This seems to indicate a greater degree of casualization, of the work force. (We have other evidence of such casualization, such as the growth in the numbers of registered and unregistered non-factory enterprises and growth in employment in such enterprises even while employment growth in the private factory sector has become negative.)[12]

Table 2   Percentage of Hindus and Muslims in total population and urban population of India 1961-81

	Percentage of total population						Percentage of urban population					
	1961		1971		1981		1961		1971		1981	
	Hindus	Muslims	Hindus	Muslims	Hindus	Muslims	Hindus	Muslims	Hindus	Muslims	Hindus	Muslims
India (a)	83.4	10.7	82.7	11.2	82.6	11.3	76.4	16.1	72.2	16.2	76.5	16.3
Andhra Pradesh (b)	88.4	7.5	87.6	8.1	88.7	8.5	75.8	19.4	75.3	19.8	2.2	19.1
Assam	66.4	23.3	72.5	24.6	—	—	78.7	12.5	86.5	11.2	—	—
Bihar	84.7	12.5	83.4	13.5	83.0	14.1	79.1	17.6	78.8	17.5	79.7	17.2
Gujarat	89.0	8.4	89.3	8.4	89.5	8.5	77.3	17.0	78.5	16.2	80.3	15.5
Haryana	—	—	89.2	4.0	89.3	4.0	—	—	91.1	0.8	91.4	1.4
Himachal Pradesh	—	—	96.1	1.4	95.7	1.6	—	—	87.2	2.1	88.9	2.8
Jammu & Kashmir (c)	28.4	68.3	30.4	65.8	32.2	64.2	33.2	62.4	34.7	30.5	33.2	62.2
Karnataka	87.3	9.9	86.5	10.6	85.9	11.0	75.0	19.2	73.4	21.0	73.9	20.5
Kerala	60.8	17.9	59.4	19.5	58.1	21.2	59.6	20.6	58.2	22.0	58.2	22.0
Madhya Pradesh	94.0	4.1	93.6	4.4	93.0	4.8	78.9	15.3	79.2	14.9	80.5	14.1
Maharashtra	82.2	7.7	81.9	8.4	81.4	9.2	72.2	15.0	71.2	15.9	71.2	16.1
Manipur	—	—	50.9	6.6	60.0	7.0	—	—	85.1	1.4	78.9	6.1
Meghalaya	—	—	18.5	2.6	18.0	3.1	—	—	48.3	2.7	41.1	2.9
Nagaland	—	—	11.4	0.6	14.3	1.5	—	—	54.9	3.9	36.7	3.3
Orissa	97.6	1.2	96.2	1.5	95.4	1.6	89.5	7.2	90.9	5.4	91.6	5.1
Punjab (d)	63.7	1.9	37.5	0.8	36.9	1.0	76.2	1.1	66.4	1.3	64.1	1.3
Rajasthan	90.0	6.5	89.6	6.9	89.3	7.3	77.5	15.8	76.8	16.5	78.2	16.2
Sikkim	—	—	68.6	0.2	67.4	0.9	—	—	65.0	1.02	64.7	3.9
Tamil Nadu (e)	89.9	4.6	89.0	5.1	88.9	5.2	83.2	10.0	82.8	10.1	83.0	9.9
Tripura	—	—	89.6	6.7	89.3	6.7	—	—	96.3	3.1	96.5	2.6
Uttar Pradesh	84.7	14.6	83.8	15.5	83.3	15.9	68.0	29.2	67.9	29.5	69.6	28.5
West Bengal	78.8	20.0	71.3	20.4	77.0	21.5	86.5	11.5	87.2	11.3	86.2	12.2

Sources and notes : As for Table 1.

Table 3   *Number of unemployed by the usual status criterion (excluding subsidiary occupations) from 1972–73 to 1987–88 (in million)*

	Rural		Urban	
	Male	Female	Male	Female
1972–73				
(27th round of NSS)	1.5	0.3	1.6	0.5
1977–78				
(32nd round of NSS)	1.8	1.8	2.0	1.3
1983				
(38th round of NSS)	2.2	0.5	2.5	0.6
1987–88				
(43rd round of NSS)	3.0	2.3	3.0	1.0

Source: National Sample Survey Organisation (NSSO): Key Results of Employment and Unemployment Survey, All-India (Part-I), NSS 43rd Round (July 1987–June 1988, Department of Statistics, Ministry of Planning, Government of India, January 1990, Statement 39, (p.113).

Of course, unemployment in rural and urban areas is not spread evenly across the states. Nor does the rate of unemployment by itself indicate the degree of insecurity of the poor. It can be argued that in regions where the proportions of the poor are low, various informal social mechanisms, and the prospect of a relatively high-wage casual work may sustain the morale of the poor. But such a general statement cannot be fully trusted without further investigation. What I am doing here is to pull in certain kinds of data relating to the living conditions of the poor to see whether the degree of insecurity as such provides an approximate index of the proneness of the region to communal violence.

In table 4 we have reproduced the percentages of persons in the lowest three expenditure classes (in terms of per capital expenditure) in rural and urban areas in the major states of India during the forty-third round of the NSS (1987–88). (The population is divided into twelve expenditure classes in both rural and urban areas; but since prices and money incomes tend to be higher in the urban areas, the lowest expenditure class and the highest one (open-ended) both have higher cut-off points for urban areas. For rural areas, the outer limit of the lowest three expenditure classes is Rs 95 per capita, and for urban areas it is Rs 135 per capita.)

Table 4   *Percentage of population in the lowest three expenditure classes (in terms of monthly per capita expenditure) in rural and urban areas of major states of India in 1987–88*

States	Rural: monthly per capita expenditure less than Rs 95	Urban: monthly per capita expenditure less than Rs 135
Andhra Pradesh	23.4	31.7
Assam	12.2	16.4
Bihar	29.3	40.5
Gujarat	13.8	16.0
Haryana	7.8	15.0
Himachal Pradesh	5.4	5.4
Jammu and Kashmir	8.7	12.0
Karnataka	25.8	20.2
Kerala	9.8	14.0
Madhya Pradesh	32.9	28.0
Maharashtra	24.0	21.0
Orissa	25.4	27.4
Punjab	5.1	12.2
Rajasthan	19.1	22.5
Tamil Nadu	29.2	27.0
Uttar Pradesh	26.4	35.3
West Bengal	19.0	25.9

Source: National Sample Survey Organisation (NSSO): Key Results of Employment and Unemployment, All-India, NSS 43rd Round, Statement 8.

One inference follows directly from table 4. In both relatively urbanized and non-urbanized states, there is a large proportion of people who can be regarded as desperately poor by any standard. (Here, I am not entering into a technical discussion of the comparison of degrees of poverty in real terms as between different states: relative price structures, absolute price levels, and differences in the consumption baskets of the poor all enter into the picture.) The only major states in which the proportion of the very poor as defined above is less than ten per cent of the rural population are Haryana, Himachal Pradesh, Jammu and Kashmir and Punjab in the North and Kerala in the South. Some of the populous states, such as Bihar, Madhya Pradesh, Orissa and Uttar Pradesh in northern and central India, and Karnataka and Tamil Nadu in the south have more than twenty-five per cent of the rural people in the three lowest expenditure classes. Maharashtra and Andhra Pradesh have their corresponding figures lying between twenty and twenty-five per cent. Low figures of population in the lowest expenditure classes of Assam are more in line with those of the north-eastern states than with those of the other eastern states. (This largely explains the attraction of immigrants to Assam from Bangladesh and from other neighbouring states within India.)

If we look at the figures of the population in the lowest expenditure classes in urban areas, we find that they vary largely, though not wholly, with the corresponding figures for the rural areas of the respective states. The figures for the proportion of the poor in the urban areas tend to be higher—in some cases, for example, Andhra Pradesh, Bihar and Uttar Pradesh considerably higher—than for the corresponding figures of the rural areas. The exceptions to this are Himachal Pradesh, Karnataka, Madhya Pradesh, Maharashtra and Tamil Nadu. But since in the case of Madhya Pradesh the proportion of the urban poor exceeds twenty-five per cent of the total urban population, this is little comfort. It does seem, however, that the above-average industrial growth of Karnataka, Gujarat and Maharashtra has helped keep the numbers of the urban poor lower than they would otherwise have been.

We will add another table of figures to illustrate the asymmetries of the grid against which the deadly politics of communalism and casteism is being played and then begin to draw out some of the social, political and ideological implications. Table 5 reproduces the statewise figures of the urban unemployment rate and the total numbers of unemployed in urban areas as estimated by the forty-third round of the NSS (1987–88). For this purpose, we took the usual (principal) status criterion of unemployment. One of the most striking features of the array of figures in table 5 is that urban unemployment rates among males are the highest in the two states governed by the Left parties, namely, Kerala and West Bengal. These two states also have the two largest masses of unemployed females in the country. The number of unemployed women is low in most of the north Indian states, not because women face alluring prospects of employment, but because female participation rate in the work force outside the households is low.

Let us now look at the rough grid of communal and casteist violence in

Table 5 *Usual status unemployment rates (as percentages of the workforce) and numbers of persons unemployed (in 000s) by sex in urban areas of major Indian states in 1987–88*

States	Unemployment Rates (%)		No. of Persons Unemployed	
	Males	Females	Males	Females
Andhra Pradesh	6.4	9.0	269	134
Assam	5.3	28.4	41	25
Bihar	6.4	3.3	190	11
Gujarat	4.7	2.2	169	12
Haryana	4.6	9.6	55	13
Himachal Pradesh	6.9	10.5	7	3
Jammu & Kashmir	4.7	15.5	22	10
Karnataka	5.6	4.1	209	47
Kerala	14.1	33.8	239	211
Madhya Pradesh	4.3	5.6	158	47
Maharashtra	6.5	5.0	496	88
Orissa	7.1	14.0	87	27
Punjab	4.8	14.7	84	28
Rajasthan	4.7	1.4	119	9
Tamil Nadu	7.3	9.1	413	175
Uttar Pradesh	3.4	2.9	250	25
West Bengal	9.0	21.4	492	188

Source: NSSO : Key Results of Employment and Unemployment Survey, All-India (Part-1), NSS 43rd Round (July 1987–June 1988) Statement 40.

recent years against the information about insecurity and poverty culled so far. Uttar Pradesh and Bihar would seem to fit a hypothesis that links the potential for communal violence to the incidence of poverty. Moreover, the massive numbers of unemployed men confined in over-crowded urban slums also provide frequent occasions for the flaring up of tempers or for deliberate mobilization of ignitable materials required for such flare-ups. But Gujarat does not conform to this stereotype at all. The state has witnessed some of the worst communal riots in recent years.[13] Yet, the incidence of poverty and the incidence of urban unemployment among males in Gujarat are below the average for the major Indian states (the all-India average computed by the NSSO and reproduced in table 3 seems to be biased downward because of a large weight accorded to the north-eastern states—out of proportion to their population). One clue to all this is to be found in the general climate of opinion among the upper classes (and castes) of Gujarat, which have practised a policy of social Darwinism over a number of years.[14] 'If the existing local population cannot be exploited at low wages, and if labour can be obtained from elsewhere at lower wages, the local exploitable population might as well die off.' This is the implicit ideology of the thrusting, predatory commercialization process almost everywhere in India. But its ideology can be seen nakedly in operation in Gujarat, in the consistent and open violation of most of the minimum wage and social security regulations, by local capitalists with the deliberate connivance and collusion of the state apparatus.[15] This is also the state that witnessed one of the worst carnages instigated by members of the upper castes protesting against reservation of some jobs for the backward castes; this casteist carnage later turned into communal violence in which again the poor suffered most of the casualties and loss of belongings.

Is there any way of countering this ideology? Activists in Gujarat have tried public interest litigation. The Government of Gujarat was the first state government (apart from Tamil Nadu) to try and reserve jobs for backward castes other than scheduled castes and tribes, and there has been a proliferation of non-governmental organizations taking up the cause of the women, the poor and the tribals. But most of these moves have again and again been swamped by casteist riots and communal riots engulfing major cities and towns of Gujarat and have even spread to the rural areas.

Let us look at neighbouring Maharashtra. There, in spite of a high rate of industrial growth and burgeoning of trade related to West Asia, massive urban unemployment continues to persist. Rural male unemployment rates in Maharashtra however, are pretty low according to the forty-third round, much lower, say, than in Kerala and West Bengal. In the wake of a major drought in Maharashtra, the Government of Maharashtra launched the Employment Guarantee Scheme, which has been hailed as 'perhaps the first programme which guarantees the right to work as a basic right in a developing country'.[16] Yet rural wages in Maharashtra often remain far below the minimum legal level, workers wait vainly for the employment guaranteed to them, and the proportion of the people in the lowest three expenditure brackets was twenty-four per cent (see table 4)—much higher than in Kerala and West Bengal, both states that have done far worse in terms of industrial and commercial growth than Maharashtra. Maharashtra has been repeatedly embroiled in massive communal riots, mostly in and around Bombay, but these have also spread to other areas from time to time. Admittedly, the number of urban unemployed males (UUM) in Maharashtra is the largest among all the major states. But Maharashtra with 496,000 UUM is closely followed by West Bengal with 492,000 UUM and we have to remember that the latter's population is considerably less than that of Maharashtra. The ideological and political aspects of communal violence acquire significance when we see that despite the poor record of urban unemployment, at least since the middle of the 1970s, West Bengal can claim the best record in terms of keeping communal peace.

Let me now put forward several propositions without claiming more than that the picture presented above provides only a suggestive support for them. The first proposition is that in most states of India, the insecurity of the poor, as indicated by their meagre daily earnings when they are lucky enough to find a job, the threat of unemployment to which they are continually exposed because of predatory commercialization,[17] and the continual threat of disease and death under which they spend their daily lives maintain a fertile ground for *agents provocateurs* to prod them into divisive conflicts of all kinds.

The second proposition is that the overcrowded conditions of most cities and the competition for valuable urban space which can be monopolized, speculated with, divided and redivided to profit the greedy, made them powder-kegs for generating various petty conflicts. Adroitly exploited, such petty conflicts can be made to snowball into a major communal conflagration.

The third proposition is that any measures that improve the chances of upward social mobility for the poor and accord them increased bargaining power against the rest will help to make the environment less congenial to fomenting communal violence. These measures include pro-peasant land reforms that effectively eradicate landlordism, a continuous campaign for universalizing literacy, removing the special position of women as both the victims and hostages of communal violence and hostility and making them fully equal citizens with men, and providing everybody with a guarantee for the basic necessities of life. The first three sets of measures will themselves reduce poverty and insecurity of life by giving more land to the small peasants who will cultivate it more intensively by raising productivity through the spread of literacy among workers and by releasing the productive powers of women, a large number of whom are immured within walls as the ultimate victims of exploitation, and the residuary legatees of the all-oppressive systems. A uniform civil law which abolishes the special pre-bourgeoise privileges enjoyed by propertied Hindus (under the Mitakshara system) in most parts of India, and render their positions of vantage relatively immune to competition from other groups which are not similarly placed will increase the chances of upward mobility of disadvantaged groups. A civil law that makes women equal sharers in property and the fruits of work with men will also liberate the energies of fully half of the population. (India shares with West Asia the dubious distinction of having one of the worst records of treatment of women in terms of work, health services and literacy.)

But this package of social and economic reforms must be accompanied by a basic but comprehensive social security system which will guarantee that nobody need starve to death or die of exposure to cold and heat, or from easily preventable diseases. This system will be necessary because unemployment will not go away soon, landlessness or propertylessness will continue to increase, and we cannot depend on market forces alone to raise wages to the minimum standards laid down, as we saw from the examples of Gujarat and Maharashtra.

The importance of a civil law which distances itself from arbitrary religious criteria needs to be emphasized again. The landlord lineages and trader lineages of northern and central India have effectively used non-market power and the power of restrictive organizations and practices to keep their vantage positions. Intermediary rights were abolished in many states. But landlordism survived wherever land ceiling laws and tenancy legislation were weak or were badly implemented. But that landlordism now required the exercise of political power, including local administrative and police authority, and in turn shored up the political power of landlord lineages in a nominally democratic society. Muslim landlords in Uttar Pradesh and Madhya Pradesh lost their pre-eminent positions. Many migrated to Pakistan, and those who remained found it difficult to maintain their position through lineage ties or links to the local administration and the police. The migration of their co-religionists in erstwhile strategic positions in administration and their weakening ability to maintain patronage networks for their dependents sapped their muscle power and their shouting prowess, both of which counted in an imperfect democracy.

With declining fortunes of Muslim landlords, the continued erosion of the livelihood of Muslim artisans and the diminished opportunities for public employment for a community which suffered renewed educational backwardness in states such as Hyderabad and Uttar Pradesh, areas where the Muslim elite had been earlier the dominant section, the major avenue of upward mobility for Muslims could have been trade. Here the dominant position maintained by particular groups of Hindu traders with the help of their early start and the special advantages conferred on them by the Mitakshara law of property inheritance and partition erected strong barriers against the entry of not only non-trading Muslim groups (that is, all except Bohras, Khojas and Memons) but also against Hindu castes or ethnic groups which had not acquired a major position of vantage. In states in which trade was not already monopolized by all-India lineages of Hindu traders, new trading (and industrial) groups came up by using the resources of local politics and various government subsidies and contracts. Tamil Nadu and Andhra Pradesh would provide many examples of such upward mobility. This avenue was not and is not generally open to Muslim groups, although some particular groups or individuals may be cited as exceptions. This means that, without conscious public action to counter the trend, the vast majority of Muslims in urban areas can only hope to hold on to what they have, or worse, expect to come down in the world. This pauperized mass, along with their Hindu brethren in similar situations, then become available as the frontline operators in smuggling, drug-peddling, protection rackets and other illegal or semi-legal activities that thrive in a regime of predatory commercialization. They also, of course, become available for manipulation by politicians who use communalism for their own ends.

Using impoverished Muslims and Hindus as the infantry of contraband trade is the most obvious aspect of predatory commercialization that I referred to earlier. The point about the process of commercialization that is occurring in India today is that there is no social institution or mechanism to ensure the minimal needs of the losers in the game. Although commercialization as a process is fairly blind, there are various institutional structures that different groups use in order to find footholds for advance on the slippery terrain. The use of intra-caste and intra-clan networks, the use of trade unionism with close-shop policies by employees in many public and private organizations, the wielding of political and muscle power by lineages of big landlords and rich peasants—all these permit particular sections of the community to keep their existing positions and allow other members to get into the protected riches. In this situation of prevailing insecurity, especially for the poor of the minority communities, it is easy for communalist organizations and politicians to pose as the champions of the minorities. They can launch schools, colleges, hospitals to cater especially to members of minority communities. However marginal these gains may be, they still loom large in relation to the efforts of a government which does little to succour the poor. Many religious institutions also, besides seeking to provide a psychological solace, dole out alms and medicines and provide other real or illusory services and thus strengthen their hold on the consciousness of the poor.

The greatest threat to communal peace in India today is the communalization of politics. The state of West Bengal in recent years provides one clear case where an ideological battle supported by the state administration has been able to stem the tide of communal violence. However, the ideological base of such struggles needs to be strengthened by a massive effort to secularize people's consciousness; and this ideological deepening needs to be sustained by changes in the legal apparatus, the social structure and the political arrangements that will make the whole society attuned to the needs of the poor, and the requirements of sustained economic growth whose effects are diffused through all the layers of the social system. No state can be an island in an all-India context; nor can pure ideological work be sustained in the long run without changes in the material conditions of living.

I will end this paper by making concrete some of the implications of the propositions just put forward. The major ideological influence on the consciousness of the poor in our country still stems from religion. However, such ideological influences were not immutable. Hinduism has been at best a congeries of faith and practices, with intermittent attempts to reassert the authority of some ancient text, or to invent a new tradition in the name of either reform, devotion or orthodoxy, while popular practice has again and again strayed beyond all those carefully constructed boundaries. Brahminical Hinduism has also had one of the most unegalitarian ideologies and social hierarchies associated with it, viz., the caste system, including the practice of characterizing a vast number of people as untouchables (or, even 'unseeables' as in the case of the Nayadis of south India). As a result, religions whose ideologies preach equality before God, at least for men, has claimed adherents away from this amorphous mass of Hindus: this has certainly been one factor responsible for the steady increase in the number of Muslims in South Asia. For very similar reasons, vast numbers of Dalits converted to Buddhism in the 1950s.

The Arya Samaj, and the modern political movements such as the Rashtriya Swayamsevak Sangh (RSS), the Vishwa Hindu Parishad (VHP) and the Bharatiya Janata Party (BJP) have tried to create a militant Hinduism in the mirror image of a militant Islam. Hinduism is not a religion with a single creed or with a single focus of authority. Not only are there multiple interpretations of sacred texts but new sacred texts have been created within the fold of the religion every few centuries. The disputes between Shaktas and Vaishnavas in Bengal or between the Veera Shaivas and traditional Brahminical Hindus in the South have been on occasion no less acrimonious than between Muslims and Hindus. Moreover, a Hindu often harbours beliefs and traditions which are mutually contradictory with one another. The attempt to impose a single belief-system or a single authority structure on the people belonging to such a religion (or rather such a congeries of religion) is likely only to produce a new sectarian division at a tremendous cost to the society and polity. The onslaught on the fabric of the Indian polity mounted by the RSS, the VHP and the BJP in their attempt to impose a single ideology on Indian Hindus and by extension on the rest of the population has been a prime cause behind the flaring up of communal violence in recent years. Their ideological onslaught is bound to fail for at least two reasons. In spite of Swami Dayanand Saraswati's preaching against caste, the insignia of caste are treasured highly for both narrow materialistic reasons and for reasons of status by members of higher castes, as the recent anti-reservation movement has demonstrated with gruesome vividness. The second reason is that a majority of the Hindus would be unwilling and perhaps even unable to convert themselves into monocredal people of the book or with a single historical tradition, especially when most of that tradition is based on myth—some of it concocted before their very eyes.[18]

It is necessary, ideologically, to confront the ventures of both militant Hinduism and militant Islam. That confrontation is not achieved by writing learned essays in English or even in the vernacular. Perhaps the liberal and radical propagandists of secularism can take a leaf out of the practices of the Faraizi and Taiyuni movements in Bengal in the nineteenth century. The preachers affiliated to these movements literally became 'fish in the water' (as Mao Tse-tung advised his followers to become in a later and much bigger movement), lived at the level of the common people and tried to spread Islam by using vast numbers of vernacular tracts (as well as ill-understood texts of the Koran in Arabic) and frequent formal and informal meetings.[19]

Militant and reformist Islam preached equality before God, and gave the poor a collective identity as an *umma*, but unfortunately left the women in a permanently inferior position even in terms of religion and, of course, in terms of rights to property and income. In other respects, the practice of societies dominated by a theocratic Islamic ideology has remained as unequal and as undemocratic as ever. If militant Hinduism succeeds in its endeavour, it will produce at best the same results as reformist Islam attained, and at worst, will also perpetuate caste-based inequalities in the bargain.

A militantly secular ideology has to be diffused into the people's consciousness, and the defaults of the religion-oriented ideologies which promise paradise to the poor after death, but nothing at all on earth, have to be clearly pointed out. The political activities of most of the left-oriented parties have studiously avoided such substantive issues of ideology. The cadres have also tended most of the time to distance themselves however marginally from most of the poor villagers and the town-dwellers. Secularism has meant for most of them allowing all religious claimants to acquire more and more public space at the cost of other citizens. This sort of tolerance cannot be extended indefinitely without the claims over public spaces of different religions coming into conflict as they have already done with tragic consequences. (Associated with many of the so-called religious activities are very narrow private interests such as claims over prime land occupied by temples or mosques or the right to raise protection money in the name of subscriptions—but I am leaving such issues aside.) Are these cadres ready to take up the cause of secularizing people's consciousness with the same zeal and commitment as the sadhus and the fakirs have done in the past?

Finally, in all the states including those such as Kerala and West Bengal, which have had some success in resisting communalism, we need a strong positive growth of employment and of the incomes of poor people for secularism to gain any ground. Pro-peasant land reforms and universal literacy will go a long way towards creating the conditions for such growth. Such social changes will also directly hit at the conditions that allow communal violence to be provoked.

Notes

1. This is apparently how the communal conflict originated in the walled city of Delhi in 1974.

   See Gopal Krishna, 'Communal Violence in India: a Study of Communal Disturbance', *Economic and Political Weekly*, vol. 20, nos.2 and 3, 12 and 19 January, 1985.

2. R. Dasgupta, 'Poverty and Protest: a Study of Calcutta's Working Class and Labouring Poor (1875–1900)', in A.N. Das, V. Nilakanth and P.S. Dubey (eds.), *The Worker and the Working Class,* Public Enterprises Centre for Continuing Education: New Delhi, 1984.

3.   According to official data during the ten years, from 1954 to 1963, an average of sixty-two riots took place annually and the number of those killed in these riots was forty on an average. From 1964 to 1970 the number of communal riots rose to an annual average of 425 and the number killed increased even faster, to a figure of 467 persons killed annually. With some improvements from 1971 to 1978, the situation again deteriorated drastically from 1979. If we take the killing of Sikhs in the wake of the assassination of Indira Gandhi into account, the figure in the 1980s must have averaged more than 600 a year.

See P.R. Brass, *The Politics of India Since Independence, The New Cambridge History of India*, IV. 1, Cambridge University Press: Cambridge, 1990, Table 6.3; N.S. Saksena: 'Anatomy of Communal Riots', *Indian Express*, New Delhi, 31 March 1990. With increasing politicization of communal issues, the figures of communal incidents and deaths from communal riots have become far more unreliable in recent years. But our discussion in the text suggests that earlier also, a purely personal, sectional or economic conflict was often presented as a communal incident. Such mistaken identification can be the source of further communal conflicts.

4.   Partha Chatterjee, *Bengal 1920–1947*, vol. 1, *The Land Question*, Calcutta, Centre for Studies in Social Sciences, Calcutta, and K.P. Bagchi & Co., 1984; P. Hardy, *The Muslims of British India*, Cambridge: Cambridge University Press, 1972; J.R. McLane, *Indian Nationalism and Early Congress*, N.J. Princeton University Press: Princeton, 1977; G. Pandey, 'Rallying Round the Cow: Sectarian Strife in the Bhojpuri Region, 1888–1917', in R. Guha (ed.), *Subaltern Studies*, vol. II, Oxford University Press: New Delhi, 1982; idem. 'The Bigoted Julaha', *Economic and Political Weekly*, vol. 20, no. 5, Review of Political Economy, 29 January 1983; Parimal Ghosh, *Emergence of an Industrial Labour Force in Bengal: a Study of the Conflicts of the Jute Mill Workers with the State 1880–1930* (unpublished Ph.D. dissertation, Calcutta, 1984); Suranjan Das, 'Communal Violence in Twentieth Century Colonian Bengal: an Analytical Framework', *Social Scientist*, vol.18, nos.6–7, June–July 1990; Tanika Sarkar, *Bengal 1928–1934: The Politics of Protest*, Oxford University Press: New Delhi, 1987.

5.   For more detailed discussion and some references, see A.K. Bagchi, 'Reflections on Patterns of Regional Growth in India Under British Rule', *Bengal Past and Present*, vol. 95, part I, no. 180, January–June 1976.

6.   This apparently originated as a movement among the Kuka Sikhs of Punjab in 1870 or so. But it was taken up as a slogan by Dayanand Saraswati and his followers. It then assumed the character of a movement in virtually all parts of North India in the 1880s and 1890s. It thrived often on the patronage of the Hindu zamindars and Maharajas. A major part of the early Congress leadership was imbued with an ideology of Hindu revivalism of which cow-protection was a part. See, in this connection, Mushirul Hasan, *Nationalism and Communal Politics in India*, Manohar: New Delhi, 1979, ch. II.

7.   Paul R. Brass, *Language, Religion and Politics in North India*, Vikas: Delhi, 1975, ch. 3. See also F.S. Robinson, *Separatism Among Indian*

Muslims: The Politics of the United Provinces Muslims, 1860–1923, Vikas: Delhi, 1975. According to Brass, Muslims in the United Provinces before 1900 held more than a disproportionate share of the government jobs open to the Indians, and they were also better educated in terms of western learning than the Hindus. According to Robinson, they also formed a disproportionate share of the landholding aristocracy of the province, especially in its western part.

8. For an account of the demographic changes and changes in the position of Muslims in Uttar Pradesh, see Brass, *Language, Religion and Politics in North India,* ch. 3 and 4.

9. For a graphic description and analysis of the Bhagalpur riots, see People's Union for Democratic Rights, *Bhagalpur Riots,* Delhi, April 1990.

10. Usual Principal Status: a person is considered according to this concept is he/she was available for but without work for a major part of the year. Weekly Status: a person is considered unemployed according to this concept if he/she, though being available for work, did not have work even for one hour during the reference week. Daily Status: it is a measure of unemployment in terms of person days of unemployment of all the persons in the labour force during the reference week. Planning Commission, *Employment: Past Trends and Prospects for the 1990s,* Working paper, Planning Commission, New Delhi, May 1990, p. 14.

11. These findings are based on the 32nd, 38th and 43rd Rounds of the National Sample Survey and have been summarized in *Employment: Past Trends and Prospects for the 1990s,* Planning Commission. The only exception to the increasing trend is the measure of unemployment by Daily Status, that is, measured in terms of person days of unemployment of all the persons in the labour force during the reference week.

12. See Appendix table 3.2, in Government of India, *Economic Survey 1989–90,* Ministry of Finance (Economic Division), New Delhi, 1990.

13. For descriptions and analysis of communal riots in Gujarat, see A.A. Engineer, (a) 'Ahmedabad: From Caste to Communal Violence', *Economic and Political Weekly,* vol. 20, no. 15, 13 April 1985; and (b) 'Communal Fire Engulfs Ahmedabad Once Again', *Economic and Political Weekly,* vol. 20, no. 27, 6 July 1985; and Sudarshan Iyengar and Sujata Patel, 'Gujarat: Violence with a Difference', *Economic and Political Weekly,* vol. 20, no. 28, 13 July 1985.

14. See, for example, J. Breman, *'Even Dogs are Better Off'*; *The On-going Battle Between Capital and Labour in the Cane Fields of Gujarat* (mimeo), Indian Council of Social Science Research, New Delhi and Institute for Social Science Research in Developing Countries, The Hague, April 1990; Sujata Patel, 'Gujarat: Contract Labour and Public Interest Litigation', *Economic and Political Weekly,* vol. 18, no. 51, 17 December 1983; and Mathew Kalathil, 'Gujarat: Everyday Discrimination Against Tribals', *Economic and Political Weekly,* vol. 18, no. 47, 19 November 1990.

15. For a discussion of the linkages between caste, class and dominance in Gujarat, see I.P. Desai. 'Should "Caste" be the Basis for Recognising Backwardness', *Economic and Political Weekly,* vol. 19, no. 28, 14 July

1984; Ghanshyam Shah, 'Caste, Class and Reservation', *Economic and Political Weekly*, vol. 20, no. 3, 19 January 1985; and Upendra Baxi, 'Caste, Class and Reservations (In memoriam I.P. Desai)', *Economic and Political Weekly*, vol. 20, no. 10, 9 March 1985.

16. Sarthi Acharya, *The Maharashtra Employment Guarantee Scheme: a Study of Labour Market Intervention* (mimeo), New Delhi, ILO (ARTEP), May 1990, preface.

17. Degrees of poverty and infant mortality rates both in urban and rural areas are closely related. See *World Development Report, 1990*, Oxford University Press for the World Bank, 1990, p. 30. When talking about unemployment, we have to remember that most of the poor face a positive threat of unemployment and starvation practically all the time. The threat may be caused by drought, floods, disabling disease, sudden loss of assets through seizure by money-lenders and so on. Thus while some people stay desperately poor all the time, there are others who may move out of poverty in one year to find themselves again pushed below subsistence levels of living the next year. For a study of this kind of instability around the poverty line, see ibid., p. 35, which summarizes the findings of a study of 211 agricultural households in drought-prone areas of central India between 1975 and 1983 carried out by the International Crops Research Institute for the Semi-Arid Tropics (ICRISAT) based in Hyderabad.

18. I cannot here resist reproducing a story (in free translation) from Charuchandra Datta's *Purano Katha* (1343 B.S. or AD 1936, reprinted, Vishva-Bharati: Calcutta, 1962, p. 24) which illustrates the contradictions and the amorphousness of popular Hinduism: 'On a rainy and stormy night a (Muslim) *fakir* took shelter in a dilapidated temple, which still housed a Shiva-*linga*. The *fakir* did not know the *linga* from any ordinary stone. He sat down on it, and ate some *kababs* he was carrying. The rain and the storm continued to rage. A Hindu peasant also ran into the temple to get some relief from the inclement weather. He was flabbergasted by the sight of the *fakir* with his white beard, and became transfixed in the doorway from fright. The *fakir* did not open his mouth, but the god was less kind. In a dreadful accent the *linga* spoke thus, "My dear fakir, move your feet a bit. Let me go and break the neck of the Hindu. How dare he, a low-born fellow, enter my temple with muddy feet and dirty clothes?"'

19. For accounts of this mode of preaching and reform, see Rafiuddin Ahmed, *The Bengal Muslims 1871–1906: a Quest for Identity*, Oxford University Press: New Delhi, 1981; Abul Mansur Ahmed, *Amar Dekha Rajnitir Panchash Bachhar* (Bengali), Nowroz Kitabistan: Dhaka,1970, ch. 1.

Notes on the Contributors

S. Gopal is Emeritus Professor of Contemporary History at the Jawaharlal Nehru University, New Delhi.

K.N. Panikkar is Professor of Cultural and Intellectual History at the Jawaharlal Nehru University, New Delhi.

Sushil Srivastava is in the Department of Medieval and Modern History of the University of Allahabad.

A.G. Noorani is a lawyer and well-known writer on public affairs.

Mushirul Hasan is Professor of History at the Jamia Millia Islamia in New Delhi.

Neeladri Bhattacharya is at the Centre for Historical Studies in the Jawaharlal Nehru University, New Delhi.

Romila Thapar is Professor of Ancient History at the Jawaharlal Nehru University, New Delhi.

Aditya Mukherjee is at the Centre for Historical Studies in the Jawaharlal Nehru University, New Delhi.

Asghar Ali Engineer is the director of the Institute of Islamic Studies in Bombay.

Amiya Kumar Bagchi is the director of the Centre for Studies in Social Sciences in Calcutta.

Chronology

1528 The Babri Masjid built by Mir Baqi, a nobleman of Babur's court.

1855 The Hanumangarhi episode. Hindu–Muslim conflict as a consequence of an attempt by Muslims under the leadership of Shah Gulam Hussain to oust the Hindu Bairagis from the Hanumangarhi temple on the grounds that the temple had supplanted the mosque. The Muslims were defeated. The dispute was not over the Babri Masjid.

1857 Soon after the Revolt, the Mahant of Hanumangarhi takes over a part of the Babri Masjid compound and constructs a *chabutra*.

30 November: Maulvi Muhammad Asghar of the Masjid submits a petition to the magistrate complaining that the Bairagis have built a *chabutra* close to the mosque. (Similar complaints are made in 1860, 1877, 1883 and 1884.)

1859 The British Government erects a fence to separate the places of worship of the Hindus and the Muslims. The Hindus are to enter from the East gate and the Muslims from the North.

1885

29 January: The Mahant files a suit to gain legal title to the land in the mosque and for permission to construct a temple on the *chabutra*.

24 December: The Mahant's suit and appeals are dismissed. His claim for the proprietorship of the land in the compound of the Masjid is also dismissed by the Judicial Commissioner.

1886

25 May: The Mahant appeals again to the highest court in the province.

1 November: The Judicial Commissioner dismisses the Mahant's appeal again.

1936 An inquiry conducted by the then Commissioner of Waqfs under the UP Muslims Waqf Act, and it is held that the Babri Masjid was built by Babur who was a Sunni Muslim.

1949

22–23 December 1949 : In the night an idol of Rama was installed by the Hindus inside the mosque. The Government proclaims the premises as disputed area and locks the gates.

1950

16 January: A suit is filed by Gopal Singh Visharad in the Court of the Civil Judge, Faizabad, praying for a declaration that he is entitled to worship in the Ramjanmabhumi.

24 April: The District Collector of Faizabad, J.N. Ugra, files a statement in court that the property in suit has been in use as a mosque and not as a temple.

1951

3 March: The Civil Judge orders that the idols should remain. The High Court confirms this order on 26 April 1955.

1961

18 December: The first civil suit by Muslims is filed by the Sunni Central Waqf Board for the delivery of the possession of the mosque by the removal of the idols and other articles of Hindu worship.

1984

7 and 8 April: The Vishwa Hindu Parishad (VHP) sponsored Dharma Sansad in a session at Vigyan Bhavan, New Delhi gives a call to liberate the Ramjanmabhumi.

To create national awareness in support of the liberation of the Bhumi the VHP organizes a *rath-yatra* of Sri Rama Janaki Virajman on a motorized chariot from Bihar on 25 Sept 1984 to reach Ayodhya on 6 October 1984. But Indira Gandhi's assassination later that month leads to a suspension of the *yatra*.

1986   Umesh Chandra Pandey files an application in the court of the munsif seeking the removal of the restrictions on the puja. The application is turned down.

1 February: K.M. Pandey, District Judge, Faizabad, orders the opening of the locks to the Hindus for worship. The Muslim community is not allowed to offer any prayers.

March : The Babri Masjid Action Committee (BMAC) is formed. This is followed by a countrywide Muslim 'mourning'.

12 May: The Sunni Central Waqf Board files a writ petition against the District Judge's order.

1987

11 December: The State of Uttar Pradesh applies to the Allahabad High Court that the hearing of the two writ petitions be deferred and the four civil suits be withdrawn from the court of munsif sadar and tried by the High Court.

March: At New Delhi's Boat Club three lakh Muslims gather to demand handing over the Babri Masjid.

April: The Hindus gather at Ayodhya to pledge the liberation of the shrine.

1988

December: The Babri Masjid Action Committee splits to form Babri Masjid Movement and the BMAC.

1989

November: The Shilanyas is held at Ayodhya on 9 November and the foundation of the temple is laid the next day. The plinth is dug 192 feet away from the mosque.

On 11 November the VHP leaders declare that the construction of the temple is being deferred and it would be decided in January 1990.

December: A coalition of the Janata Dal, the Bharatiya Janata Party and the Communist Party of India forms the Government at the Centre after the general elections.

1990

15 February: The new government constitutes a committee to talk to the various groups and find an amicable solution.

October: A *rath-yatra*, from Somnath to Ayodhya led by the BJP leaders starts.

The BJP withdraws support to the Janata Dal Government.

In the Shilanyas procession and the *kar seva* on 30 October performed amidst tight security, several people are killed and injured in the police action.

November: The BJP and the VHP decide to resume the *kar seva* on 6 December.

APPENDIX

The Archaeological Evidence

In November 1990, the newspapers reported a talk by Prof. B.B.Lal in which he is said to have revealed that during excavations, fifteen years ago in 1975, in the area adjoining the Babri Masjid the excavators had found some pillar-bases. Earlier, in October 1990, Prof. B.B.Lal had made a similar statement in the RSS magazine, *Manthan*. This information together with interpretations of the carved stone pillars used in the Babri Masjid were then claimed as 'conclusive evidence' of the existence of a Hindu temple at the site of the present Babri Masjid (supposedly located at the birthplace of Rama). It was further claimed that this temple was deliberately destroyed and replaced by the mosque in 1528. It was argued that the pillar-bases were foundational to rows of pillars some of which can now be seen in the mosque. The temple was dated to the eleventh century, using the stratigraphy of the excavated pillar-bases and the decorative motifs sculpted on the stone pillars in the mosque and elsewhere.

These claims of 'conclusive evidence' have been made repeatedly by Dr S.P.Gupta (who however was not a member of the excavating team), in a number of newspaper articles. One was published in the *Indian Express* of 2 December 1990. Reactions to these claims by historians and archaeologists were carried in the *Indian Express* of 5, 6 and 13 December. The debate has been extended and carried in other newspapers as well.

Apart from the question of the acceptability of the evidence and its interpretation by Dr S.P.Gupta (on which there are two detailed comments given below), the issue also raises a question of archaeological method and procedure which archaeologists feel has been violated in the publicity sought by the claims. It is normal that in archaeology, as in most branches of learning, significant findings are mentioned in a preliminary report but are discussed in full in a detailed report which is published. Any claims to major new evidence would have to depend on the availability of a detailed report. It is only when other archaeologists have seen the full report and judged the method of excavation and interpretation of the data, that a claim can be assessed. In the case of this excavation at the Babri

Pillar at Faizabad similar
to pillars used inside the
Babri Masjid.

(*Photograph by
S. Srivastava*)

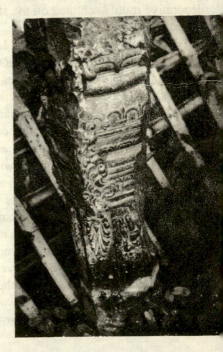

Pillar at the foot of the
grave of the local saint
Musa Aashikan.

(*Photograph by
S. Srivastava*)

Masjid, the excavator Prof. B.B.Lal, has not so far published a detailed report. Furthermore, in his preliminary report (*Indian Archaeology—A Review 1976–77*), he states, 'After the early historic deposit there is a break in occupation, with considerable debris and pit formations before the site was again occupied around the eleventh century AD. Several later-medieval brick-and-kankar lime floors have been met with, but the entire late period was devoid of any special interest.' This is the period in which it is now claimed that a Hindu temple of the eleventh century was destroyed in the sixteenth century. There is no mention of the pillar-bases even in his later preliminary report in 1979–80.

The debate in the media has touched on many points. The following comments are more specifically addressed to the archaeological, architectural and iconographic evidence referred to in the debate.

A Comment by Dr Suraj Bhan
Department of Archaeology, Kurukshetra University, Kurukshetra

The trenches dug outside the compound wall of the Babri Masjid to the south by Prof. B.B.Lal have yielded two rows of squarish pillars made of bricks standing to a height of 2 feet less than half a metre below the surface of the mound. The northernmost pillars found in the trench are not fully excavated. This pillared structure was constructed in the eleventh century as inferred from the association of the typical pottery of the period. The Muslim glazed ware pottery pieces generally ascribed to a period between the thirteenth and fifteenth centuries were also found from the upper levels of the above trenches marking the end of the brick-pillared structure.

Fourteen black stone pillars, dated on stylistic grounds to the eleventh century are used in the Babri Masjid. This was constructed according to a Persian inscription located in the mosque in AD 1528. Besides this evidence, reference has also been made to two pillars and a doorjamb of this stone, which have also been found at different places on the Ayodhya mound far away from the Babri Masjid site. The stone pillars are carved with figures of *yakshas, salabhanjikas, dvarapalas*, creepers, *purna ghata,* etc.

The argument in support of a temple considers all these stratigraphically unassociated structural pieces—brick pillars in trenches, black stone pillars used in the Babri Masjid and black stone pillars and a doorjamb found at two different parts of the mound—as an integral part of one and the same structure, namely, a 'Hindu Temple'.

On the basis of this disparate archaeological evidence it is asserted that a 'Hindu Temple was built at the controversial site in the eleventh century which continued to be used till the very end of the fifteenth century. Then suddenly, in the early sixteenth century, it was demolished and its debris was partially used in the Babri Masjid.'[1]

It must be stated emphatically that these assertions are not tenable and the conclusions which follow are wrong because the assumptions are faulty.

(i) It has been assumed that the brick pillars in the trenches excavated outside the compound wall of the Babri Masjid in the south and dated to the eleventh century, belonged to a 'Hindu Temple' on the ground that these served as 'bases' of the black stone pillars (re-used in the Babri Masjid) carved with figures of semi-divine beings related to the 'Hindu' pantheon. The conjecture that the stone pillars (of the Babri Masjid, etc.) originally formed an integral part of the brick-pillared structure excavated in the trenches, is absolutely unfounded because no stone pillars, broken or unbroken, were found stratigraphically associated with the brick pillars (supposed to belong to a Hindu Temple) in the trench. Nor was any evidence found of Hindu ritual objects or sculptures stratigraphically associated with the brick-pillared structure supposed to be a 'Hindu Temple'. Besides, the carvings on the stone pillars reused in the Babri Masjid, or found elsewhere, do not specifically relate to Rama or to Vaishnava temples. Such figures are found carved on Buddhist, Jaina or Shaiva architecture as well. The brick-pillared structure by itself reveals no architectural features of a temple, nor do the brick pillars, supposed to be the bases of the stone pillars, have any sockets in which the stone pillars could be fitted.

(ii) That the brick-pillared structure extended underneath the Babri Masjid further north is neither proved nor relevant because the structure cannot be identified as a Hindu temple.

It is evident from the above, that the brick pillars found in the trenches and the stone pillars used in the Babri Masjid had nothing in common and belonged to two different structures of the eleventh century. There is no evidence to identify the brick-pillared structure in the trenches with a 'Hindu Temple'. The black stone pillars found in the Babri Masjid and elsewhere may not belong to a single structure or a temple as indicated by the differences in the carvings of the pillars.

(iii) Although the brick-pillared structure in the trenches as well as the black stone-pillared temple structures seem to have been constructed in the eleventh century AD, these may not have come to an end simultaneously. The introduction of Muslim glazed ware pottery dating from the thirteenth to the fifteenth centuries, in the hurriedly excavated upper levels of the trenches, may suggest the end of the brick-pillared structures anywhere between these centuries but does not suggest that the so-called temple existed in the sixteenth century until it was 'destroyed' in AD 1528.

There is absolutely no evidence in the form of tell-tale marks of the use of tools in the demolition of the brick-pillared structure by a human hand. In all probability the structure seems to have collapsed on its own and was not demolished.

The black stone-pillared temple structures, whose location and stratigraphical context are as yet unknown, could have ended any time between the eleventh century and AD 1528 when these pillars were re-used for constructing the Babri Masjid. It cannot be said with any definiteness that the stone pillared temple structure was demolished by human hands in the absence of any marks that suggest the battering of the pillars with iron tools.

(iv) Lastly, it may be pointed out that it is not within the scope of archaeology to give calendrical dates for a structure. Nor can it tell us anything about who 'destroyed the temple' or whether it was the same persons who constructed the Babri Masjid. Such questions can only be answered with the help of a written record.

To conclude, the excavations at Ayodhya both by A.K. Narain of the B.H.U. (1969–70) and by B.B. Lal (1975–80) have yielded the Muslim Glazed Ware pottery dating between thirteenth and fifteenth centuries in the last period. In fact the excavations at the Jain Ghat have revealed six structural periods associated with the medieval times dating from the thirteenth century onwards. The digging in the south of the Babri Masjid outside its compound wall also yielded a thick deposit associated with Muslim Glazed Ware pottery pieces *immediately* below what is supposed to be the general floor of the Babri Masjid. This deposit of Muslim Glazed Ware overlies the floors associated with the brick-pillared structure and dating back to the eleventh century AD. These evidences have established beyond doubt that the introduction of the Muslim Glazed Ware marks the occupation of parts of Ayodhya mound called Rama Kota locally and in the revenue records and in the Babri Masjid area at least two centuries before the construction of the Babri Masjid. As such any possibility of the brick-pillared structure supposed to be a Hindu Temple being demolished in the early sixteenth century and the mosque being constructed at the same site in 1528 is ruled out. Such an inference will be in contradiction of the evidence procured by the archaeologists through their excavations.

A Comment by Professor R. Champakalakshmi
Centre for Historical Studies, Jawaharlal Nehru University, New Delhi

There are fourteen pillars, which are at present found built into various parts of the Babri Masjid. Of these, two are found built into either side of the entrance. These pillars do not represent a pair as they normally should, for the pattern of the carvings or decorative sculptures on them is dissimilar, i.e. not identical.

In the interior of the mosque twelve pillars are found. Of these, two each are built into either side of the arched openings or entrances into the three chambers of the mosque. Eight of them are dissimilar, the pattern of carvings or decorative sculptures being quite different from each other. The other four have similar carvings but they do not necessarily occur in a particular grouping.

Thus these pillars show that they are an assorted lot and hence cannot be described as *in situ* or in a row which may indicate their structural alignment. They seem to belong to some other structure, and to have been later used by the builders of the mosque. This has given rise to the assumption that they must have been part of a temple at the very same site and that it was a Rama (Vaishnava) temple which was destroyed to make way for the mosque. An attempt is also being made to link these pillars with the 'brick pillar bases' supposed to have been revealed during the excavations of 1975–76 near the mosque at Ayodhya, but reported in a newspaper article only in December 1990. It is claimed that these pillars were originally supported by the 'brick pillar bases' and removed and used in the building of the mosque. Curiously, it is also pointed out that the alignment of the 'brick pillar bases' can be shown to continue into the present mosque where the pillars are now found, meaning that the pillars now in the mosque are *in situ*. These statements are quite clearly contradictory to each other and hence questionable. There are also other pillars or parts of pillars found scattered in the vicinity of the mosque, some as far as half a kilometre or one kilometre away. They carry similar carvings.

The dominant motifs in the carvings are floral, conventionalized or stylized lotuses, palmettes and other patterns woven out of foliage. The second important motif is the female figure, generally in the form of a *vrikshadevata* or *salabhanjika*, often shown standing on a lotus, itself stylized and issuing out of a vase or what is called a *kumbha* or *purna-ghata*, i.e. a pot. There are thus no iconic representations in any of the pillars, with the single exception of a figure holding a *trishula* in its left hand, which is found on the lower part of what may be described as a doorjamb now located not in the Masjid but in a structure at the site called Sita-ki-Rasoi at a little distance from the mosque. This will be taken up later for a detailed description and identification.

The predominant motifs thus would be the floral and conventional lotus carvings and the female figure. The latter, in particular, is prominent in some pillars, including the one lying some distance away from the mosque. The female figure is standing on a lotus issuing from a vase *(purna ghata)*. This motif may be traced back to early Buddhist art as represented in Sanchi, Bharhut and other places (first century BC and first century AD), where it symbolizes Maya, the mother of the Buddha and also stands for life and prosperity.[1] The lotus is associated with early Buddhist and Jaina art and iconography from the early historic period (third century BC to third century AD). In Buddhist art it was a part of the 'tree of life and prosperity' and this is illustrated by the occurrence of stylized lotuses as decorative motifs and in the tree of life issuing from a pot or *purna ghata*. The tree, apart from the lotuses, also consisted of a stem with the figures of birds, animals and human beings (often as couples or *mithuna* and sometimes only as female figures) issuing from it on either side. Garlands and jewels are often found hanging on either side of the stem. Significantly, some of these 'trees' issue from the footprints of the Buddha and end up at the top with the *triratna* and *shrivatsa* symbols[2] (standing for the Buddha, Dharma and Sangha). Occurring in a period when the Buddha was not yet represented in anthropomorphic form, this tree of life is often described as the earliest conceptualization and visualization of the Buddha (footprints: Buddha's feet, the stem with motifs: his body, and the *triratna*: his head). This motif undergoes interesting variations in the decorative sculptures of all periods and of various religious sects. As we see it in these pillars, it is a decorative female figure often in the *tribhanga* posture or a dancing pose standing on a lotus issuing from a pot, which also has other foliage issuing out of it and flowing all over. It is a motif common to all religious art and may well have been even a part of pillar decorations in secular structures.

The *vrikshadevata* or *salabhanjika* often holding the branch of a tree may also be traced back to early Buddhist art in Sanchi, Bharhut and Mathura.[3] Later this figure also becomes a common decorative motif in all structures, Jaina, Shaiva and Vaishnava, sometimes figuring prominently as bracket figures as seen at Khajuraho (Shaiva), Halebid (Shaiva), Belur (Vaishnava) and the Jaina temples of Gujarat.

The only pillar (doorjamb?) which has anything that may be called a religious motif is the one found in the Sita-ki-Rasoi. On its lower part it has a figure with a *trishula* in its left hand. The figure may be a *dvarapala* and the *trishula* would indicate a Shaiva association. However, two other features which this figure shows have been claimed as typical Vaishnava features: its crown which is described as *karandamukuta* and the garland which decorates it and which has been described as a *vanamala* as it is a long one reaching down to the knee.

It is incorrect to attribute the *karandamukuta* to Vaishnava images alone, for it is not characteristic of or peculiar to Vaishnava images. In fact, it hardly occurs in the Vishnu icons which have a characteristic *kiritamukuta*. The *karandamukuta* is prescribed for female deities (goddesses) and minor deities and attendants[4] including *dvarapalas* of all religious affiliations. It occurs on Ganesha icons also as well as on non-religious figures like royal figures.[5]

As for the garland, while the *vanamala* or *vaijayantimala* is associated with Vishnu icons, the long garland as a decorative element occurs in most of the Pala, Sena sculptures of the tenth to twelfth centuries AD, be it Vaishnava, Shaiva or of any other pantheon. In the medieval sculptures of Bengal, Khajuraho, Rajasthan and in south Karnataka (Halebid, etc., of the Hoysala period) this element is a prominent decorative motif in all sculptures. It is also worn by dancers and musicians[6] and by the river goddess Ganga in medieval art.[7]

In the case of the present figure, it may also be identified as a garland-like *yajnopavita* or sacred thread, worn over the left shoulder and coming under the right arm. Such *yajnopavitas* reaching down to the knee or even below the knee are found in Shaiva images, in flower garland form as seen in *dvarapalas* of the Shaiva temples[8] and even on Shiva as Natesa and Gangadhara.[9] Apart from a garland-like sacred thread, what are called *vastra-yajnopavita* are also worn by such figures.[10] Surya images are often decorated with such long garlands or *yajnopavita* in garland form.[11] The figures of Avalokiteshvara (Buddhist-Bodhisattva) are also shown with the jewel form of the motif worn in the *yajnopavita* fashion.[12]

It is also noteworthy that the lower garment with its *katisutra* (a sash-like cloth tied around the waist) sometimes appears like the garland reaching the knee. The *katisutra* is worn around the waist with loops and knots, the loops flowing down to the knee. This is a common feature of both the Shaiva and Vaishnava figures.[13]

Hence the figure on the lower part of the pillar is not necessarily a Vaishnava *dvarapala*. Above all the presence of the *trishula* is the main factor in establishing the figure to be anything but Vaishnava. For no Vaishnava *dvarapala* can be and has ever been shown with the *trishula* as an attribute.

Above the figure of the *dvarapala*, the pillar/door jamb has a vertical row of male and female figures and some decorative foliage. Again the female figures are of the dancing female or *vrikshadevata* type and are both decorative as well as symbolic of life and prosperity like the early 'tree of life' design. Their occurrence on doorjambs is common to all structures, including secular ones.

Another motif found in many of these pillars is the schematic garlands hanging around the pillars on their upper part well below the capital. This again is a feature common to all structures, religious and secular. Such decorations are found in *kirti-toranas* (gateways commemorating fame or victory) and in Jaina (Dilwara) and Shaiva temples (Khajuraho and Bhubaneshwar). In Bhubaneshwar it is a part of the entrance *torana* of the Mukteshvara temple.

The pillars in the mosque can thus be seen to be an assorted lot and can on no account be described as *in situ*. Firstly, they are not found in identical pairs at the entrances or with identical decorative features in a particular alignment. Secondly, they are of a height of not more than 5.6 or 6 feet. Thirdly, one of the pillars has the palmette motif upside down and may have been built into the wall upside down. Fourthly, in two of the pillars in the mosque, there is clear evidence of their upper parts—the portion representing the capital—being unfinished as this part shows no clear hammer dressing or chiselling, not to speak of carvings. The capital portion in the other pillars show some carvings, which include a stylized neck in the form of a ribbed element and an abacus carved with petals.

The unevenness of the upper parts of some pillars also raises the question whether they are complete pillars as they stand now. As they are found at present, they also seem to have no specific load-bearing function. Hence to assign to them a specific function and alignment would be highly unscientific. It could even be suggested that they were ruins of a structure in the vicinity of the mosque or at some other site in Ayodhya, which the builders of the mosque found convenient to use in their structure. Such a structure could have been a *mandapa* (a pillared pavilion), but considering the height of the pillars, it could also have been a veranda or balcony of a structure, which was non-religious (secular) for given the nature of the decorative features on these pillars, they could occur in both religious and secular structures.

Thus the evidence for the existence of a Hindu temple and more particularly a Vaishnava temple dedicated to Rama at the very same site as the present mosque is *far from conclusive*. Any attempt to use the available evidence as conclusive is questionable.

Notes

(References to well-known centres and their monuments are too many to be listed here. Hence the following are to more specific instances.)

1. John Marshall, *Guide to Sanchi*, Reprint, Delhi, 1955; Ludwig Bachhofer, *Early Indian Sculpture*, 2 vols., Paris, 1923.

2. John Marshall, A. Foucher and N.G. Majumdar, *Monuments of Sanchi* vol II and III, Delhi, 1940.

3. ibid.; Bachhofer, op.cit.; Nihar Ranjan Ray, *Maurya and Post-Maurya Art*, Calcutta, 1975, figs. 45 & 46.

4. C.Sivaramamurti, 'Geographical and Chronological factors in Indian Iconography', *Ancient India*, no. 6, January 1950, p. 30; See also C. Sivaramamurti, *South Indian Bronzes*, figs. 26, 30, 49(b), 68(a), 72(b), 80(a), 86; Also R.Champakalakshmi, *Vaishnava Iconography in the Tamil Country*, New Delhi, 1981.

5. C.Sivaramamurti, op. cit., 1950, fig.15 (2c); fig. 81(a)

6. *The Struggle for Empire, History and Culture of the Indian People*, vol. V, Bharatiya Vidya Bhavan Series, K.M.Munshi (ed.), fig. 112 (Dancers and Musicians from Harshagiri).

7. C.Sivaramamurti, op.cit., *(Ancient India*, no. 6) pl. II, fig.C.

8. ibid., fig. 21(a) and (b), pl. XXV, (c) and (d). (Gwalior and Dacca) (pl. IV(c) for Ganesa).

9. ibid., pl. XXVII

10. ibid., fig. 7.

11. ibid., pl.III: C and E

12. *The Struggle for Empire*, the figure of Avalokiteshvara from Nalanda.

13. C.Sivaramamurti, *South Indian Bronzes*, Lalit Kala Akademi, New Delhi, 1963, pl.

14. *The Struggle for Empire*, fig. 51 from Vadnagar and fig. 33 from Khajuraho.

Index